AUSTRIA – LAND OF ENCHANTMENT

Where lies a land that can with this compare?
Look around, whichever way your glances turn,
It smiles as on a bridegroom smiles the bride.
With meadows shining green and grain like gold,
Made gay with saffron's yellow, flaxen blue,
Spiced fragrantly with flowers, precious herbs,
It sweeps through ample valleys, broad and vast -
A rich bouquet, so far as eye can see,
Held in the Danube's silvery embrace! -
Then climbs aloft to vineyards on the slopes,
Where serried rows of lustrous grapes ascend,
Full-ripened under Heavens's radiant sky;
While forests dark for hunting rise on high.
And God's own gentle breath suffuses all,
And warms, matures and makes the pulses throb,
As no man's pulse can throb on chilly plains.
And so the Austrian is free and frank,
He bears life's pain, life's pleasures openly,
Not envious, oft though he envied be!
And what he does is done with chearful mien.
Perhaps in Saxony or on the Rhine,
There may be folk more versed in bookish lore;
But in what counts before the sight of God:
An open eye, straightforward common sense;
In these the Austrian outstrips his brothers,
Franz Grillparzer   Thinks his own thoughts and leaves the talk to others.

Austria
Land of Enchantment

The Land and Its History

Translated with the collaboration of
Donald Gutch, Antony Kemp,
Carol Renner, Alison Thielecke,
and Margaret Wasmeier,

and edited by

Otto Hietsch

Emeritus Professor of English, University of Regensburg

EDITORIAL NOTE

Bezauberndes Österreich, the parent volume for the present English one, this year again happily confirms its wonted flagship rôle. The staff of contributors continue to be Andreas Albrecht ('Wien'), Josef Brettenthaler ('Ein Land im Wandel der Zeiten,' 'Salzburg,', 'Tirol'), Karl Heinz Burmeister ('Vorarlberg'), Georgine Veverka ('Burgenland,' 'Kärnten,' 'Niederösterreich,' 'Oberösterreich,' 'Steiermark'), and Hanns Jäger-Sunstenau ('Wappenbeschreibungen'). Recent political, economic, social and, not least, cultural developments, though, have been duly recorded, some less important paragraphs abridged or deleted, and pertinent illustrations added in many places.

Austria - Land of Enchantment, the old and new companion volume, of course reflects all those changes. Special care has been taken to elucidate the respective background and to offer explanations whenever historical or strictly regional terms might baffle native English-speaking readers around the globe. For similar reasons, a rather detailed Index has been appended, to act as a quick guide to the key figures and subjects discussed and to bracket waywardly scattered items together.

By and large, however, the English pages follow the German setting very faithfully; this also applies to the pieces of poetry found throughout the pages, most of which were translated here for the first time. Where possible, an effort was made to preserve the historical flavour of metre and diction. An even more compelling caveat was lucidity of style and ease of expression; after all, "an honest tale speeds best being plainly told."

The history of this volume has unfolded upon three stages: among the vine-clad hills of the Wachau, facing King Richard the Lion-Hearted's unceremonial seat of residence in Lower Austria; in the shadow of Tyrol Castle and all its mountain glory; and, of course, in this ancient Castra Regina, on the northernmost bend of the legendary River Danube.

There a team of five from the English Department of Regensburg University readily banded together to add their share, each one taking a certain chapter. These were the people who did the spadework of translation on 'Vienna,' 'Styria,' 'Upper Austria,' 'Tyrol,' and 'Carinthia' (to whom credit is given in this order above).

Jean Ritzke-Rutherford and Deborah Lehman-Irl reread several manuscripts and suggested a number of valuable improvements, for which I am thankful. Randall Thomas did likewise, forgetting time and temptations to add polish and sparkling wit to many a page that might otherwise have remained dull and lustreless. It was a pleasure to have such accomplished stylists by one's side through the untold sessions of search for the proper word or phrase.

This trio of verbal dexterity was ideally complemented, on the production side, by the publishers, a close-knit family quartet, and especially by Roland Schmid, whose judicious advice and unstinting assistance were ever ready blessings to fall back upon. Throughout those months of summer and autumn sunshine, Ingrid, my dear wife, the most willing of helpmates, cheerfully shared my frantic existence in order to speed this work to conclusion. May the result of our joint labours reward her!

CONTENTS

Winds of Change over Austria   6

Burgenland   22
Burgenland

Carinthia   42
Kärnten

Lower Austria   64
Niederösterreich

Upper Austria   84
Oberösterreich

Salzburg   104
Salzburg

Styria   126
Steiermark

Tyrol   146
Tirol

Vorarlberg   164
Vorarlberg

Vienna   182
Wien

Austrian Coats of Arms   204

In nomine sancte et indiuidue trinitatis. deo diuina preordinante clementia Imperator augustus. Noueri...

...norum tam presentium quam et futurorum. qualiter nos dignis petitionibus dilectissimi nepotis nostri baioariorum ducis heinrici annuentes quasdam...

...contractu heinrici comitis filii luitpaldi marchionis in loco niuuanhova dicto idest cu eade cuppe et in p...

...aquis aquarumue decursibus. venationibus Zidaluueidun piscationibus molendinis mobilibus et inmobilibus uiis et inuiis exitibus et reditibus quesitis et in...

...sup gremiu frisingensis aecclesiae. ad seruicium sancte mariae eiusque sancti confessoris atque pontificis corbiniani. cui nunc fidelis noster rota sca...

...peruum proprium concessimus firmamusque tradidimus nostra imperiali potentia. Eo modo eoque tenore ut eadem prefata frisingensis aecc...

...sui successores libero deinceps perfruantur arbitrio. haec omnia tenendi. commutandi. et quodquod voluerint inde faciendi...

...firmiori stabiliorque ut est sancte dei aecclesiae filiis speciem credatur. hanc cartam inscribi iussimus. Anulo...

...sigillari iussimus.

signum domni ottonis [monogram: OTTO] inuictissimi Imperatoris augusti.

Hildibaldus episcopus et cancellarius uice uuilligisi archiepi recognoui.

Data kl nou. Anno dominicae Incarnationis DCCCCXCVI. Indictione X. Anno uero tertii ottonis regnantis XIII. Imperii...

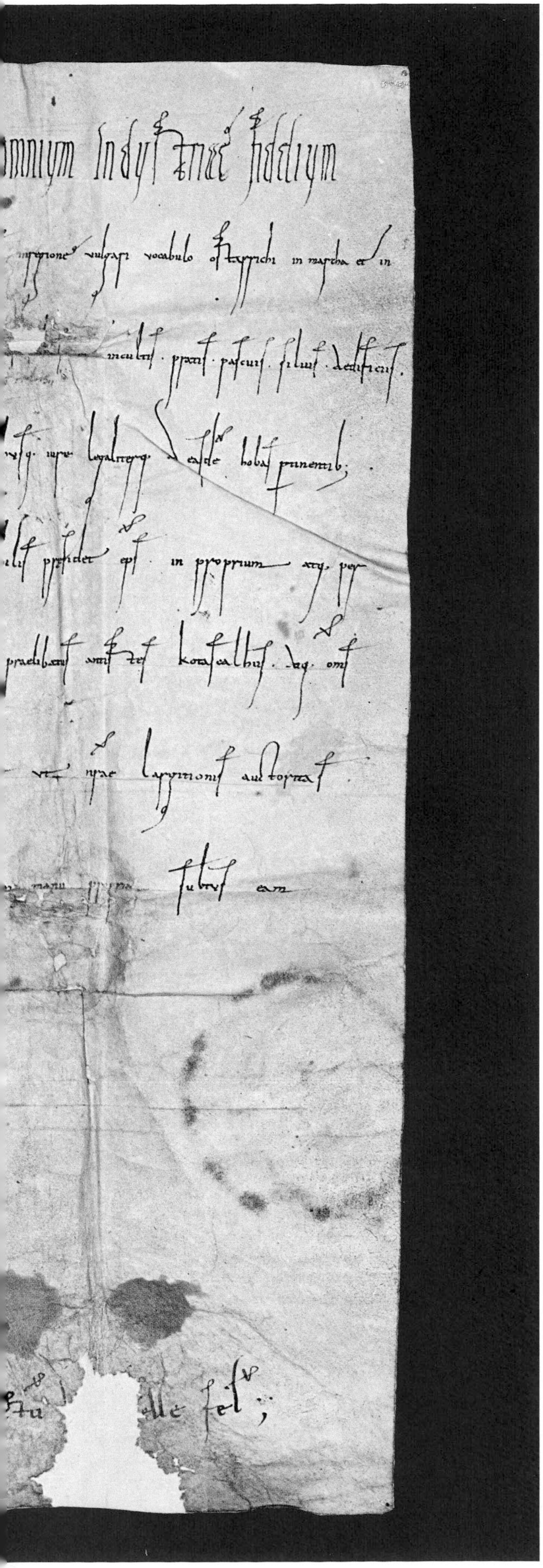

Winds of Change over Austria

In an Endowment from Emperor Otto III to the Bavarian bishop of Freising, dated 1 November 996, a strange name appears officially for the first time; it is possible, however, that it had been in common use before that:

Ostarrîchi.

Translated, this means the 'Realm in the East.' What pompous term for a narrow strip of land between the River Enns and the Vienna Forest, whose boundaries, amidst constantly reiterated threats, were only slowly pushed eastwards through the labours of ploughmen and monks! Yet, at that time, this territory, in all probability, must already have been regarded as something special, for a poet writes of it:

This land of Ostarrîchi has its honour and dignity.

And elsewhere we find,

Well leave henceforth your questions be:
You did a parfit Austrian see!

In the year 996, then, it so happened that Emperor Otto III made over some territory near Neuhofen on the River Ybbs to Bishop Gottschalk of Freising. That area, in the vernacular, bore the name of *Ostarrîchi*, which in Neo-Latin is 'Austria.' So Austria, in 1996, was duly justified in celebrating the millennium of that famous title deed, and there were several exhibitions making the event stand out in bold relief to the viewers.

The traces of man's earliest presence on Austrian soil in the Alpine foothills, and even more conclusively on the Danube, date back to the Early Stone Age; and yet only in 1970 was a surprising discovery made: until then it had been believed that mankind,

The *Ostarrîchi* Deed of Endowment, dated 996, according to which the Bishop of Freising was granted a piece of land near Neuhofen on the River Ybbs by Emperor Otto III. It contains the first mention of the name *Austria* in the vernacular (see top right-hand corner, second line).

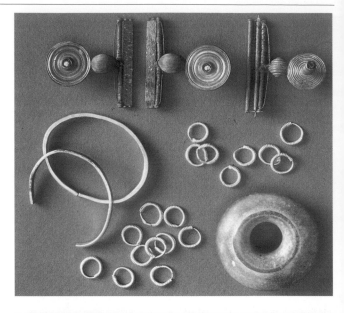

Exhibits from the Celtic Museum at Hallein, Salzburg:
Top left: A bronze manikin fibula, dated between 450 and 370 B.C.
Top right: Ornaments found in a woman's grave, about 500 B.C.
Bottom left: Annular eartenware bottle, fifth century B.C.
Bottom right: A bronze bird fibula, dated between 450 and 370 B.C.

up to about the year 4000 B.C., had not dared to venture into the mountains at all. However, but a decade ago, in a natural tunnel at an altitude of some 5,000 feet, crudely made tools were found amongst the numerous bones of prehistoric bears on Mt. Schlenken near Hallein, in Salzburg's Osterhorn Range. Using the most up-to-date methods, their age was determined to be at least 50,000 years. So this find is important to a proper understanding of Austria's prehistory.

In the Late Stone Age, from about 4000 B.C., the land was already spottily settled, even in the more inaccessible mountain valleys. Precious salt was being mined; and on a few lakes, pile-dwellings appeared whose function, according to the most recent research, might be regarded as that of trading-posts, as points at which goods were transferred from land to water, and vice versa.

The Metal Era, i. e., the Bronze and Iron Ages, followed, and in part we now know the origins of the people who settled the land of the present in-habitants of Austria. They stem from the Veneti and the Illyrians. The latter were prominent during the Early Iron Age (800-400 B.C.).

Prehistorians call this entire phase of development "Hallstatt Culture," after the main site of discovery in Upper Austria. At a burial ground in the Salzberg area of Hallstatt, more than 2,000 graves were unearthed; extensive finds were further made at Hallein, where the Illyrians had also dug for salt.

The Illyrian Hallstatt Culture was superseded by that of the Celts. This race occupied an area stretching from the South of England across France and over the Alps into the lowlands of Northern Italy. The Celts were splintered into many tribes and yet they became, at times, a danger to the mighty Roman Empire, although they never joined forces to form a homogeneous dominion.

In what is now Austria, they founded their Kingdom of Noricum. Only in the last few decades has the scholarly world fully recognized the sophistication of their culture in all its dimensions and made it an object of intensive study. In this respect, some exceedingly interesting exhibits are to be seen in the Celtic Museum at Hallein.

Then, at the beginning of our era, the Romans reached out towards the Celtic lands. As for the region of the Alps, the Roman Empire had, for some time, had connections with her northern neighbours, through various trade relationships and finally through a sort of "defence treaty." Now they advanced into the Alps and as far as the Danube, and carved out of the occupied lands their provinces of Noricum and, in the west, Raetia.

In the following four hundred years of Roman rule, typical qualities of the Roman way of life were imparted to the area to a great extent. A network of excellent roads was built, civilian settlements came into being; elsewhere, villages or towns arose out of the garrisons of the Roman legions; merchants and tradesmen crossed the land, foreign goods, previously unknown manual skills and antique cultural influences were introduced.

But disturbing signs of inward decay, issuing from the mother country, were already perceptible against the outward splendour of imperial might; and soon a quiet, and at first apparently unimportant, power group was to assert its claim for spiritual supremacy: the Christians. The new doctrine even pushed its way over the Alps, and here and there small early Christian communities were formed.

But in the middle of this development, starting from the fourth century, another event erupted violently into the scene, the Great Migration of the Peoples. The Huns had set in motion the major Germanic tribes in the European area between the Black Sea and the Atlantic, and the Roman Empire collapsed under the Teutonic attack. Misery and violence

Carnuntum, the strongest Roman fortification along the Danube in the provinces of Pannonia and Noricum.

continued to be widespread until, after the passage of various peoples through the Alps and along the Danube valley, Bavarian and Alemannic tribal groups settled there permanently. Again Christianity was reintroduced, and the missionaries brought rich benefits for the secular culture in its wake.

The monastic pioneers of this early period, together with the new settlers and the old remaining Celto-Romanic inhabitants, were responsible for what has become known as the First Colonization. To begin with, it covered the Alpine foothills and then reached out along the rivers into the mountains. Only much later, in the eleventh and twelfth centuries, forced by the swelling population and the subsequent need to find new farmland, did it penetrate into the tributary valleys. Farmhouses were now built at high elevation, the shady sides of valleys attracted inhabitants, and forested areas began to be cleared.

During this second spell of colonization another group of well-known monasteries appeared, particularly in Lower Austria, in the granite plateau of the large Northern Forest. Amongst these, the Cistercian Order, known as the "White Monks," took the lead. Clearing of forests was done on a large scale, and viticulture was intensified.

But let us go back for a moment to the beginning of the sixth century. The realm of the Franks spread out from the Rhine and attained the height of glory in the Universal Empire of Charlemagne (768-814); that ruler also put an end to the former independence of the Bavarian dukes, and thus made his influence felt in the southern German and Austrian territories. We cannot help being thrilled with a sense of history on hearing that this mightiest of all sovereigns should have received the fairy-tale Prince Harun al-Rashid's greetings and gifts of homage from thousands of miles away. And yet, folklore has it, the same Charlemagne sleeps on in the Bavarian-Austrian borderland, in the depths of Untersberg near Salzburg, until the time when the Empire's need is greatest, and he will come again to sit in judgment of Good and Evil.

It was also Emperor Charlemagne who freed the Eastern borderland from a new but continuing threat, the Avars. He took from them the land which is today in Lower Austria and, at the beginning of the ninth century, proclaimed the entire Eastern region to be the Avaric March, also called in later times the Carolingian, or Ottonian, March. This province began at the River Enns; its originally proposed eastern boundary probably should have been the River Raab (Rába), but rarely did it ever extend far beyond the Vienna Forest. Instead, the boundary was pushed across the Danube, west of the River Kamp in the north and hence towards the large woodland area. But eastwards from the Vienna Forest there stretched a wilderness of waste land and low-lying river meadows, a no man's land in military terms and with regard to settlement.

It was simply dubbed Avaria, but had a number of other names. It was mistaken for the territory formerly held by the Huns and called *terra Hunnorum*, the 'land of the Huns'; another name was Slavinia, after the Slavs who lived there and were subject to the Avars. In the eastern parts, the old Roman name, Pannonia, lived on.

A further borderland of the Frankish Empire was Carantania, which included present-day Carinthia, Styria, and also parts of East Tyrol, Salzburg, and Upper und Lower Austria. In 1122 the Carinthian March broke away and later, in 1180, joined with other areas to form the Duchy of Styria, which fell to Austria in 1192. It was only in 1335, however, that Carinthia passed to the Habsburgs who thereby increased their hereditary dominions and their dynastic power. But in the south-east of the Empire, there were other consequences which arose from the Emperor's victorious campaign against the Avars. We must retrace our steps once more. By the end of the sixth century Slavic groups, the Alpine Slavs, had already penetrated into parts of present-day Styria, Carinthia, and the mountain land around Salzburg, and they had driven wedges of settlement right into the Alpine foothills. Through the founding of a major realm in the seventh century (under Samo, probably a Frankish merchant), points of contact were even formed between northern and southern Slavs in what is today's Waldviertel, the section of Lower Austria stretching from the left bank of the Danube to the borders of Czechia. When the Carolingian Eastern March came into being, this marked the end of a bridgehead that had already begun to function as a cultural and political clearing-house from the Baltic to the Adriatic.

However, after the death of Charlemagne, the Empire fell apart. Again there was the threat of a Slavic alliance when an additional menace cast its shadow: the Magyars, a race from the Ural Mountains between Europe and Asia, had moved into Hungary; exploiting the weakness of the Empire, they carried their devastating raids into the West year for year. The people, stirred by unforgotten memories of earlier reigns of terror, called them "the Huns."

In the late spring of 907, lacking a central Imperial army, Luitpold of Schyre, the ancestor of the Wittelsbach family, led a Bavarian army to fight against the Magyars. He suffered a crushing defeat near Pressburg (Bratislava); the flower of knighthood lay strewn on the battlefield, and amongst the dead was Archbishop Theotmar of Salzburg. It meant the end of the political structure which Charlemagne had founded. Although the Eastern March was never formally handed over to the Magyars, the land was a deserted waste: the villages had been destroyed, the people had fled or been murdered. The turning-point did not come until the year 955. On August 10, the day of St. Lawrence's feast, Emperor Otto the Great "wiped the floor" with the Magyars in the Battle of Lechfeld so decisively that, according to legend, only seven of his opponents ever returned to their homeland.

In any case, it remains as historical fact that after this event the danger from the East was averted for good and that the people and the ruling house under the saintly Stephen I (997-1038) adopted Christianity; Hungary was thus integrated into the European cultural world. The second, "Ottonian," Eastern March came into being. As mentioned above, when the old *ôsterlant* received the name *Ostarrîchi*, it had already been through a long ordeal, but also had a glorious past behind it. Now Count Burchhart of Regensburg was entrusted with the leadership of the new March. He is perhaps identical with the "good

Emperor Charlemagne, as painted by Albrecht Dürer about 1512 (Museum of Art History, Vienna). A mighty monarch, he was the first to enjoy a fame of truly European dimensions; he died at Aachen (Aix-la-Chapelle) in 814, at the age of 71.

A page from *The Lay of the Nibelungs*, the most important heroic epic in the Middle High German. This is from one of the two manuscripts found in 1775 and 1778 in a palace in Vorarlberg (see p. 174); now in the Princely Fürstenberg Court Library, at Donaueschingen in the Black Forest.

The Imperial Crown of the Holy Roman Empire, which has been in Vienna since 1804 (temporarily in Nuremberg from 1938 to 1945), was probably made for Otto the Great in 962. Its form is a combination of the secular crown and the ecclesiastical mitre (represented by the hoop).

margrave of Bechelaren" (Pöchlarn), mentioned in *The Lay of the Nibelungs*. This greatest of German heroic epics was possibly composed, and passed on in fragments by oral tradition, during the Great Migration. Not until about 1200, probably in the Austrian Danube valley, or not far from it, was the story finally written down and united to form one great poem.

Shortly afterwards, the first margrave became involved in a power struggle over the throne of the German Empire and was deposed as a result. The succession went to the Babenbergs, a ruling family who were destined to prove uncommonly beneficial to the land for the next three hundred years. With the eastward expansion of settlement their dynastic seat of residence continued to move down the

Danube in the course of the centuries; from Pöchlarn to Melk, then to Tulln, and finally into the Vienna Forest and its last foothills on the edge of the great plains. The boundary now stretched as far as the Rivers March (Morava) and Leitha, but ethnically extended even further east into present-day Burgenland.

The most notable character of this period of Babenberg rule was undoubtedly Margrave Leopold III (1095-1136). He was related by marriage to the Salic Imperial house of that time and won dominion over the town of Vienna. This action proved a decisive step in the development of an independent Austrian principality. Leopold III was canonized in 1485 for his services to the Church (including his generous endowments to the Monastery of Kloster-

A detail taken from the Babenberg Family Tree portraying Leopold III. (1095-1136) with his sons Adalbert and Otto, the future Bishop of Freising; in the background are, from left to right, the monasteries of Kleinmariazell, Klosterneuburg, and Heiligenkreuz, which the margrave had richly endowed during his lifetime.

For an overall view of that Family Tree in its ramified glory, see p. 187.

neuburg and his establishment of the Monastery of Heiligenkreuz), and he has been the patron saint of Lower Austria since 1663.

The Babenberg duke, Henry II Jasomirgott ('God willing'), was forced to renounce Bavaria, the land of his fathers, in 1156, for domestic political reasons; however, subsequently his portion of Austria was issued with the special rights which were to give Austria a favoured position within the Empire from that time on - the so-called *Privilegium minus*. Henry II also transferred his residence down to the town on the Danube. While the Babenbergs held court *am Hof* (and a modern square of that name is a fitting reminder), the Imperial Palace of the Habsburgs was built by the former city wall, where it still stands today. Thus the importance of Vienna grew noticeably, and alongside Cologne it was ranked among the largest towns of the Empire. In 1237 the Emperor pronounced it an Imperial City, and the Babenberg lands to be "immediate," or subject to him alone. Walther von der Vogelweide, when casting his mind back to his early years as a poet, is full of praise for the Viennese court where he "learnt the skills of Song and Story." The last of the Babenbergs, however, was to sink like a dying star. Frederick the Quar-

Walther von der Vogelweide, the famous minnesinger, born about 1170. We see the poet taking the characteristic posture in which one of his reflective pieces, "I sat upon a stone," begins.

relsome defeated the Hungarians at the River Leitha, but the victor never returned from battle.

In the meantime, there was no German Emperor either. The Interregnum, "chaotic times when the throne stood bare," proved not altogether unfavourable for Austria, for the Bohemian King Přemysl Otakar (Ottocar) took over the orphaned country and administered it in his own way, not at all badly. Thirty years later he lost his land and his life in the Battle of Marchfeld to the newly elected monarch, Rudolph of Habsburg. The Babenberg possessions in Austria, Styria, and Carniola became Imperial fiefs of the Habsburgs; and in due course Carinthia and Tyrol followed suit. Only Salzburg remained as an independent ecclesiastical principality.

However, from now on, it was the Habsburg family which, with some exceptions, produced the German Emperors. At the same time, they also extended their dynastic power in the south-east in the form of hereditary dominions. Astute diplomacy and a clever marriage policy enabled them to unite the German-speaking Alpine and Danube territories with Hungary and Bohemia. In the course of the fifteenth and sixteenth centuries the Habsburg family split into several branches when the inherited lands were divided; these were re-united by Leopold I in the century thereafter. In the sixteenth century, the Spanish branch of the family won most of the lands of the New World. In Charles V's empire "the sun never set"; but in the long run, these world-wide possessions could not be retained.

Then the Reformation, the Counter-Reformation, and the Thirty Years' War all rocked the Empire, and with it Austria. But now the main opposition to

Cavalry attacking in the Thirty Years' War, an oil painting by Otto von Thoren (Austrian National Library, Vienna).

the country came from the East, into which it jutted like a bastion. As early as the fifteenth century, Austria's relationship to the Ottoman Empire alternated between war and deceptive years of peace, with struggles mainly over sovereignty and possessions in Hungary. During this period, in Lower Austria as well as in the remote valleys of Styria and Carinthia, the simple folk, naïvely unconcerned about politics, were continually plagued in a most shocking fashion by the "scourging and scorching" of the Sultan's hordes. With Ottoman strength at its greatest, the Muslims wanted to take control of the entire Occident, in particular the "Realm of the Golden Apple," i. e., Rome and the Papacy.

Vienna, then one of the strongest fortresses in the Empire, was an obstacle to the Turkish plans: contemporary strategy could not allow for a further push west, while leaving such an important place unconquered. For this reason, in 1529 and 1683, the two sieges of Vienna, the Imperial capital, and its successful defence were of vital consequence to the whole of Europe.

But then, at the beginning of the eighteenth century, the tables were turned: desperate defence action changed into a glorious offensive. The flags of Prince Eugene flew over Belgrade, the "White City," the gateway to the Balkan Peninsula. In the Peace Treaty of Passarowitz (1718) Austria made her largest territorial aggrandizement. The strength of the Turks in Europe was broken at last, even if several major gains were to be lost a few decades later and it would take another one hundred and fifty years for the Balkan Christians to liberate themselves.

Settlers from Southern Germany now cultivated the Banat and Transylvania, which had been depopulated during the long war years; at the Tsar's invitation, they founded their villages in the formerly Turkish holdings from the Ukraine to the Volga. And while the European nations, in particular Great Britain, were acquiring colonies overseas, Austria felt her mission to be on the Continent - to gain an influence in the South-east, and to become a respected force of order there. This was a rôle, though, which not only aroused strong nationalistic feelings in the countries thus dominated, but which made for increased tension and, much later, led to the catastrophe of the First World War and the fall of the Empire.

The eighteenth century brought Austria the culmination of artistic creativity in the form of the Baroque, especially in the field of architecture. On the political scene, however, the quarrel over the future supremacy in Central Europe began to be visible with the growing importance of Prussia, even

Prince Eugene of Savoy (1663-1736), one of Old Austria's greatest generals, portrayed by Johann Kupetzky, a contemporary painter (Museum of Army History, Vienna).

during Maria Theresa's reign. But yet another momentous happening was to delay the final confrontation. The unbridled genius of Napoleon tore the European map to shreds; thrones were toppled, old confederations were dissolved, and new ones created in their place at the stroke of a pen. Impressed by the happenings, Francis II abdicated from the throne of the Holy Roman Empire in 1806, mainly in order to adjust to the new realities. After bringing all the Habsburg territory together under the name "The Austrian Empire," he called himself from then on the "Emperor of Austria" and "King of Bohemia and Hungary."

At that time, this multinational state, later fourteen nations with a population of over 53 million, ventured upon an amazing test of strength. Austria became the head of the coalition against the Corsican, and at Aspern in 1809 defeated his army, which had never been beaten in open combat before. Hence, she served as a fine example for the peoples to follow, kindling their will to fight their way to independence. These years, from about 1800 to 1814, were deemed Austria's "heroic age" in Imperially biassed literature. We, today, look back more soberly, but are forced to recognize that this land which had been bled to exhaustion had a back-breaking burden to bear. Although the Wars of Liberation brought about the downfall of Napoleon, at the same time they cemented Metternich's policy; the old conditions continued unchanged for many years, as did the Holy Alliance. In the long run, this was bound to cause difficulties, for the spirit of the Enlightenment and of the French Revolution had lived on in the nations throughout the Napoleonic era, and now these sentiments were augmented by fervent national ideas.

In Austria, it was a period in which any political activity whatsoever appeared suspicious or even illegal; and people thus retreated to the fields of domesticity and the arts. This is the Biedermeier epoch, a time when the Viennese Waltz was casting its spell, when the public was charmed by Raimund's fantasies and Nestroy's influence had begun to be felt in the theatres of the capital. Painters of the Romantic were discovering Old Vienna and environs, and enthusiastic artists were able to imbue others with their passion for the glory of the Alps. The origins of today's tourist trade, specifically in the Salzkammergut, in Salzburg and Tyrol, can be traced back to these early travels through the mountains. The fact that such giants of music as Franz Schubert or even Ludwig van Beethoven are sometimes identified with the Biedermeier era merely because they lived during this period rests upon a somewhat superficial view of things; nor does Franz Grillparzer fit in here, despite his random literary expressions of loyalty to the Metternich policies.

But there is a strange divergence from, or a paradox to, the still common concept of this "race that moves to dance and music." During the same Biedermeier era of pleasant hominess, other Austrians were quietly opening new vistas of technical innovation. A man named Ressel invented the ship's propeller; Madersperger discovered the marvel of the "Sewing Hand," and with that the principle of the sewing-machine; shortly afterwards, Mitterhofer modestly carried his version of the first typewriter from South Tyrol to Vienna - a journey lasting several days - only to receive a mere 200 florins, and later another 150, as a consolation prize.

It was an Austrian who designed the original steam-engine in the distant vastness of Russia; and Karl von Ghega headed the line of great Austrian railway engineers by making it possible for trains to push their way over the Semmering mountain pass for the first time.

The list of Austrian inventors who themselves "never hit the headlines," but whose ideas made others rich, is almost endless. A prime example of this strange side of the Austrian mentality is the engineer and aulic councillor, Otto Nussbaumer (1876-1930), who in 1904 at the Graz Technical College succeeded in giving the world its first wireless transmission of music. Siemens, the international firm, wrote to him regarding the possible exploitation of his invention, but he never even answered. Then, long after radio had marched triumphant into people's lives, and others had made their fortunes from it, friends one day asked him whether he did not regret his attitude, to which he replied, "I only wanted to see if it worked, and it did!"

During the Biedermeier era, the flames of nationalism rose increasingly higher amongst the various peoples in the Austrian Empire, and the Revolution of 1848 added fuel to the fire. From then on, the spark of discontent was never to be extinguished until the dissolution of the monarchy. Nestroy, usually looked upon solely as a spirited joker, once wrote:

The people's excessive nationalistic pride is coquettish: each race believes itself to be the pace-setter, and other

When the 23-year-old Maria Theresa was crowned Empress in 1740, there was considerable unrest in the country, and the Empire was on the verge of breaking up. The sovereign showed remarkable courage, tenacity and political skill, not least in her dealings with the arch-enemy Frederick II of Prussia. She gave birth to 16 children, and her actions were always dominated by her heart, her motto being, "A mediocre peace is better than a glorious war."

On the Marchfeld, Archduke Charles succeeded in defeating Napoleon for the first time, in May 1809. He thus set an example for others to join Austria in shaking off the Corsican's yoke. That inspiration must, in a way, have also been felt by Peter Krafft, a young contemporary of the battle, whose Classicist painting (now hung in the Vienna Museum of Army History) reflects both the glory and the devastation of War; for the Austrian victory, though spectacular, had also been a costly one.

races just the followers; in the same way, each human being only calls every other man a follower because he considers himself to be setting the pace...

The peoples of the Empire now strove with all their might to be rid of the "chains of monarchy." Only later did they realize that with the Danubian Monarchy a large economic unit of world-wide political importance and a dynamic force in its own right had been destroyed. Of course, one should not overlook the fact that the age of such dynastic regimes was simply over. It is, however, also a fact that the old Danubian Monarchy had permitted a secure life and political elbow-room to all its peoples through a currency which remained stable for decades - a situation the "liberated" were afterwards incapable of achieving for themselves.

The Revolution of 1848 succeeded, for the time being, in doing away with the obsolete Metternich System, which had existed for over thirty years: the "Coachman of Europe," who had held the reins of European politics for so long, had to flee the coun-

try into exile in Britain, but was allowed to return unharmed some years later. For the beginning, however, the proposals of the youngest parliamentary member, 25-year-old Hans Kudlich, were accepted under the impulse of initial enthusiasm: the peasant population in the Empire was freed from the quasi-medieval system of landlordism through the so-called Land Release. For a good many millions of people this meant a great upheaval of their entire former social relationship and economic circumstances.

Numerous other attempts and initiatives towards changing public life were apparent in these twin years of unrest, 1848-49; but then Emperor Francis Joseph, who had just taken the throne at the age of eighteen, once more fell back upon the old strict tenets of Absolute Rule. The Revolution was halted, and active participants were severely punished.

Only after fifteen years, under pressure of grave foreign political affairs, did a fundamental change come about, introduced by the "Fratricidal War" of 1866. In the north, Prussia had once again gained

The barricades in the Michaelerplatz during the night of 26-27 May 1848, painted by J. Ziegler (Museums of the City of Vienna).

power. More and more urgently the question was being raised who should take the lead in the German Confederation, which in any case was no more than a loose association of states, founded after the German Empire had been dissolved during Napoleonic times. Bismarck pressed for a "strictly German" solution, with Prussia as a leader - a solution which completely excluded multinational Austria.

During the War of 1866, even though the Austrians were generally successful on land, and particularly at sea, under Admiral Tegetthoff (as for example in a naval engagement off Lissa Island against the Italians, who were allied with the Prussians), hopes of an overall victory were dashed on the northern front, at Königgrätz (Sadowa), in Bohemia. As a result, Austria was forced to withdraw from the German Confederation, and thus proceeded to dedicate her attention more fully to Balkan politics, a new orientation which was destined to lead to world war fifty years later.

Pressured by defeat and general discontent, the Emperor had to concede substantial reforms and constitutional amendment. In particular, the Hungarian half of the Empire was granted more latitude by this policy.

Modern social and educational laws were passed, and the Imperial Primary School Act of 1869 took Austria to the forefront of European education. Austria-Hungary, as the Monarchy was from now on called, trod its own path, but was a military ally of the Second German Empire, which had come into being in 1870-71.

However, the brotherhood-in-arms during the First World War was not simply the result of treaties, but also rested on the feeling of interdependence shared by the German-speaking peoples. The War was lost, and a 53-million-strong Empire disintegrated into the Succession States.

"Austria - that's what's left over," said the French statesman Georges Clemenceau during the peace negotiations at Saint-Germain. By "left-over" he meant the new small republic with about six million inhabitants, from which South Tyrol, Southern Styria, parts both of Southern Carinthia and Lower Austria had been excluded; by way of compensation, only a meagre slice of what had been Western Hungary was allotted, and this became Burgenland. For geographical and historical reasons, the new state system was quite unskilfully designed by the victors' wishes; and it was only due to the dogged determination to survive that Austria could assert itself at all during the wretched post-war years, possibly because her people, let us face it, are less "brisk and rigid" than persevering.

So the country overcame this extremely difficult period; the monetary system, disrupted by heavy inflation, was reorganized by Federal Chancellor Ignaz Seipel, between 1922 and 1924. But in the thirties, like so many other states, Austria was drawn into the fatal downward spiral of world-wide depression. The consequences were strong political tensions as well as ideological and economic struggles on the homefront. This country, "wanted by nobody," appeared too bourgeois-conservative to some, too suspiciously socialist to others, and not nationalistic enough to the rest. Thus the temporary affinity for Germany which followed seemed to fulfil many desires and aims of past centuries. Such leanings must be understood in the light of the history just shown and, above all, of the external and internal plight of the First Republic. In this respect, there is nothing to be excused or kept secret, at least not by those who lived through the times and are striving to retain an objective viewpoint.

The pressure from the German Reich, now a National-Socialist country, increased during the years 1933-38, the more so as its following grew within Austria's own borders, spurred on by disastrous economic conditions. The Austrian government tried to face the danger along authoritarian lines by establishing a "Christian Corporative State"; again, this met with rejection from left and right. After several years of development things came to a head, and the problem was solved from outside: German troops invaded, and Austria was annexed to "Greater Germany." It was this event which, but one year later, embroiled Austria in the inferno of the Second World War.

The War was lost. Austria suffered heavy losses of population, and endured destruction of all kinds. The country was occupied by four powers. (The Russian Zone of Occupation comprised Lower Austria, Burgenland, and the northern part of Upper Austria, the Mühlviertel; the British Zone was Carinthia and Styria; the French, Tyrol and Vorarlberg; and the American Zone Salzburg and Upper Austria, excluding the Mühlviertel.) All four powers occupied Vienna, each having control of certain districts, and all represented in the First District.

Again, post-war reconstruction proved most difficult, but it also showed what enormous inner strength could be drawn from this country and its people. Though UNRRA and the Marshall Plan both offered valuable support, in the main it was the Austrians themselves who, in spite of severely limited possibilities, brought about achievements that would have done full credit to any large state. Excellent statesmen made the country's rise from the depths of despair possible. The Austrian Treaty of 1955 at long last enabled the country to resume the course of time-honoured Austrian diplomacy. The occupying powers duly left, and with the acceptance of the concept of "permanent neutrality" Austria gained international status and goodwill, which has since been confirmed in many ways.

Vienna, Salzburg, and other cities have repeatedly been the meeting-places of statesmen of the World Powers during critical situations in sundry areas on the globe; important positions in international associations have been held by Austrians. The voice of this small country is well received all over the world. Completely new and most positive developments evolved after 1945, especially in economics. Austria built up her industries on an unprecedented scale; major branches of trade and manufacture were nationalized, and tourism flourished as never before. It was finally possible to build the many highways whose designs had often been on the drawing-board for dozens of years; important power-stations were erected; and on a cultural level, especially that of music and dramatic art, Austria picked up the pieces of her old traditions and triumphs to bring about new successes.

The sketchy outlines for a unification of all European countries are becoming more and more distinct. Some states soon became aware of the drawbacks of isolation, chiefly in the field of economy, and at first joined the Organization for Economic Cooperation and Development (OECD); Austria, in fact, has been a member from its inception, 1948. In 1959 several states, among them this country, combined to form the European Free Trade Association (EFTA), by way of counterbalancing the European Community (EC). On 1 January 1995, Austria became a member of the European Union (EU), and as such enjoys equal rights in all the committee work, looking after her interests, and actively aligning her future, on that European platform.

Let us, at this point, close our short summary of the history of Austria, and quote from a poet who more than a century ago foresaw the position Austria was to retain in spite of all the winds of change:

> *A small world though, yet Austria proves best*
> *As touchstone for the big world put to test;*
> *If her internal scales are poised and light,*
> *'Twill follow that the rest is balanced right.*
>
> Friedrich Hebbel

Burgenland

The Austrian Burgenland is a bit of a puzzle. Besides being the youngest province in the Republic of Austria, it also causes every visitor to raise the question of why exactly it should be called "Burgenland." The most common explanation points to the great number of castles in the area. This is a misleading idea, however, for the name in fact originated from the expression *Vierburgenland*, the land of four boroughs, a reference to the four districts, or comitats, under Hungarian control: Press*burg*, Wiesel*burg*, Öden*burg*, and Eisen*burg*. After the First World War, Pressburg was allotted to the newly created Czechoslovakian Republic and re-christened "Bratislava," while Ödenburg (or Sopron) stayed with Hungary: the remaining territory became then simply known by the name of "Burgenland."

the Alpine foothills dipping down to the Pannonian Plain, is one of the oldest centres of prehistoric settlement on the entire Continent. Archaeological discoveries have established that modern Burgenland was already colonized in the Stone Age at a time when the first settlers were striving to cultivate the land around Lake Neusiedl, a large and yet fairly shallow lake well-known throughout Europe. These prehistoric farmers left scattered evidence of a difficult struggle behind. Excavations of neolithic longhouses at Neckenmarkt, in central Burgenland, give proof of this. Drassburg is regarded by experts as the most important archaeological site, widely known through the discovery of a figurine, the so-called Venus of Drassburg. Today this familiar fertility symbol is considered to be one of the most outstand-

Austrian troops entering Burgenland in 1921, after the territory was given to the new Republic under the Treaty of Saint-Germain.

The country possesses a wealth of history, although at first glance it might not seem so at all to the casual visitor. Let us begin with the most recent past. The right of self-determination was demanded and won by the German population in Western Hungary under the Peace Treaty of Saint-Germain-en-Laye after the First World War. In 1921, this area was duly passed on to the Republic of Austria without a plebiscite. Burgenland, which extends across

ing exhibits of the Burgenland Museum. Despite her many rivals in the history of art and archaeology, this Venus remains the second oldest sculpture of a woman found by Austrian archaeologists up to the present (cp. p. 66). In addition, cult objects dating back to the Hallstatt Period were unearthed in the vicinity of Donnerskirchen and Loretto, while astonished scientists brought to light an entire Celtic settlement near Sauerbrunn.

The Celts were forced out by the Romans, in Burgenland as elsewhere in Europe; and the new rulers, in the years when Christ was born, began to erect their province of Pannonia, with the Danube then for centuries forming a natural border to the north as well as to the east. This area was unusually fertile and, even before the Romans came, had proved itself to be an important political and military factor; trade connections also appear to have had more than merely local dimensions. For it would be mistaken to imagine these prehistoric people as uncivilized hordes, living at an existential minimum in complete isolation from the rest of the world. As early as the later Old Stone Age, the tribes had established trade routes over which amber, obsidian, lapis lazuli and, later on, rare metals such as tin were transported. One such major route, the "Amber Road," cut across present-day Burgenland, leading westwards past Lake Neusiedl and on to the Adriatic.

When the Romans incorporated this important region into their empire in 11 B.C., they not only extended the network of roads but also introduced the cultivation of wine, fruit and vegetables. They set up craft centres as well as schools. The settlements of Carnuntum (Petronell) as well as of Julia Scarbantia and Claudia Savaria, now known as Ödenburg (Sopron) and Steinamanger (Szombathely), attained the status of Roman towns. Excavations at these sites show that the Romans, however far from the capital, nevertheless decorated their temples and villas with statues and reliefs. Many works of art perished during the Great Migration of the Peoples, although some were buried by layers of earth that kept them intact, to be brought to light centuries later. One example is the so-called Emperor's Villa at Bruckneudorf with its mosaic floors, which are rightly considered among the highest in quality, and best preserved, north of the Alps. Such works of art show that the Romans created a culture to which the world is still indebted today.

History never rests. As a well-known Greek philosopher says, "Everything is in a state of flux." Consequently the Romans, too, did not remain untouched by tumultuous events. The uprisings of the Marcomanni and Quadi as early as the second century A.D. were indicative of the growing unrest amongst the tribes beyond the *limes*, as the Romans called their defensive frontier against the "barbarians." At that time, however, Rome was still strong enough to ward off invasions of its territories south of where the Danube happened to form the *limes*. Only after her empire was undermined by civil wars and internal strife did the protective wall in the far north fail to guarantee security. In short, the Romans were

Avaric belt-clasp, cast bronze with gold-plating and griffin design. Discovered at Podersdorf, on the eastern shore of Lake Neusiedl.

thus at the mercy of those bellicose neighbours they had so long and unjustly held in contempt.

The Migration of the Peoples, then, was a period of tempestuous unrest which dealt a death blow to the Roman Empire. This period counts as one of the darkest in European history. What took place after the retreat of the Roman occupation forces is open to speculation. We only know that in the more than three centuries of the Great Migration, one tribe after the other, Teutons, Slavs, Huns, Goths, Langobardi (Lombards), and Avars, crossed through the former Roman provinces. When the Battle of the Catalaunian Plains put a halt to the Huns' advance into Europe in 451, the Gepidae and Langobardi took over the Carpathian Basin and the erstwhile province of Pannonia. When the Avars pushed on into Europe from the steppes of Asia, they defeated the Gepidae in 567, whereupon the Langobardi withdrew to Northern Italy and founded a new state there. The Avars, a diminutive, yellow-skinned people, soon ruled over the countries along the central reaches of the Danube. As there is a dearth of more extensive written records, much of the research into the life and culture of this tribe must depend on the analysis of archaeological excavations. Only recently, chance has led to remarkable discoveries: the rich burial grounds at Mödling in Lower Austria, and the Burgenland finds around Zillingtal, Leithaprodersdorf and Gross-Höflein. Archaeologists have unearthed exquisite gold jewellery; for not only do all children of nature delight in personal ornament, they also regard it as a talisman to protect them against evil demons. Of course, a great deal of material was also found which provided scholarship with concrete information on the burial rites of this far-travelled race. The Avars laid their dead warriors to rest in complete armour; and chieftains were even buried together with their war-horses, in addition to the usual grave-furnishings. Such evidence proves that the conventional picture of the Avars as a "marauding pack of barbarians" can no longer be accepted as entirely valid. Historians later filled whole libraries with books about these combat-loving horsemen, who eventually had to make way for a stronger tribe - as is the law of history. Towards the end of the eighth century Charlemagne conducted three campaigns against the Avars, all of which brought him victory. From 803 onwards, the Franks began with a systematic colonization of Pannonia. The newly acquired Eastern March of the Franks and Bajuwari was soon to become a reservoir of western culture and Christianity. Even the reins of government and the administration of the Realm rested in the hands of the Imperial Bishops. Today we must take into account the fact that the Church at that time represented the true political and social power, and its activities pervaded all aspects of public life.

Yet even the special protection of the German Emperor could not guarantee a lasting peace for the Eastern March; once more the terrible memories of the invasions of the Huns and Avars were evoked in the Occident. The Magyars had broken away from the steppes of the Ukraine and advanced westwards in sweeping raids. Historians of the time describe these savage horsemen with nothing but raging indignation; they regarded them as descendants of the Huns, spawn of the Devil, more bloodthirsty than a pack of wolves.

For a long time, the whole of Europe was floundering for a proper defence against the apocalyptic scourge of the Magyars, who burnt many settlements to the ground and indeed depopulated entire regions. Moreover, the German Emperor was forced to pay tribute to the Magyar people, until in 955 Otto I's glorious victory on the Lechfeld (south of Augsburg) finally put an end to the warring and raiding of these barbarians of the steppes. At long last, the Hungarians bowed to the influence of the Christian western world. They gave up their nomadic life and, what is more important, their highest military leader, who later became King Stephen I, won safety and recognition for the new Kingdom of Hungary, especially by his conversion to Catholicism. Stephen refused to be crowned by the German Emperor and received both title and throne from the hands of Pope Sylvester II - a fact which might well be understood in the light of the fierce desire for independence on the part of the Magyar tribes: the kingdom was thus subject to no worldly power, but only to the Pope as spiritual guardian of the entire Christian world. Stephen's crown was destined to become a symbol of freedom for the state of Hungary.

King Stephen, canonized at the end of the following century, spared no effort to be in political control and to encourage the economic development of his country. He invited foreign colonists to come in, a varied lot from all walks of life - noble knights, missionaries, handicraftsmen, and peasants. These "hospites" were granted certain privileges and enjoyed the protection of the monarch, a good many among the nobility indeed receiving from the Hungarian kings vast tracts of land as gifts in Western Hungary. Such title deeds, in fact, initiated the growth of extensive manors throughout Western Hungary and the Burgenland. However, Fortune's wheel was bound to turn. The danger of an invasion from the East was brewing. Around 1241, bands of Mongolian raiders broke into the densely populated area around Lake Neusiedl and ravaged the countryside. The invaders made havoc of what farmers had laboured for decades to achieve.

But then came the Turks. They surged into Central Europe, where their attacks led them to the Vienna Basin, and in 1529 right to the foot of the walls of the Imperial capital. Stories of their atrocities swept before them. Wherever in fact the attacking hordes appeared, destruction was left behind - trampled fields, charred ruins, devastated villages, churches and bridges, some of which would never be restored. No power on earth could check the Turks; they smashed all opposition.

Countless stories of Turkish savagery, murder and arson tell the sad tale of the sorely tried population. Even today many chapels, wayside shrines and crosses are traditionally said to have been erected in gratitude for God's protection from the Turkish menace. Nearly every community in Burgenland has some building or landmark to commemorate the Turkish encounter.

Still more than a hundred years were to pass before the Ottomans suffered a major setback. Once again Burgenland was the scene of murderous conflict. On 1 August 1664, a battle took place near Mogersdorf in which the united Christian armies and the Ottoman troops were pitted against each other. Today, a white cross with an inscription marks the site of the decisive victory of the Christians under the command of the Imperial Generalissimo Montecuccoli:

To heroes valiant one and all
Who in 1664 did fall
They bravely forced the Turkish hand
For God, for Emperor and Fatherland.

Rauscher Lajos 1881

The most distinctive feature of St. Stephen's Crown, worn by the kings of Hungary since the thirteenth century, is its slanting cross. King Charles IV (in Austria, however, Emperor Charles I) was the last ruler to be crowned with it. In 1945, after the turmoil of the Second World War, it passed into the hands of the United States, and was returned by Mr Carter, its then President, to Hungary in 1978 (National Museum, Budapest).

In 1683, Kara Mustafa, the Turkish Grand Vizier, laid siege to Vienna with some 200,000 troops. His mission proved abortive, and he was garrotted by order of Sultan Mahomet IV in December of that year.

Again, barely two decades later, fire-scarred farms and devastated villages lined the route which Kara Mustafa's hordes had taken on their way to Vienna, Hanns Tschany's *Hungarian Chronicle, from 1670 to 1704* gives a detailed account of the events of the year 1683: "Everywhere people are fleeing. They have either taken their possessions with them, or left them buried in the ground or walled up in niches. But most of it falls into the hands of the Turks. Exile, slavery, and death threaten the remaining population. Entire villages are going up in flame.... Only Ödenburg, Eisenstadt, Rust, Donnerskirchen, and Mörbisch have escaped the worst by buying Turkish protection and paying homage to Thököly, the ringleader of the Hungarian rebels allied with the Turks."

As is well known, the defenders of Vienna were able to ward off the deadly assault as before. Then, in 1697, the Turks suffered their heaviest defeat at Zenta and were forced to relinquish the Hungarian territories. One to gain special distinction in those campaigns of the Empire against the archenemy was Prince Eugene of Savoy.

Soon, however, the West Hungarian farmers had to fear for their lives again when the *Kuruzzen* began their incursions in 1704. These were bands of insurgents whose name was a corruption of the German word *Kreuz(fahrer)*, suggesting their religious rancour towards the Habsburgs, against whom they felt called upon to "crusade." They reduced to naught everything that had so carefully been built up in the intervening years. ("Kruzitürken!", a swear-word blend reminiscent of those two causes of multiple misery may well continue to be heard sometimes from the lips of an indignant Burgenlander, or East Austrian, to this very day.)

Under such adverse circumstances, it seems almost a wonder that Burgenland should have been able to develop its own folklore and culture - one amply authenticated by the stupendous collections of the Provincial Museum as well as by the continuity of living tradition.

Due to its hereditary rôle as an embattled border province, cultural centres of life did not evolve until relatively late. As a result, the oldest witnesses to the past are not towns, monasteries and churches, but fortifications. From the twelfth century onwards, one castle after another was built in the mountainous country to the south, forming a mighty ring of defence against the East. Possibly the most formidable stronghold, the castle of Landsee, stood amidst the surrounding hills; once dubbed "The Honour of the Land," it still counts as one of the largest in Central Europe. Similarly important border posts were Schlaining and Güssing Castles, the latter recorded for the first time in a document of the twelfth century. The magnificently preserved Bernstein Castle was surrounded by powerful bastions in the Italian manner during the Renaissance period. Today it is a well-appointed hotel; and with a little help from their imagination, guests might even make the acquaintance of a genuine ghost of the castle. According to rumour, at midnight "Red Ivan," a red-headed knight in full armour, is said to have often frightened inquisitive visitors with evil peals of mocking laughter.

Schlaining Castle, one of the mightiest strongholds in Burgenland.

Probably the most famous castle, and certainly one of the most beautiful in the province, is Forchtenstein, an imposing defence of bastions, ramparts, casemates, and a moat, whose foundations date back to the end of the thirteenth century. However, there were several alterations in the course of time, the last by order of the Esterházys, who had Turkish prisoners drill the famous castle well through 465 feet of sheer rock.

Countess Elizabeth Báthory-Nádasdy, one of the most cold-blooded psychotic murderesses in world history who, on the strength of her own records, tortured to death some 650 young girls.

Like Forchtenstein, Lockenhaus was also doubtless a centre of courtly medieval life. But the Castle Chronicles record little of minstrelsy and knightly tournaments; instead, they present an account of unparalleled horror. Even today the name of the lady of the castle, Elizabeth Báthory-Nádasdy, is enough to make the human mind cringe at the depths to which inhuman depravity can descend. Although to outward appearances a dark beauty of almost delicate build, she was nevertheless one of the cruellest psychotic murderesses in history, who by her own testimony brutally slaughtered some 650 young girls.

When Báthory was eventually brought to trial in 1610, perversions of unimaginable savagery came to light. "The Countess of Blood" used to begin her amusements by pressing red-hot keys or coins on the palms of her victims' hands, and she often seared their faces with smoothing-irons. To avoid attracting attention, she had the poor wretches' mouths sewn shut. For there had almost been a scandal when Báthory pursued her lethal pastimes even in her Vienna town house, and the monks of a near-by monastery were nightly jolted out of their sleep by the piteous screams of the tortured girls.

However, only the henchmen were sentenced to die at the stake, a fate probably well deserved. Elizabeth Báthory, by virtue of her station in life, was automatically spared interrogation by torture, and was merely sentenced to exile. There is no indication that she even showed repentance for her crimes.

Indeed, the Baroness is not the only member of the Nádasdy family whose name sullied the Lockenhaus Chronicles with blood. Her grandson, Francis III Nádasdy, became involved in the Magnates' Plot of 1666 against Emperor Leopold of Austria and, in 1671, the conspirator was duly beheaded in Vienna. His body was laid to rest in a sumptuous marble sarcophagus in the crypt of the Augustinian Church at Lockenhaus.

Small wonder that up to the present no writer of travel accounts has been able to by-pass Lockenhaus Castle. As early as the Biedermeier period, that great epoch in romantic folklore, Franz Seraph Weidmann devoted a particularly "spicy" chapter to the site in his book about Burgenland. He described the fortress as "a chaos of passages, chambers, and halls amidst the colossal debris of walls and towers." What would such a castle be without its own ghost? At least the lingering memory of gory ancient crimes should cling to the ruined walls.

Eisenstadt - once called Castrum Ferreum

The first documentary evidence of a local castle dates back to 1118. At this time, according to Bishop Otto of Freising, a noted historian, the Babenberg Margrave Leopold III destroyed a *castrum quod ferreum vocatur*, 'a castle called the iron one.' While the *castrum ferreum* may quite possibly have stood on the site of the present palace, it was by no stretch of the imagination the type of late medieval castle familiar from picture-books; on the contrary, it was little more than a minor fortification, a modest defence post. The founder of this "iron defence" is said to have been none other than Prince Giletus, claimed by the Esterházys as the mythical ancestor of their dynasty.

The Palace as we now see it, however, was actually built at the command of Prince Paul Esterházy. Under his rule, the medieval fortress was completely rebuilt and richly furnished. The commission was given to no less a man than Carlo Martino Carlone, the master builder from Como in Lombardy. Also his assistants, Sebastiano Bartoletti and Antonio Carlone, did their utmost, and the prince's suite and reception halls were soon resplendent in full Baroque glory. The façade of the new Esterházy Palace, now painted the uniform yellow colour introduced by Empress Maria Theresa, once gleamed in blue, pink, and white. The stucco design is the workmanship of Andrea Bertinelli, a North Italian master. The grotesque stucco masks grimacing beneath the ledge of the main façade soon gave rise to the popular view that they were caricatures of over-zealous court officials who, during the absence of their Lord, withheld the hard-earned wages of the stucco workers. The cheated craftsmen supposedly immortalized all these officials under the cornice for revenge.

As in all noble residences of the Baroque period, the Eisenstadt palace grounds represent a remarkable example of historical landscape gardening. When Maria Theresa once honoured the town with a visit, Prince Nicholas wanted to give the high-born lady a sleigh-ride right in the middle of summer. The magnificent setting really was transformed into a winter scene in the middle of July for the Archduchess of Austria: some resourceful theatre property-man had conceived the brilliant idea of "icing" the park with salt.

"I can do anything the Emperor can do," was the motto of Prince Nicholas I Esterházy, also known by

The Gothic Main Hall in Lockenhaus Castle, one of the oldest and historic-ally most interest-ing fortresses of this province.

An old view of Eisenstadt, a copper engraving from Braun's *Beschreybung der vornehmbsten Welt,* Vol. 6 (1616): Eisenstadt was then a well-fortified bor-der town, complete with moat and wall and battlements, prepared to brave the gathering storms from the East.

The imposing Esterházy Palace in Eisenstadt, especially during the eighteenth century, was the congenial setting for that princely dynasty to hold court; in it, Joseph Haydn, the famous composer, played a signal rôle.

The Haydn Concert Hall, the main attraction for visitors to Esterházy Palace, continues to offer the proper ambience for major cultural events to this day.

the epithet "the Splendour-bearing." He had a reputation throughout the Empire for entertaining on a lavish scale, both at Eisenstadt and at Esterháza Castle, the "Hungarian Versailles" off the southeastern end of Lake Neusiedl. And indeed, life at the court of Eisenstadt differed little from that of a world metropolis. There was one party after another; coteries of artists were in permanent residence; and opera, theatre and marionette performances were the order of the day. His Serene Highness even had his own House Orchestra, whose most famous conductor was Joseph Haydn. Eisenstadt owes its reputation as the "town of music" to the immortal work of this master, who was active here from 1761 to 1790. Haydn was a passionate and effusive artist, and the Baroque period loved music, movement and drama as well as the inexhaustible means of expression found in the fine arts.

The Church, the aristocracy, and the upper middle class were patrons of the arts, and also placed value on outward ostentation. Thus, it is entirely justified to call Eisenstadt a "lesser Salzburg." The face of this Baroque town, with its warm and sunny character, has changed little down to the present day.

It is one of the few Austrian towns to emerge virtually unscathed from the Second World War; it has even been spared the ugly excesses of modern construction in recent decades. That is the reason why Eisenstadt has remained something quite unique - a town rich in history, art and architecture, and in piety and the joy of living.

Lowly Villages and Lordly Manors

Not only do the towns of Burgenland abound in many valuable cultural monuments; but also smaller places, brightly scattered over the countryside, have managed to retain their own character in spite of time. The drowsy villages with their whitewashed farm dwellings seem to lie dormant in a spell of enchantment, caught between the vineyards. Their churches are usually surrounded by a stone wall with a picturesque gateway. In accordance with an unwritten law, a column dedicated to the Virgin Mary is to be found in the immediate vicinity. A castle or manor, naturally dominating the scene, stands on a rise above the settlement or amid a fluvial plain. Fortified places like Kobersdorf, Deutschkreutz, Potzneusiedl, Gattendorf, and Kittsee tell the story of the ancient feudal grandeur of Hungarian dynasties.

One of the most beautiful is Halbturn, a Baroque hunting-lodge built at the beginning of the eighteenth century from the plans of Lukas von Hildebrandt, the famous architect. A fire, which broke out in 1949, spared only the central section with its renowned ceiling fresco. This painting is one of the masterpieces of Franz Anton Maulbertsch and depicts the glorification of the Sun-God as the Bearer of Spring. Today Halbturn Castle provides an appropriate setting for province-wide exhibitions that are known to be excellently organized.

No less than the charming villages with their sloping vineyards drenched by the sun, Lake Neusiedl and its environs has few rivals for its scenic beauty and fascination. The countryside around this most westerly European lake of the steppes is a wildlife sanctuary, and largely part of the Lake Neusiedl National Park which also reaches out onto Hungarian territory. Some 250 species of birds inhabit the marshland which, with its primitive flora, stretches for miles. The great white heron, the scooper, and the spoonbill are among those best known.

Here the wide open spaces and untouched character of the land provide the visitor with a foretaste of the steppes further east - a memorable experience for every lover of nature. No words can describe the severe charm of the local *Puszta* scenery.

Halbturn Castle, designed by Lukas von Hildebrandt, ranks as the most notable example of Baroque secular architecture in Burgenland, and indeed as one of the finest of its kind throughout Austria. Its historic function was that of a hunting-lodge, with Emperor Charles VI as a regular guest.

A reed-covered cottage of Illmitz, a farming and fishing village first documented as early as 1217.

From time immemorial these people have sensed the singularity of their way of life. Their closeness to nature has made them prone to imbue plants, animals, and even the entire universe, with qualities both human and demonic, and to interpret the unexplainable in terms of the fantastic. Therefore, it seems only natural that the origin of Lake Neusiedl has been embellished with a legend. In the Seewinkel area to this day, the story can be heard that there

ried, and the deceived wife plotted revenge. In the end, the Princess of Forchtenstein managed to have the girl and her match-making mother drowned in the village pond. But lo and behold! The water rose higher and higher until the whole area was flooded. The Prince was, of course, inconsolable and had the famous pilgrimage church of Frauenkirchen built in atonement for the murder. Only then did the waters recede, to form what is now Lake Neusiedl.

Lake Neusiedl is subject to considerable fluctuations of its water mark and has, in fact, several times completely dried up.

was a fertile valley centuries ago in the place where the lake now lies. Prince Giletus of Forchtenstein once became lost here; this popular and well-known legendary figure was adopted by the as yet relatively young Esterházy family, to give themselves the appearance of ancient and noble descent. According to the folktale, Prince Giletus fell in love in the Maiden Valley with an angelic young beauty called Mary. Unfortunately, the Prince was already mar-

Nothing is known about the historical origin of Frauenkirchen. The first document in which the name *Zenmaria* (short for 'At [Our Lady] Mary's') is mentioned, dates back to 1324. As in the great majority of popular fables, there is a grain of truth here, too, for there were periods when the lake virtually disappeared, only to refill after some time. Thus the legend woven around the origin of Frauenkirchen must surely be regarded as an attempt to

interpret such inexplicable phenomena. As a matter of fact, settlements really did form repeatedly on the bottom of the lake during long dry spells; these, of course, had to be abandoned when the ground water began to rise again.

The mystery of the water-level of this lake of the steppes has not only captivated the story-tellers; to the present day, science continues to search for a definitive explanation. The surface tributaries of Lake Neusiedl can in no way compensate for the amount of water lost through normal evaporation. The people have cudgelled their brains and come up with their own explanation for the phenomenon: "Lake Neusiedl must surely be connected to the Danube by an underground river." This belief is reflected in the story of "The Cooper's Mallet," which is told in many versions throughout Burgenland, and which basically goes like this:

Once upon a time a young cooper from Neusiedl set off on his travels. He journeyed far and wide in the world, and in Regensburg at last he boarded a ship which was to take him back home. At first the trip was uneventful, but at Grein one of the dreaded Danube whirlpools seized the ship and sucked it down into the deep. Although the cooper was able to save his life at the last moment, his knapsack and mallet were engulfed by the raging current. Grateful to escape with his life, the journeyman returned to his native village and set himself up as a master-cooper there. One day, long after he had forgotten his shipwreck, while walking round Lake Neusiedl, he noticed an odd bulgy object floating in the water. He pulled it on land and was astounded to find that he was holding his old knapsack in his hands after so many years.

Some such variant of the legend, incidentally, must have reached the ears of a British party negotiating those dangerous whirlpools of the Danube, back in the year 1664. Its chronicler, John Burbury, records that the river "runs most impetuously, and the water whirles about so in several places, as if through some Tunnel it emptied it self into a Gulph." We are then told about "the Watermen," assuring their no doubt awe-stricken listeners, "that part of the Danube ran there under ground, disburthening it self afterwards in Hungary, where it made a great Lake, and this was confirmed, they said, by sinking a great Pole, with a proportionable weight fastened to it, which was afterwards found again in the Lake aforesaid."

Strangely enough, the results of recent scientific research appear to confirm such superstitions by and large. For a great amount of ground water flows into the lake from the north, above all from the gravel

area on the east bank; and even the bottom of the lake emits water as well, some of it with a high mineral content.

Burgenland has a wealth of such tales, both mythical and supernatural and we encounter colourful folklore wherever we go. Some time-honoured customs not only testify to the remembrance of traditional sacrifices made by our ancestors long ago to fierce water-demons, but also give us a clue to the mythical significance of pagan water-spirits. Even today, at Illmitz, the "Old Man," an ornamental cake made in a human shape, is served on Christmas Eve. In a festive dinner ceremony, the head of the "Old Man" is cut off and thrown into the house well as a token of a human sacrifice to appease the well-spirits. The moorland farmers east of Lake Neusiedl practise a very similar custom; here, tradition demands that a christening party passing over a bridge throw a loaf of bread into the water, to secure the favour of the spirits below for the newly born.

The Healing Powers of Nature

But Burgenland is not only enticing for its idyllic small towns, sleepy villages, and beautiful lakes for boating and swimming: this delightful countryside can also be a definite health benefit, with its numerous medicinal spas.

The "Old Man," an ornamental loaf of bread baked for special occasions.

Bad Tatzmannsdorf, for instance, can look back on many thousands of years of history. The healing powers of its springs were indeed known in the Bronze Age. Its planned development did not take place until the seventeenth century, but quite soon Tatzmannsdorf enjoyed a reputation similar to that of Franzensbad in Czechia. Millions of patients were cured of vascular diseases here, or went back home with considerable improvement in their conditions.

As in Tatzmannsdorf, a busy social life grew up around the acidulous mineral springs of Jormannsdorf, Oberschützen, and Kobersdorf. Hungarian, Styrian, and Austrian nobility once gathered here to take the waters. Güssing is equally endowed with recognized health springs, and "Paul's Spring" at Sauerbrunn was known even before Roman times and is highly recommended for bladder and kidney complaints.

A Toast to the Local Wine

However, many guests who come to drink the waters in Burgenland come not so much because of the healing powers of the acidulous springs, but in search of the pleasant little wine-vaults where they can refresh themselves with a drop of something delicious. Anyone who has paid a visit to the rathskeller at Rust will gladly bear out the truth of the inscription over the archway, "I do feel fine/When full of wine." And even the Privy Councillor Goethe appreciated the quality of choice Rust vintages, of which it is rumoured, probably not without reason,

> *A surfeit of such wine goes to the head,*
> *Which two full days feels like a lump of lead.*

This Burgenland speciality is as valuable as the dried-berry wine gathered from choicest grapes. The world would certainly be a poorer place without this tasty fruit of the vine, which has been produced in Burgenland for two thousand years. Here is a story to be told. The first wine was already cultivated in the area before the birth of Christ, but viniculture did not reach its height until three centuries later. For this reason, legend credits Emperor Probus (276-282 A.D.) with the establishment of Pannonia's reputation for wine. He ordered better varieties of grape from the south, the vineyards were cultivated in the Italian manner, and many an improvement was made.

After the retreat of the Romans, Burgenland was subject to bad times; and it was only when the Magyar tribes were finally pacified that wine-growing achieved the level it had once enjoyed.

By the fifteenth and sixteenth centuries, Burgenland wines were already being exported to Bohemia, Moravia, Silesia, Poland, Germany, Switzerland, and England, and today viniculture is still one of the most important branches of industry in the land.

Ancient wine presses as well as beautifully carved barrels bear witness to a venerable tradition among wine-growers.

Saints, Witches, and Villains

The Burgenlander's relationship with God and His saints, from whose goodwill or displeasure, after all, life and successful labour seemed to depend, was clearly modified by a natural familiarity with ideas which sprang from a fertile imagination. Thus, for instance, St. Urban was invoked to keep frost out of the vineyards. Livestock and the fruits of the fields were entrusted to the care of St. Wendelin. Drinking consecrated "St. John's wine" was supposed to guard against evils of every kind and was regarded as a proven folk-remedy for man and animal alike. Martinmas, November 11, is a special feast-day for the wine-growers: by then the young wine, though yet "dusty," has matured, and the vintners welcome one to a "wine christening," where drinking the health of those present with a first glass of the new growth is a time-honoured custom. Cheers!

But the Burgenlander's particular patron saint is the Holy Virgin. As early as the fourteenth century, devout Christians were making the pilgrimage to Maria-auf-der-Heid, i. e., 'St. Mary's on the Moor,' in the Seewinkel. In many cases, pilgrimage chapels were built above or close to sacred springs popularly thought to have cleansing and healing powers. In the year 1626, in a field near Ollersdorf, a spring is said to have burst from the ground with a mighty roar. And when an image of the Virgin Mary was miraculously found in the waters, the village was quickly blessed with a brisk influx of pilgrims. The Holy Well of Ollersdorf can be seen to this day, and pilgrims like to take home a little jar of "miracle water."

Count Francis Nádasdy, who was later to lose his life in a political gamble, undertook the rebuilding of the monastery and church of Maria Loretto after a devastating attack by the Turks. The parish chronicles relate how the ill-fated count, with his head under his arm, still haunted the old ruins for years after his violent death.

The foundation-stone of the first church built at Loretto was laid in 1651 by a Baron Hans Rudolf von Stotzingen. Returning from a pilgrimage, the baron brought with him a copy of the "Black Madonna," a devotional portrait from Loretto in Italy, and had a chapel erected in honour of this "miraculous" image of the Virgin. The layout of the shrine in Burgenland is an exact replica of its Italian model, which, according to a pious legend, was the house of the Holy Family, transported by angels to the province of Ancona.

The Calvaries in Eisenstadt and Frauenkirchen are probably the clearest expression of this popular cult of the Baroque. Such artificial hills are meant to symbolize the mountain of life, Adam's grave, and the site of the Crucifixion, at one and the same time. A similar degree of dedicated piety is to be seen in the Passion Plays, which continue to be staged in Burgenland, in the magnificent natural theatre of the "Roman Quarry" near St. Margarethen. And just as they did in the devout Baroque period, the whole community relives the experience of the suffering of Christ.

In the waning Middle Ages as well as in the Baroque era, popular piety assumed almost hysterical forms, but it was possibly a mere coincidence of circumstances that witch-trials reached a tragic climax at the same time. In any case, it should be remembered that until recently heathen beliefs were far from extinct. An inclination towards magic was clearly evident in the Baroque worship of saints, and the veneration of relics bore strong similarities to heathen idolatry. To be sure, people called themselves "Christians," just as their ancestors had done for generations, but they preserved a fundamental spiritual substance closely akin to the "old" religion. The various superstitious ideas about the powers of witches and warlocks by no means originated with the Baroque; nor did they arise when the Germanic tribes were converted to Christianity, although even then church canons were fulminating against sorcery, soothsaying, and the invoking of spirits: such practices had existed long before the advent of Catholicism.

Even today, witchcraft must still be seen as a largely unexplored phenomenon; the little that we do know about witches chiefly stems from documents left behind by their relentless persecutors, for the ordinary people of the time - and this includes the majority of magicians, both male and female - could neither read nor write. Indeed, what intelligent person would have risked his life to help them by acting as their spokesman?

The court records of the little market town of Pinkafeld clearly show how witches were regarded by the lawmakers and judges. For example, they tell the story of "Old Dotty," who was brought to trial in 1688. She had allegedly caused the death of both people and animals by her black magic and, much worse, had tried to steal a baby. Kidnapping was one of the major charges frequently raised against witches. This is understandable when we look at some of the ancient recipes for witches'-brew: the body of an unbaptized child was thought to yield indispensable ingredients for such concoctions. The physician and alchemist Paracelsus believed that a mixture of "minced babyflesh, poppy, ground-cherry, and hemlock" could work wonders. Another brew consisted of "the fat from a child, cinquefoil, nightshade, and bat's blood." These recipes conclusively prove the use of herbal drugs which could produce hallucinations and dreams very similar to those confessed by witches stretched on the rack. Of course, under the physical and mental tortures of the rack, the accused admitted everything their tormentors wished to hear. But we must bear in mind that a knowledge of herbal properties and benefits was essential for the survival of the ordinary working woman; and these were, after all, the basic ingredients of the notorious witches'-brew. Modern biochemists, physicians, and botanists are once again discovering, through painstaking and strenuous research, the powers of natural medicine by which these people made their living. Herbs were bought to supplement a meagre or an indeed entirely inadequate diet, as well as to heal wounds and sicknesses.

Witches'-brews also played a significant rôle in the second Pinkafeld witch-trial of 1699. We can quote from the fanciful account of a witches' Sabbath. The three accused "witch-women" related that a hierarchical order was even observed at the regular witches' gatherings in Burgenland: the more distinguished ones were allowed to ride in the devil's carriage, whereas the common women had to run behind and act as cooks and scullery-maids at the feast.

Obviously, a country replete with fairy-tales, legends, and ancient folklore is clearly bound to preserve the romance of the highwayman. In Burgenland, the legendary chief of the highway robbers was Nicholas Schmiedhofer, the son of a woodcutter from Edlitz, in Lower Austria. To the people he must surely have embodied the struggle of oppressed serfdom against feudal despotism and exploitation of the peasantry. Like Robin Hood, he was a thief untrue to his type, who robbed from the rich and gave to the poor. He remained a nuisance for a long time until at last Emperor Francis formed a special commission to capture Nicholas Schmiedhofer and his "merry men." The gallows was re-erected for the execution, a perfect occasion for a festival. To mark this day in the minds of the young, and to remind them of the traditional rights and privileges of their native town, crescent rolls were distributed amongst the children and the older citizens were given wine to drink.

"The woodcutter boy," who was responsible for at least 48 petty thefts, 54 robberies, and 14 murders with robbery, showed true remorse in the face of death. Indeed, as he was being dragged up the gallows, he begged the crowd for forgiveness and urged the youngsters to take warning from his example.

Beauty has its Uses

In spite of all the fanciful elements in his view of the world, the Burgenland farmer has both feet on the ground, economically as well as culturally. The cultural wealth of the province does not lie exclusively in its history and art treasures; the ordinary people themselves contribute greatly to the face of culture. So, for centuries cottage industries and handicrafts have been the main occupations of the Burgenland people, alongside farming and wine-growing. Pottery, wickerwork, and wood carving produced articles for daily use found in every country household, and thus formed a valuable contribution to folk culture.

Unfortunately, cottage industry is slowly, yet surely dying out today. The linen-baskets, breadbaskets, and beehives earlier made in the farmhouse during long winter evenings have now been supplanted by factory products. A search for a chairmaker will probably be in vain, even though in times gone by the "Chairmaker of Tschurndorf," who peddled his wares from village to village with ten to fifteen chairs on his back, was a common sight. Nor is it likely that you will find a woodcarver who could match the artistic woodwork seen on the front wall of the giant wine-casks in the vaults of old manors and monasteries. At one time, the landed gentry took great pride in decorating their wine-barrels with costly wood carvings. Religious motifs, symbols, mottoes, coats of arms, and other designs were the most popular. Every visitor to the famous Burgenland wine cellars is also likely to recognize the truth of one such inscription:

Why long on earth for many treasures?
We can forgo, or give up, pleasures.
On two scores, though, men won't resign:
They love their women, and they love their wine.

Folk art, and particularly pottery, holds its own against the other economic and industrial fields in Burgenland. It only goes to show that man's environment determines to a great degree the manner of his cultural creativity. The choice of working materials in Burgenland was, as everywhere, dependent on availability. For example, a healthy cottage industry and a rich pottery trade can thrive because of the rich deposits of clay in the Oberpullendorf Basin. At present, pottery is mainly produced at Stoob, which is also the seat of the only technical college for ceramics and stove-making in Austria. A similarly important branch of industry is the so-called serpentine grinding. This ornamental or semi-precious stone, resembling jade, is quarried near Bernstein Castle and lends itself to shaping into pieces of jewellery, jugs, vases, and bowls. These miniature works of art are among the most popular souvenirs taken home by foreign visitors.

Finally, in addition to deposits of serpentine and clay, the famous quarry at St. Margarethen should not be forgotten. The Romans had recognized the superb quality of this sandstone nearly 2,000 years ago. Excavations at Carnuntum, Vindobona, and Julia Scarbantia have provided us with the earliest proof of a more than merely regional use of the stone. Soft sandstone, which is as easy to fashion as wood, was also a favourite raw material for the sculptors of Gothic architecture. Right until now, any restoration work on St. Stephen's Cathedral in Vienna will draw its material from the so-called St. Stephen's Wall. Further, sandstone from St. Margarethen is also employed in the Austrian capital for the Minoritenkirche ('Church of the Minorites') and the Kirche Maria am Gestade ('Church St. Mary-on-the-Bank'). Centuries later, the same, easily worked material was used for the ornamental figures of the buildings along the Viennese Ringstrasse. Even the road-metal for the permanent way of the railway line across the Semmering Pass was made from Burgenland sandstone.

Today, the Roman Quarry is well known as an international meeting-place of culture. This bizarre natural setting not only provides a stage for famous Passion Plays, but also for a symposium which every year attracts sculptors to this tiny town in Burgenland from all over the world.

Burgenland thus seems to have all the necessary potential for being a cultural and economic factor in the history of Austria and Europe, and yet it is an area of depression today. Wine-growing, farming, and handicraft provided a livelihood for centuries, but neither these nor even modern industry can now supply a sufficient number of jobs. Many workers commute from here to Vienna, Lower Austria, and Styria. Approximately 37,000 Burgenlanders emigrated overseas, especially to the United States, from 1899 to 1935. A few returned to their home grounds; and to this very day, it can hardly be denied that the people of Burgenland are torn between "the desire to leave and the yearning for home."

The potter's craft adds an indispensable feature to man's everyday life in the area.

Carinthia

It is the variety and the ever-changing wealth of the scenery, the contrast between grandeur and charm which characterize sunny Carinthia, with its perpetually snow-topped mountains and glaciers, its rugged rock-faces framing the flowery Alpine meadows, and its thundering waterfalls and romantic glens. Mountain lakes, glittering blue, green and silver, are one of the special features of this region which, in the truest sense of the word, is a centre of tourism.

The fact that visitors come here from many different countries has meant that Carinthia has taken pains to offer visitors relaxation and diversion. Summer pastimes include swimming, rowing, sailing, motor boating and motor racing. In the famous Wörther See, bathing is possible even until the end of October; also the other lakes, those of Millstatt, Ossiach, Faak, and Klopein, no matter what their names, are all exceptionally warm. Even the Weissensee, in spite of the fact that it is about 3,215 ft. above sea-level, has a temperature of 25°C (77°F) in summer.

From December till March, the whole province is a haven for winter sports. There are tempting bobsleigh- and toboggan-runs, ski-runs and skating-rinks; and to add to the variety, there is also ice hockey and curling, which all goes to show that this region offers a wide variety of choices. Needless to say, Carinthia proves an ideal playground for mountain-climbers.

Seldom does the stranger feel so quickly at home as he does in Carinthia. The people of Carinthia love the small pleasures of life and enjoy music and song. Justifiably, they are said to place the highest value on a quiet and peaceful existence:

> *The Carinthian clings to his soil,*
> *He never ventures away;*
> *At home he would rather labour and toil,*
> *The good earth will give him his pay.*

Yet it is certainly not a lack of drive or energy which prompts the Carinthian to remain true to his homeland, come what may, but rather a love for his beautiful country.

Tauriscan Gold and Norician Steel

The only thing that can possibly rival the almost inexhaustible variety of this province of Austria is its eventful past, which takes us right back to the dawn of human history. In the stalactite caves of the Griffener Burgberg, tools from the Early Stone Age have been found. A comprehensive record of the Late Stone Age has been made possible by a relatively

large number of finds. On the Kanzaniberg which, until today, is of almost cultic significance, there was already an important settlement at that time. Here clay brands have, in fact, been brought to light which experts on prehistory assume were used to mark and thus decorate the body. Similar "tattooing" is customary among many primitive peoples even in our day. Lead figures from the Hallstatt period and the ox-drawn carriage of Frögg, which played a rôle in religious ceremonies, are some of the most

ancient relics we possess of a people's way of life and their fertility cult.

With the influx of the Celtic tribes, an era of great importance began in the history of Carinthia. The Celts occupied not only Hallstatt as we know it today, but also large areas elsewhere in the Eastern Alps. In the one place they were attracted by the salt reserves, in the other by the rich deposits of iron ore. The Carinthian Erzberg ('Ore Mountain') near Hüttenberg was to provide the famous "Norician steel," the Jaukenberg the lead. The inhabitants, of Veneto-Illyrian origin, who had older prospecting rights, were simply driven out.

Yet neither salt, nor lead, nor iron could equal the noblest of elements, "the king of all metals": such and others were the verbal forms of adulation later used by the alchemists when referring to gold. The presence of gold in the mountains of the Hohe Tauern was also to have a profound influence on the history of Carinthia, and even more so on that of Salzburg.

Even in the second and third centuries B.C. the area of the Eastern Alps was the centre of brisk trade; and as merchants with an eye to business always have to adapt to the economic system of their trading partners, the Celts abandoned their original system of barter and began to mint coins, following the example of the Romans. They were also skilled in making beautiful jewellery from the Tauriscan gold. In 1874 on the Maschalpe in the Rauriser Seidlwinkel a magnificent neckband with an ornamental clasp was discovered. It is a treasure that would certainly enjoy pride of place in any museum today, had it not, during the turmoil of the Second World War, taken the fancy of a private collector.

Such immense wealth was bound to excite their neighbour's envy. In fact, Rome observed the Nori-

cians' every action with suspicion. In the second century B.C. a good opportunity for closer contact with the Celts at last presented itself to the Romans. Livy then places on record that, in 186 B.C., parts of a very large tribe (probably those called "Noricians" later on) had entered Italy with peaceful intentions, possibly from Carinthia; they duly established an oppidum in the area of what was to become Aquileia, but Rome nimbly saw to it that the place had no future. Nevertheless, there is evidence of diplomatic relations between the two, which indeed led to a treaty of friendship. Its contents, though, were rather ethical in character, and there was but a modicum of mutual commitments: it did not cost Rome any legions, yet it brought her closer to the Norician mineral deposits. The Celtic tribes, imbued with an overweening thirst for conquest, were, on the other hand, quite proud to call themselves "friends of the Roman Empire" - a title which Rome could easily afford to bestow.

"This friendship" took concrete shape as Norician wealth in the bestowers' minds. When, around about 113 B.C., the tribes of the Cimbri and Teutoni advanced into the regions which are now Styria and Carinthia, it was clearly in Rome's interests to protect their so-called friends. However, the decisive battle near the legendary city of Noreia ended in a

crushing defeat for the Roman legions. At the time, ancient historians recounted that tribes of Teutonic origin had annihilated the inhabitants of Noreia. One can safely assume it to be probable that the victors proceeded to behave in a manner similar to their conduct in 105 B.C. at Arausio. There they had torn up the garments of the fallen legionaries and trampled them in the mud, had smashed their armour and drowned their horses, while the survivors were strung up in the trees, so that "the victor should have no booty, and the vanquished receive no mercy." An amazing discovery in the Wendic Hills not far from Marburg (Maribor) helps to confirm the suspicion. Here archaeologists found a collection of bronze helmets belonging to the Noricians, one of which bore an inscription dedicated to "Heergast, the god of war."

Rome's defeat at the hands of the Cimbri and the Teutoni, however, did not mean that her ambitions were in any way curtailed as regards the extension of power. On the contrary, now the friends of the Roman Empire were, step by step, incorporated into the federation. Under the emperor Claudius, the "Regnum Noricum", as the Celts called their state, became a Roman province after 41 A.D. The provincial government at Virunum, situated in a plain (on what is now known as the Zollfeld), unfortified and difficult to defend, was moved to Teurnia about the middle of the fifth century A.D. Teurnia, by contrast (the present-day St. Peter im Holz), was a hill settlement, with all the inherent strategic advantages. Eugippius, using its Late Latin name form, speaks of Tiburnia as "metropolis Norici", the capital of Noricum. It is safe to assume that, by the fourth century, both Virunum and Teurnia were already diocesan towns. These bishoprics were last mentioned in 591; they then fell victims to the advancing Slavs.

Yet surely none of these towns could vie with the fortified Celtic metropolis on Mt. Magdalen. The mighty walls, the temple ruins, the public baths, and the market square where trade was carried on have all been revealed by the spades of the archaeologists. In this light, it seems scarcely credible that the name of such a settlement should have been omitted in antique documents. Today we know no more than that, long ago, the political and religious centre of the Celtic Kingdom of Noricum must have been located on Mt. Magdalen.

Druids and Christian Bishops

The first Christian priests, who had already disseminated the new teaching in the province of Noricum

Besides skiers, snowboarders have now been gripped by "the ghoulish weird passion of dashing downhill through lots of swishy smooth snow."

during the Roman period, knew full well that the heathens could only be converted if they were able to retain the broad outlines of their traditional religious concepts. That is why they merely endowed heathen customs with Christian meaning, and in

in order to provide a protective wall around the heart of the Empire. As early as 970 there is documentary evidence of a *Marchwart* (governor) from the House of Eppenstein, who was responsible for the *Marchia Carantana*.

Early Christian inscription on a tomb from Virunum, with a portrayal of the Good Shepherd.

this way the Catholic faith was able to penetrate the old concepts of worship to an ever increasing degree. Nor did the first Christians even have to give up their familiar surroundings when they went to sacrifice. The old places of worship, such as the temple precincts of the Celtic regional god Jouenat on what is today known as Mt. Hemma, were simply transformed into bishoprics at the turn of the fourth century. Of course, a bishop was resident in each of the two main cities of Noricum, Virunum and Teurnia, from the fourth century onwards. At that time church organization corresponded with state administration, and the boundaries of the diocese coincided with the ones of the city.

In those centuries the church served both as a place of worship and as a fortress of refuge. In spite of this, the early beginnings of Christianization seem to have disappeared again at the time of the Great Migration of the Peoples. Many Christians from Noricum probably joined the Romans from the Danube who, in 488, set off in the direction of Italy with the body of St. Severinus.

The March becomes a Duchy

Now the reorganisation of the German Empire was carried out with renewed zeal. As is well known, border provinces, or *Marken* (marches), were created

The Boy from Mt. Helena is the Roman copy of a Hellenistic sculpture. The life-size votive statue was found as early as 1502 and inspired Albrecht Dürer's "Adam." Now in the Art History Museum of Vienna.

Not long after, in 976, Emperor Otto II raised Carantania to the status of a dukedom. This was the hour in history when the Duchy of Carinthia was born, even if only because Henry II of Bavaria, nicknamed the Quarrelsome, once more did full credit to his name by taking up arms against his cousin. Until then Carantania had been part of the Duchy of Bavaria, and it was only as a result of Otto II's decree that it became the first autonomous territory among the present-day federal provinces of Austria.

The Duchy of Carinthia included the scattered dependencies founded from here - the Carantanian March on the River Mur, as well as the Marches or Counties of Carniola, Cilli (on the Sann), and Pettau (behind the Drava Forest, in the south-east of Lower Austria). Most important, however, was the link with the March of Verona which henceforth, until 1151, was administered by the Dukes of Carinthia in personal union. Along with Verona, the Marches of Friuli and Istria were added to the Duchy of Carinthia.

Late Roman floor mosaic from the former cemetery church of Teurnia. The donors were the Ostrogothic governor Ursus (literally, 'The Bear') and his wife, Ursina. This work of art contains both Christian and pagan symbols (dating from about A.D. 500).

Celtic-Roman excavations on Mt. Magdalen (until 1583 known as Mt. Helena), a hill rising above the Zollfeld, north of Klagenfurt.

A nook of the cloister at Millstatt. The old and famous Benedictine abbey was founded in the second half of the eleventh century. Up to its decline and dissolution by the Pope (in 1469), Millstatt was a major centre for medieval monastic culture.

Idols and Saints

In this period, when things were flourishing both economically and politically, creative art also enjoyed its first heyday.

Romanesque art found expression in monumental monastery buildings such as the impressive Benedictine abbey of Ossiach, which was endowed by a Bavarian nobleman called Ozi in the early years of the eleventh century. It is at Ossiach that the Polish king Boleslav II is said to have found his final rest in 1089, after ten years of atonement as a monk for the murder of the Bishop of Cracow. The legend has been preserved in a fresco. Similarly, the monastery at Millstatt also houses something of particular interest. Here a glass coffin can be seen which, according to folk belief, holds the earthly remains of Domitian, the legendary duke of Carinthia. Like all the great figures during this period he, too, was a dynamic promoter of Christianity who, tradition has it, ordered about "a thousand statues of idols" sunk in the lake now called Millstättersee. Apparently it is these *mille statuae* that have given the settlement its name. And thus Millstatt is widely felt to be one of those places where Christianity was closely connected with heathendom.

So it will hardly surprise us to learn that even Gurk Cathedral marks the Christian consecration of a heathen shrine of worship. The highly revered "Hemma Stone," from which the Carinthian patron saint is said to have supervised the building of the monastery, is nothing other than the altar of a Celtic goddess of fertility. Even the grave of the chaste lady was not spared when it came to fertility rites, for pilgrims who were pregnant could not be prevented from creeping beneath the sarcophagus in order to have an easy delivery. However, by the Romanesque period a purer and stricter form of Christianity was firmly established. St. Hemma is no longer one of those "demigods" who were merely put in the place of heathen idols, as, for example, St. George; she is a historical figure who has been found worthy of sainthood as a result of her suffering. In fact, Hemma was the last descendant of a nobleman called Zwentibold to whom, in 898, Arnulf of Carinthia is known to have bequeathed a Carolingian palace; on its site, the stupendous Romanesque cathedral was later to be built.

When, in 1036, the husband of the noble Hemma was assassinated by the Carinthian duke Adalbero von Eppenstein, she was filled with despair and withdrew more and more from the world. At Gurk she endowed a St. Mary's church and a nunnery, which were consecrated by the Archbishop of Salz-

A view of Lake Millstatt, one of the attractions of Carinthia's lakeland Eden.

burg in 1043. However, the latter, so richly provided for by Hemma, saw itself dissolved by 1072, its property being used for instituting a separate Salzburg bishopric there. This status meant, however, that the Bishop of Gurk was not directly subordinate to the German king, but to the Archbishop of Salzburg. Thus the latter had the right to nominate candidates for Gurk and to invest them with worldly possessions. The result was "a minor controversy over investiture"; again and again there were complications, indeed open hostilities. Not until 1535 was there a ruling established which seemed to meet with everyone's approval. The bishop was to be chosen by the king on two successive occasions; on the third, the Archbishop of Salzburg had the right to select the bishop. In 1859 the diocese of Gurk was extended to include the whole of Carinthia. By this time, however, the bishop's residence had long since been moved to Klagenfurt.

Who possessed the power in Carinthia?

We can only properly gauge the honour of Gurk's being raised to the status of a separate Salzburg bishopric if we recall that the Babenbergs were never able to achieve this for their own city of residence,

The pilgrimage church of Maria Saal, one of the most magnificent fortified churches in Carinthia, and also the oldest one in the country on record.

history. This knowledge we owe to the Styrian verse chronicler Otacher oûz der Geul, who has handed down to us a detailed description of the festivities of 1 September 1286. That poet is, by the way, an old friend, for he is the very same Ottokar von Horneck who acts as Grillparzer's mouthpiece when holding his famous monologue "In Praise of Austria".[1]

It must truly have been a spectacular sight when the duke, in peasant costume, standing before the "prince's stone" near Karnburg, received the homage of peasant-soldiers, therewith taking the country under his tutelage. But the occasion was by no means finished with on the completion of this ceremony. It was followed by a solemn procession from Karnburg to the nearby cathedral of Maria Saal, where the prince took part in the celebration of High Mass. Afterwards everyone went to the ducal throne, where the prince sat in judgement and the fiefs were redistributed. And this seat of honour, which our forefathers laboriously pieced together out of Roman stones a thousand years ago in order to set up an imposing throne, is still "the symbol of Carinthia's unity, freedom and independence."

Vienna. Their *Ostarrîchi*, or 'Realm in the East,' was subordinate to the diocese of Passau and was to remain so up to the late Middle Ages.

The sphere of influence of the Church was, at this time, completely different, if only because the Church owned most of the land and controlled the important markets and trade centres. In the Duchy of Carinthia, dignitaries like the Patriarch of Aquileia, the Bishop of Gurk and the Archbishop of Salzburg shared the land more or less fraternally among themselves. Villach, which even in Celtic and Roman times had been the junction of overland routes in Upper Carinthia, belonged to the Bishops of Bamberg and provided them with a very lucrative living throughout the Middle Ages. The domain of the prince of the country was really restricted to the Klagenfurt Basin.

Nevertheless, the dukes of Carinthia were always adept at maintaining their subjects' belief in their "omnipotence" by means of imposing processions and effective gestures. The investiture of a duke of Carinthia was carried out with hardly less extravagance than that of one of the really great figures in

The "Carinthian Interregnum"

It may seem a curious act of Providence that about the middle of the thirteenth century so many important ruling families should have died out. In 1269, Duke Ulrich von Sponheim also deceased without legitimate issue; and to spare his people the usual altercations over the question of inheritance, he bequeathed Carinthia and Carniola to King Premysl Otakar of Bohemia.

Now it seemed as if nothing could stop the Premyslid's ascent to power. Finally, in 1272, the Bohemian king was appointed captain-general of Friaul, and thus he ruled over a kingdom which stretched from the Sudeten mountains to the shores of the Adriatic.

In the early Christian period Roman stones were built into the walls of churches and monasteries in order to "banish the heathen gods." A relief on the south outer wall of Maria Saal (but originally at Virunum) from about A.D. 100 depicts a Roman carriage.

Another Roman artifact on that church places before our eyes the legendary punishment of Hector as he is dragged along behind a chariot.

[1] To be found among the prelims, on the page facing the half-title of this volume.

The Minster of Gurk, consecrated as early as 1174, ranks among the most important pieces of Romanesque architecture in Austria. Its crypt of one hundred pillars houses the sarcophagus of St. Hemma, the Carinthian patron saint.

In the middle of the Zollfeld near Maria Saal stands a double throne made of Roman stones. The medieval Carinthian dukes not only had to swear an oath to the Estates, but also received homage, administered justice, and bestowed fiefs here.

Margarete Maultasch, Countess of Tyrol. After her husband, Margrave Lewis of Brandenburg, and her son, Meinhard III, had died, she in 1363 handed over Tyrol to the dukes of Austria, though retaining its regency during her lifetime.

Yet, there were men who had still more power, namely the German princes and the Pope, Gregory X. It depended on their approval whether the Bohemian king could, by way of fitting conclusion, also add the German crown to his trophies. We know how the story ended. The electors chose Rudolph of Habsburg, whom King Otakar's propagandists - and there was such a thing, even in those days - had derided as the "poor count" when they thought victory was theirs.

However, even Rudolph of Habsburg will hardly have had any difficulty in keeping the wolf from the door. At that time there were no really "poor" nobles, only rich ones and those, like Rudolph, who were not quite so rich.

The Meinhardiners - Adventurers on the Ducal Throne

With the fall of the Bohemian king the ducal throne of Carinthia once more became vacant: Rudolph of Habsburg, who annexed Austria and Styria as soon as he entered office, cannot have been particularly

interested in Carinthia. At any rate, he bestowed the duchy upon his loyal ally, Meinhard IV of Görz (Gorizia). True, at the decisive Battle of Marchfeld Count Meinhard did not put in an appearance until the worst was over; but nevertheless, the fact that he had shown himself willing had to be rewarded. In the very same year, 1286, Meinhard of Görz received the Duchy of Carinthia as his fief and thus rose to the rank of Prince of the Empire.

The new ruler of the country was by no means to the liking of the old established Carinthian nobility. The upshot was that there were bloody revolts against both Meinhard of Görz and Rudolph of Habsburg, to which the Archbishop of Salzburg also strove to lend his vigorous support. In 1292 the rebels seized the duke's son, Ludwig, who happened to be in St. Veit at the time. The city of residence was plundered by the mob and the fortifications were razed to the ground. However, Duke Meinhard soon had the situation under control again and retaliated brutally, which, of course, hardly helped to increase the popularity of the new ruling family.

Yet the Meinhardiners, as the Tyrolean branch of the counts of Görz were also called, took little interest in Carinthia; they had their eye on something

that would bring greater prestige and honour. Henry of Carinthia, a son of Meinhard IV, was determined to wear the unclaimed crown of the Přemyslids, at all costs. He achieved this in fact, though only by making enormous financial sacrifices, but was not able to enjoy his new prestige for very long. The House of Luxembourg was too powerful and too wealthy an opponent. Nevertheless, the tide once again seemed to turn in Henry's favour. At the double election in 1314, in his capacity as Prince of the Empire, he decided, with astute foresight, to support Frederick the Fair, and after the latter's victory he was also promptly rewarded with the wealthy North Italian provinces.

However, Henry of Carinthia wanted to make up the losses of his Bohemian escapade within as short a time as possible, and consequently tried to squeeze too much tax out of his subjects: Treviso and Padua, enraged, sought the protection of the Scaligers of Verona. When, in 1335, after an eventful life, Duke Henry closed his eyes for the last time he left "only" a daughter, whose thirst for adventure was scarcely less than his own. Margarete Maultasch ('Satchel-mouthed Meg'), supposedly called after her castle at Terlan, north-west of Bozen, was to become one of the most interesting women in Austrian history.

"... but o Habsburg, upon whom Fortune smiles, thou shalt inherit"

And as not infrequently befalls the weaker sex, Margarete Maultasch was relieved of part of her inheritance. The daughter of Henry of Carinthia was able to claim her ancestral rights only in Tyrol, for, as ill-luck would have it, the year 1330 saw the death of Frederick the Fair, whom her father had so prudently supported in the election.

Nor had the Habsburgs been idle in the meantime either, for they had secretly allied themselves with Lewis the Bavarian, the former rival candidate of the emperor Frederick. When, at this juncture, Lewis rather belatedly acquired the crown after all, he repaid the Habsburgs right royally, by giving them the Duchy of Carinthia.

From the year 1335 on, the Carinthians had no choice other than to share the fortunes of the House of Habsburg. The first Habsburg duke was followed, in 1339, by his brother Albert, who is supposed to have taken great pains to establish contact with his common subjects. He travelled through his lands, conferred new charters upon Carinthia and Carniola and, in addition, by means of shrewd measures, succeeded in increasing the royal income. Duke Albert may indeed have been a financial wizard, for, in

Carinthia at that time, there was one catastrophe after another: swarms of locusts destroyed the harvest; in 1348 there was such a severe earthquake that part of Mt. Dobratsch fell down; and at Villach the church collapsed like a house of cards, burying the

worshippers who had just gathered for the afternoon service. In the wake of these disasters followed privation, despair and pestilence. Such visitations could, on the other hand, only be interpreted as divine punishment, and thus droves of penitents and flagellants traversed the lands to placate the Almighty once more.

We are, however, likely to find out very little about the way the common folk lived from reading

The Battle of Dürnkrut, on the River March, in 1278: King Rudolph I and his entourage facing their slain adversary, Otakar II Přemysl, King of Bohemia. Coloured lithograph by Anton Ziegler.

the chronicles written at that time; they were merely part of the scenery, just like the cattle. It was only the deeds of the nobility that were considered historically relevant; for example, dynastic agreements such as the Treaty of Neuberg, whereby in 1379 the dukes Albert and Leopold, the brothers of the inventive "Founder," divided up the Habsburg domain. Albert was given control of Austria above and below the River Enns, the "iron city" of Steyr, and the lucrative region of the Salzkammergut; to Leopold fell Styria, Carinthia, Carniola, Tyrol, the so-called Forelands (or Further Austria), and the new territorial acquisitions stretching right to the Adriatic. From now on the House of Habsburg no longer wanted to be regarded as a family union, but divided itself into two separate branches, the Albertine and the Leopoldine. The old-established landed aristocracy were not prepared to sanction such a testamentary agreement under any circumstances, for they were aware of considerably older rights than those of the "foreign" Habsburgs. Soon a favourable opportunity presented itself for putting a stop to the ambitions of the rather unpopular archdukes. After the Battle of Nikopol the danger of Turkish invasion had become acute, particularly for Carinthia, Carniola and Styria. This is why, in 1396, the ambitious nobles were summoned to an Austrian provincial diet for the very first time. However, the nobility were by no means prepared to expose themselves to danger in helping to ward off the Turks. They retreated behind their fortifications, left the open country to its fate, and at the most supplied the Habsburgs with a few auxiliary troops. Yet the Estates were adept at wresting more and more important concessions from their ruler. Finally, it was agreed that there should be no further treaties like that of Neuberg, at least not without explicit approval.

The extent of the power of the Estates was most manifest when the head of the Albertine branch of the family died, leaving as his sole successor someone who was not yet of age. In accordance with the statutes of Neuberg, guardianship automatically fell to the Leopoldine Habsburgs.

This is where the all-powerful Estates had an important say in the matter. Without further ado, they placed a time limit on the guardianship, 23 June 1411; and when this date was near, the heir was simply kidnapped. Thus kidnapping is not entirely a product of our present day and age.

The uninitiated might well tend to get the impression that the Leopoldine Habsburgs opposed the Estates like an impenetrable phalanx. Exactly the opposite was the case. The first quarrels arose, of course, when the dynastic possessions were divided

up. This time three archdukes staked a claim: Leopold, the eldest, was given Austria as it then was, Carinthia and Carniola; Ernest, with the nickname "The Unyielding," received Styria; and Frederick, whom they had originally simply intended to leave out, succeeded in acquiring the Forelands and Tyrol.

This was when the quarrels really began to be heated. Ernest the Unyielding and the first-born Leopold fell out with each other so violently that neither the injunctions of the Estates nor of the German king could reconcile them.

Their subjects, too, became involved in the grim dispute and felt called upon to take sides. The feudal lords and the Viennese patricians were on the side of Duke Ernest, whereas the knights and artisans supported Leopold's aims. It seemed as if everyone had adopted the Habsburg cause. In Vienna, the city of residence, there were riots when the mayor Konrad Vorlauf had five artisans executed because they had expressed opposition to Duke Ernest in the city council. A short time after this had happened, Duke Leopold marched into Vienna and ordered the execution of Vorlauf and two of the councillors.

The killing would certainly have continued had not Leopold unexpectedly departed this life. Thus a new treaty could be made in Vienna which laid down that Albert, who had by this time come of age, should have the lands of Lower Austria, Ernest the Unyielding the lands of Inner Austria, and Frederick, Tyrol and the Forelands.

It would require too much detail to go into all the Habsburg quarrels over questions of inheritance. As for Carinthia, which was part of Inner Austria, it was a territory of merely secondary importance as far as the archdukes were concerned, and did not even have a ducal residence. At that time Carinthia, together with other lands, was amalgamated with Styria, and all the important political events took place in Graz, the city of residence.

The Habsburgs, it may be presumed, were chiefly interested in the rich ore resources of Carinthia. In localities whose names contain the element *Blei* 'lead', such as Bleiburg, Windisch-Bleiberg and Bleiberg near Villach, it almost goes without saying that there were scattered lead deposits, the mining of which was intensified in the fifteenth century by the Fuggers.

The Carinthian ore was not as abundant as that of Styria, but, nevertheless, proved important enough to turn the Habsburgs and the Archbishops of Salzburg, for whom it represented a source of wealth, into bitter adversaries. One reason for this was that the archdukes were intent upon eliminating the

Salzburg trading centre of Althofen in favour of the city of St. Veit.

Finally, there was also the famous "Tauriscan gold," about 110 pounds of which was mined each year in the fourteenth century. This is not very much by modern standards; however, at that time, mining involved very little material outlay for the owners of the mines, as labour cost them almost nothing. Sometimes the miners presumably managed to improve on their "nothing" somewhat, for between the groups of miners on either side of the Tauern ridge there prevailed what almost amounted to a state of war. They attacked each other by turns, filled up the mine shafts and dragged off the ore that was in stock.

As we know, gold mining in the Hohe Tauern had flourished under the rule of the Celts and Romans. When the occupation came to an end, the mines were shut down for hundreds of years until, in 719, mining was resumed in this area around the Sonnblick peak. In the oldest Salzburg documents, the *Indiculus Arnonis* and the *Breves Notitiae*, which date back to the eighth and ninth centuries, "gold deposits" were mentioned. Even in those days there was gold-washing in the streams of the Tauern mountains and in the upper stretches of the Salzach.

From the twelfth century Tauriscan gold must have been mined in greater quantities once again. It was taken to the mints in Salzburg, Lienz and Judenburg for further processing.

The mining and production techniques had remained unchanged from the beginning. The miners worked with mallets and crowbars; the rocks were forced apart by wooden wedges, which were made to swell by pouring water over them. Fire was used to crumble the stone. In this way, nearly a hundred miles of tunnelling had to be cut through the hard blocks of gneiss. The mines were often situated at an altitude of more than 9,000 ft. up in the mountains, so that when there was deep snow the miners could not go down into the valley even on their free Sunday.

Once in 1490, the story goes, the miners' quarters on the Ritterkar corrie were so snowed up the men thought that they had been buried alive. When the food supplies began to run short, the men began to cast hungry glances at a smith who happened to be there at the time, and they were clearly wondering whether he might not be suitable for improving the menu a little. The smith instinctively sensed the danger which threatened him, and developed the strength of a lion. In his mortal terror he fought his way through the masses of snow to reach the open; and the famished miners, then no longer on the ogre

trail, were also able to escape through the tunnel that the smith had dug.

So, the plight of the snow-trapped miners had a happy ending; and "snow stakes" 30 feet high were put up next to the Rauris parish church so that this memorable event should not be forgotten. On the whole, the miners who worked in the mountains were a pious folk, and since even having an opportunity to acquire a certain amount of wealth, they did not forget to thank the Almighty. It was when gold-mining reached its height for the first time in the Middle Ages that the venerable shrine of Heiligenblut was built.

The person who profited most from the gold deposits in the Hohe Tauern was also a man of God, namely the Archbishop of Salzburg. Certainly his residence would not now be regarded as one of the most beautiful places in the world, had not the "Tauriscan gold" provided the necessary wealth.

It is said that from the late fifteenth to the beginning of the seventeenth century there were no fewer than 2,000 miners active in Rauris alone, organized in thirty parties. The invention of gunpowder led to an intensification of the mining of gold ore; at that time, around the year 1560, the output was already some 5,700 pounds a year.

The seventeenth century, however, brought about a great change. The mining of precious metals in the Tauern mountains became unprofitable and all attempts to revive the dying industry failed.

Similarly, the significance of the Carinthian "Ore Mountain" at Hüttenberg declined. Like its Styrian namesake, it was already extremely important in prehistoric times. It supplied the Celts and the Romans with the famous "Norician steel," and in the Middle Ages iron was Carinthia's leading commodity. As early 1399, the old ducal seat of St. Veit enjoyed a trade privilege according to which every iron merchant passing through was forced to offer his goods to the citizens at a reasonable price. Only then was he allowed to continue his journey.

In the nineteenth century there were still numerous iron works and smelting works to be found by the brooks round the sites of the ore deposits in Carinthia. However, after the amalgamation of the Carinthian and Styrian iron industries, Donawitz became the main centre of production in 1881, and Carinthia had to take second place to Styria in economic affairs. Nowadays only the Ferlach gunsmith's trade enjoys world-wide fame. As early as the sixteenth century a gunmakers' guild had established itself at Ferlach, south of Klagenfurt, the successors of which now specialize in the production of high-quality firearms for hunting.

Overleaf:
The Hohe Tauern Alpine range, lofty enough to bear glaciers, is divided into four mountain systems, the Grossvenediger, Granatspitz, Sonnblick, and Ankogel groups.

The photograph offers a springtime idyll of cotton grass, tarn, and towering peaks at the open end of the Graden Valley, south of Heiligenblut.

The parish church of St. Vincent at the foot of Mt. Grossglockner was built by the owners and the pitmen of the Heiligenblut goldmine in the late fourteenth century. The name of the village is based on the legend that a relic containing Christ's Blood was found here.

Peasants have always shown an ingrained sense of duty and resolve to defend old rights, if need be by force of arms - as is shown in "The Last Reserves," a famous painting by Franz Defregger, 1874 (Austrian Gallery, Vienna).

A Target of Social Criticism

No one will now be surprised to learn that in an "industrial region" such as Carinthia notions of freedom and ideas concerned with social criticism were able to take hold very easily. First, in 1478, the bonded "Adamses who delved" planned a revolt under their leader, Peter Wunderlich.

The notions of "freedom and human dignity" also doubtless found ready adherents among the miners of the Upper Carinthian mining areas, for the work they did very clearly brought their masters considerably more profit than they were ever able to enjoy themselves.

> *Eten and drounken and maden hem glad;*
> *Hoere lif was all with gamen ilad:*
> *Men keneleden hem beforen.*
> *They beren hem well swithe heye,*
> *And, in a twinkling of an eye,*
> *Hoere soules weren forloren.*
>
> *Where is that lawing and that song,*
> *That trailing and that proude yong,*
> *Tho havekes and tho houndes?*
> *All that joye is went away,*
> *That wele is comen to weylaway,*
> *To manye harde stoundes.*

> *Hoere paradis hy nomen here,*
> *And now they lien in helle ifere:*
> *The fuir it brennes evere;*
> *Long is 'ay!' and long is 'ho!'*
> *Long is 'wy!' and long is 'wo!'*
> *Thennes ne cometh they nevere.*

Now, all at once, the call for "man's ancient rights" made itself heard. Three hundred years later the same idea was formulated more clearly as "Liberty, Equality and Fraternity."

In Carinthia things came to such a pass that the old city of residence, St. Veit, refused entry, in 1516, to a mercenary army got together by the Estates. This fact may well have strengthened the wish among the regional nobility to have a stronghold of their own that was not subject to either a secular or an ecclesiastical authority. Their choice fell on Klagenfurt which had been devastated by fire in 1514. The town, though impoverished, recommended itself through its central position as a political and military base; and being dependent on outside help for reconstruction work to get under way, Klagenfurt was the obvious choice for both parties concerned. So the Estates pleaded with Emperor Maximilian I to let them have the town on the understanding that they would convert it into a firm bulwark against all enemies, internal and external alike. And it was the Emperor, true enough, who in his Title Deed of 24 April 1518 then left the Estates the town while, at the same time, rescinding all privileges granted so far. This, in fact, was a unique case in German legal history. Once in the hands of the Provincial Estates, the town soon began to flourish, and was duly awarded the status of a regional capital.

Rebellious thoughts similar to those harboured by the "low born" may well have made the Carinthian nobles into fanatical supporters of the Protestant cause, for Luther's doctrine gave them something concrete upon which to base their opposition to the "solidly" Catholic House of Habsburg. And Habsburg was in the desperate situation of having to allow a number of concessions, for the nobility had to lend their vigorous support in warding off the Turks. This resulted, in 1578, in the so-called *Brucker Libell*, which granted the Protestant nobility of Carinthia and Styria important rights. However, this was their last great success.

With Emperor Ferdinand II, an intolerant supporter of the Counter-Reformation had come to power who set up "commissions on religious reform" - as they were called in good officialese - which travelled through the country accompanied by three hundred riflemen. Needless to say, by means of such tactics, it was rather easy to "entice" very many people back into the fold of Roman Catholicism.

As so often in the history of the world, the "weaker sex" proved to be particularly recalcitrant. The chronicles relate that the women of Völkermarkt were no longer prepared to show their husbands the obedience that was their due. The movement was led by the wife of the municipal judge, who apparently induced her fellow women citizens to refuse to fulfil even the official part of their matrimonial duties. For as long as *Frau Rat* (i. e., the respected wife of a city dignitary), who was regarded as the "most genteel" of them all, refused to return to Catholicism, then the other predecessors of Alice Schwarzer, or Betty Friedan, were not prepared to relinquish their convictions either. Well - the right man will no doubt have solved this problem, too, with a little "loving understanding."

The Dance of Death frescoes on the façade of the Charnelhouse of Metnitz (around 1500), with pictorial exempla of the omnipresence of Death. As the poem recalls, "They ate and drank, and merry made / Their whole life long they sang and played... / But health and wealth soon pass away / And joy is lost, O wellaway!"

"Understanding and Objectivity"

How seldom it is used even in the loftier realms of politics! Count Edward von Taaffe, the prominent Prime Minister of the Dual Monarchy, fondly imagined that he had found the philosophers' stone when he disclosed the following to his amazed listeners: "The secret of government in this multiracial state is simply to keep all the various nationalities equally discontented." Discontent, however, is the cause of all revolution, and the time was to come when the nations would try to break free of the hated "prison of the peoples," as it was often called, and to found independent republics.

When, after the First World War, the free democrats had a say, they hastened to announce general elections in the new "Republic of German Austria" for a constituent National Assembly. These elections could not take place in Southern Carinthia since the new state of Yugoslavia, stressing the Slav historic component of the land, laid claim to the whole of Carinthia; as it is, the Yugoslavs occupied not only the parts of the country having a mixed population, but also those with a predominantly German-speaking majority. The various military clashes in Carinthia that followed duly had their repercussions on the diplomatic negotiations in Paris, eventually leading to a plebiscite in the areas

Homage paid to Emperor Charles VI: a fresco in the Regional Parliament Building at Klagenfurt.

The Dragon is the landmark of the City of Klagenfurt. This fabulous creature, with wings and claws and able to breathe out fire, is already in evidence on the oldest civic seal dating from the thirteenth century.

of Carinthia affected; and on 10 October 1920 the decision went in favour of Carinthia, and Austria, respectively. Under the Treaty of Saint-Germain-en-Laye, however, Carinthia lost the Val Canale to Italy, and the Miess Valley as well as the area around Unterdrauburg to Yugoslavia.

After the Second World War, in the international treaty of 1955, Austria was once more to acquire the status of a "free, independent and democratic state." In Article Seven, the "rights of the Slovenian and Croatian minorities" in Carinthia, Burgenland and Styria are dealt with in great detail. The right of the Slovenes and Croatians to their own organizations and schools is expressly confirmed in writing. Moreover, the Slovenian or Croatian languages must be acknowledged as official languages, in addition to German, in administrative areas with a mixed population, while "markings and inscriptions of a topographical nature must be written both in German and in Slovenian or Croatian." What is couched

here in such carefully chosen language has, in the form of a "battle over place-name signs," for years caused dissent of the kind that has stirred up a whirlwind of words not only in the press.

Today Carinthia's bilingualism continues to present grave problems even for astute politicians, nor can they extricate themselves from a tricky situation with the same nonchalance that was allowed the sovereigns who reigned "by the Grace of God." The story goes that when Prince Metternich rebuked Emperor Francis I because there had been far too much talk at the Congress of Vienna about the peoples' rights and their national interests, he merely received the reply, "My dear Metternich, the peoples who were nonentities now have identities!"

Lower Austria

The Silvery Ribbon of the River Danube

Lower Austria is undoubtedly a land showered with plenty by Dame Nature. The majestic Danube extends like a silvery ribbon from west to east, dividing the province into two halves. Below the Danube, the Limestone Alps form a natural border in the south, while to the north the rolling hill country gradually ascends to the Moravian Massif. A particular feature of the latter are the huge lichen-covered granite boulders, standing out from the meadows and marshes as if hurled there by giants. These forbidding woodlands lying between the Danube and the Bohemian Basin were settled relatively late, in contrast to the Wachau district and the southern parts of Lower Austria.

Major Archaeological Finds

Lower Austria, so often praised in song, has a history that reaches far into the past. The first traces of human life there lead us back some 100,000 years before the time of Christ. The artifacts found in the Gudenus Cave, in the romantic valley of the Lesser Krems, furnish proof that even members of the Neanderthal race had lived here. Also from the Old Stone Age is the world-famous Venus of Willendorf, a figurine which, in its obese femininity, must have represented a fertility symbol, "the Mother Deity."

If there ever was a time upon earth that might be called "the good old days," it was the Stone Age. Man lived (to use a biblical expression) like the fowls of the air, which never sow and yet reap the harvest. To be happy, man needed nothing more than good hunting and fishing grounds. It was only with the rise of a socially structured and ordered commonwealth that the attitude towards food became one of possession.

Many tribes appear to have been favoured by fortune; others, like the salt lords of Hallstatt, were simply efficient businessmen. They amassed immeasurable wealth through the excavation of huge salt deposits, and so attracted the envy and ill will of their contemporaries. To understand the importance of this, we must realize that until quite recently salt was not only an essential condiment but also served as the most important preservative for meat and other foodstuffs.

That this civilization was one of exceptional significance is borne out by the fact that experts have named an entire epoch of mankind's history the "Hallstatt Period." Well-known witnesses of this culture are not only the extensive burial site in the Salzkammergut in today's province of Upper Aus-

tria, but other finds as well. There is, for instance, the Grossmugl, or 'Big Mound,' prince's grave near Hollabrunn, still completely intact and presently awaiting archaeological exploration.

As early as the first millennium B.C., the living space for some tribes had become too confining. About the year 400 B.C., the Celts pushed their way into Central Europe from the west. They were primarily concerned with seizing good farmland and open pastures. But no sooner did they think themselves secure than a powerful enemy arose. Thus, we know relatively little about these Celtic farmers - their conquerors, the legionary forces of the Romans, were thorough workers. Remains from the Celts include a few burial grounds and traces of their fortified refuges on hilly terrain - elevations like Mt. Oberleiserberg, Mt. Umlaufberg near Altenburg on the River Kamp, and Mt. Leopoldsberg overlooking Vienna, all tell a garbled tale that draws its substance from scraps of masonry, potsherds, and jewellery....

Roman Influences

By the birth of Christ, Rome was at its peak in power. The *Imperium* had extended its borders as far

The Heidentor (literally, 'Heathens' Gate') near Petronell-Carnuntum, the only surviving ancient building above ground. It dates back to the third century A.D.

Overleaf:
The *Tabula Peutingeriana*, a parchment roll 269 by 9 inches, is a highway map of citadels and settlements, with their respective distances in the Roman Empire and some adjoining territories, which dates from the fourth century A.D. (Conrad Peutinger, Clerk to the City Council of Augsburg, was the man who received the *Tabula itineraria* for publication from the humanist Conrad Celtis, in 1507 - hence the name of the famous scroll.)

The section in the top right-hand cor-

as the Danube and the Rhine, and had secured them against the neighbouring peoples through garrisons, well-paved roads, and observation posts. The major military camps in what is now Lower Austria were most probably Vindobona, where centuries later the cosmopolitan city of Vienna was to arise, and Carnuntum, the "Austrian Pompeii."

The configuration of the Roman *castra*, on whose sites very often trading centres of the dawning Middle Ages and, in due course, the earliest cities developed, can still be traced today. Wherever the Roman soldiers built a camp or merely pitched their tents, they repeated the traditional arrangements, based on principle of cosmic order, which they had learnt from the Etruscans. For these *castra* and *oppida*, unless the landscape constrained them to do otherwise, a square foundation was always chosen. Within the surrounding walls were laid two main roads at right angles characteristic of a holy settlement. At the intersection of this "mythical crossroads" lay the *forum*. This was a large market-place, or public place for meetings, quite often a square, on which bordered the most important civic buildings and the temple of the Capitoline Trinity - Jupiter,

ner covers some road connections in Lower Austria. Here are just three Latin-German place-name correspondences, to make it easier for modern map-readers to go on an imaginary journey along a Roman road: *Arelate* (or *Arelape*), Pöchlarn; *Namare*, Melk; *Tri[gisamo]*, ford over the River Traisen, near Traismauer (Augustiana).

Juno, and Minerva. Such a layout can be seen nowhere better than at Traismauer, then known as Augustiana. In the very centre of the *oppidum*, on the old site of the Roman temple, stands an ancient house of worship, the fabled baptistery of the Slavic prince, Privina.

As fortunate as it may be that a Roman road map from the fourth century A.D. has been preserved (actually but a medieval copy, come down to us through the zeal of the Augsburg humanist Conrad Peutinger), a dispute among experts as to the historical whereabouts of many a Roman *castrum* still exists. The most hotly debated point of discord at the moment is the presumptive burial site of a

famous early Christian saint, Severinus. According to the prevalent theory, St. Severinus supposedly resided primarily at present-day Mautern on the Danube, opposite Krems, and after his death in 482 found his last resting-place there. In about 511 Eugippius, an ecclesiastical scholar, passed down a history, the *Vita Sancti Severini*, according to which the saint was buried in his monk's cell. His corpse, we learn, was later carried back to his homeland by one of the troops guarding the retreat.

Now, whether it be due to instinct on the part of the researchers or sheer accident, an empty grave, which evidence indisputably proves to be from the fifth century, was uncovered during excavations

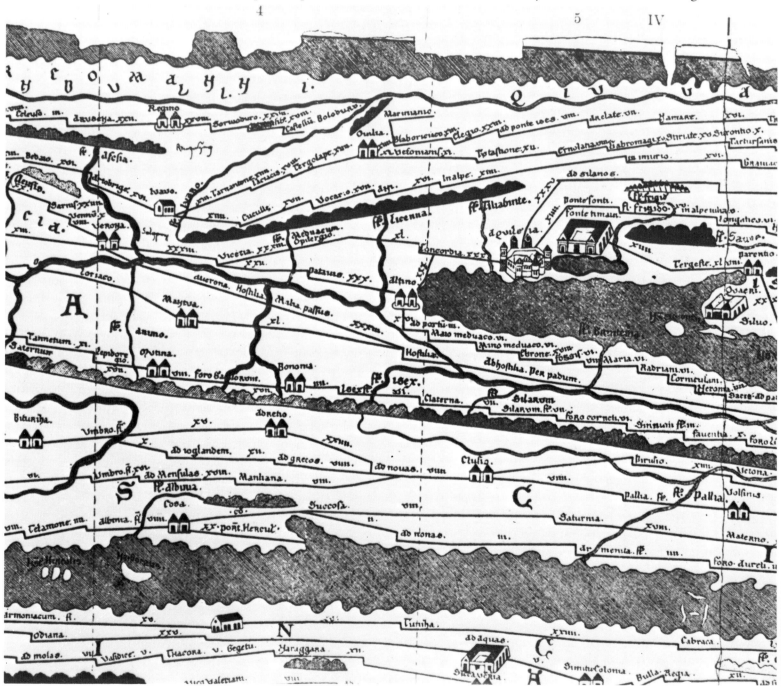

under the very old parish church of Heiligenstadt. Since the grave had not been plundered, all circumstantial evidence would seem to point to the conclusion that the body had been purposely removed.

As it is, Heiligenstadt (which had a reputation for health-giving springs until the nineteenth century, and was duly called Thermae Cetiae by the Romans) does not lie anywhere near Mautern. Rather, it lies on the outskirts of Vienna, at the foot of the Kahlenberg, where the border ran between the Roman provinces of Noricum and Pannonia in the times of St. Severinus. Should all this, then, be put down to coincidence? Hardly. The Roman walls, the removal of the body, the exact dating - these, in their sum total, are arguments that cannot be simply explained away.

Yet archaeological science and its findings will never have the cogency of written documents. It is for this reason that the centuries consequent upon the fall of the Roman Empire, the epoch of the Great Migrations of the Peoples, has been named the Dark Ages. Nevertheless, burial sites and bastions tell a story of their own. For example, the discoveries at Zwölfaxing, Mödling, and Kaiserebersdorf give impressive indications as to the prosperity and power of the Avaric tribes. Then, there are the "murder holes" on Mt. Schanzberg near Gars-Thunau, which speak of the gruesome fate of Slav colonists. In the year 1041 or so, Luitpold, the son of a Babenberg margrave, wreaked such thorough destruction with his troops that the annals of Niederaltaich Abbey matter-of-factly spoke of the victor as having returned homeward with a great wealth in spoils. In a very similar way, during the 790s, Charlemagne had done everything that the Avars "paid for their atrocious deeds." In fact, they were defeated by the Frankish army and then badly afflicted by an epidemic, which made a contemporary chronicler report to distant Kiev, "They are all dead, not one single Avar remains."

Otto the Great

In spite of this, the German colonization of the East, which now began, soon met with considerable resistance. In 881, the Franks and Bavarians for the first time clashed with Hungarian, or Magyar, cavalry *ad veniam*, 'near Vienna'; and throughout the following decades these savage horsemen from the Ural Mountains were to wield their scourge over the Danubian area. It indeed came to pass that the land east of the River Enns had to be surrendered, almost uncontested, to the Magyars. A critical turning-point, however, did occur, in 955, when Emperor Otto the Great succeeded in annihilating that Asian foe on the Lechfeld, near Augsburg. Legends of this historical battle report that only seven of those vanquished were ever to see their homeland again; and the West exulted along with the conqueror, for "none in the last two hundred years had achieved such a victory."

In fact, the good fortune of Otto the Great decisively influenced the destiny of all of the Avaric or Ottonian March, or Realm in the East *(Ostarrîchi)*, as Austria was called in those centuries. Only now could the foundations of economic and cultural development be laid. For example, in the fertile stretch of the Danube valley known as the Wachau, a virtual race had begun among the abbots and bishops from Salzburg and Bavaria to stake their claims on the sunny hills and slopes and terraces best suited for the growth of grapes. So, between Melk and Krems, both ancient settlements, well-tended tiers of vineyards ascended up on high from the water's edge, and sturdy vintage manors arose to harvest and ferment the fruit of the vine.

The fortified Teisenhofer Manor with its battlements, built in 1531, once formed part of the defences surrounding the parish church of Weissenkirchen on the Danube, but now houses the Museum of Regional History.

Overleaf: Margrave Leopold III of Austria (1073-1136), the saintly founder of several monasteries, is here shown on a stained-glass window from about 1300, in the Cistercian Abbey of Heiligenkreuz. Incidentally, the striped shield held in his left hand is an anachronism since it was not adopted by the Babenbergs until

For the protection of their peaceful labourers from the enemy, the princes of the Church ordered fortified places of worship to be erected along the river. One such instance is St. Michael, first documented as a parish church in 987; another one, Weissenkirchen or, in its historical spelling, Lichtenchyrchen - so called, we may safely assume, because the church was built not of timber but of white ashlars, thus conspicuously setting it off from many others in the area.

The most well-known of these refuges is probably the Zwiesilaburg, a fortress of God endowed by Bishop Wolfgang of Regensburg at the confluence, or "twistle" (to use a cognate English place-name adjunct), of the Greater and Lesser Erlauf. Its Roman-

about 1200. The field gules, per fess Or, is now the arms proper of Austria. (For a full description, see p. 204.)

esque nave remains intact to this day and has been incorporated, more or less harmoniously, into the modern Wieselburg parish church.

Warding off possible enemy molestations or even inroads was the main concern of the times, and the

military organisation of the newly created March lay in the hands of counts, who were feudal tenants of the German Emperor. First and foremost among the so-called margraves, or 'counts of the border country,' ranked the Babenbergs, who were to guide the destiny of the Danubian lands for fully two hundred and seventy years.

Knights, Knaves, and Minnesingers

The times were turbulent when the Babenbergs were enfeoffed with the Ottonian March. But the German Emperor could not have found more stalwart warriors or more gifted politicians for this unstable border country. Posterity has honoured them with such indicative sobriquets as "The Strong," "The Quarrelsome," "The Virtuous," and "The Glorious"; and it was with every right that they wore these distinctions. Margrave Ernest the Courageous fell in battle on 9 June 1075, near Homburg on the River Unstrut, as retainer to Henry IV. In the face of death, with a severe head injury, he threw himself into the thick of battle; the chroniclers observed admiringly that no sword-stroke found his back.

This Babenberg was, of course, not the only one to demonstrate valour and fixity of purpose. The diplomatic skill of Margrave Leopold III, "the Saint," hardly fell short of his ancestor's standards. He was in fact chosen as a candidate for the German crown after the death of Emperor Henry V.

Nevertheless, the Babenbergs were so capable in their use of family connections that they managed to rise to the rank of Bavarian dukes; for reasons of state, however, they had to lay this honour aside. The *Privilegium minus* was probably intended by way of consolation. With this famous document, dated 17 September 1156, the Austrian March was raised to a dukedom. The Duchy was vested with the exclusive right of jurisdiction within its boundaries, and received a number of financial benefits. In addition, the reigning Duke and his wife were granted the right to select their own heir in the event that they were to have no children. Moreover, the rank and title of Duchess could also be inherited - the first step, as it were, in the emancipation of the Austrian woman.

The expansion of arable land was also well under way at this time. The Babenberg monasteries of Melk and Klosterneuburg, as well as the Cistercian abbeys of Heiligenkreuz and Zwettl, were not only cultural and religious centres, but also bases from which an extensive clearing of forests now began. Paintings that show Cistercian monks at work in the fields do not, however, correspond entirely with reality. On the huge Church-owned estates there were countless *conversi*, or lay brothers, who earned little more than their daily sustenance. Somewhat better off were the bondsmen; they tilled the fields of the landowners and were required to turn over only a specified share of the crops. This form of economy was retained far into the modern era; and even now the knowledgeable wayfarer, walking around the precincts of a monastery or church, will often notice

The ornate Main Library in the Benedictine Abbey of Melk on the Danube. Arching over the painted architecture rises the heavenly kingdom of Hercules, the conqueror of Evil, a masterpiece by Paul Troger, 1731-1732.

the massive granary that was used to store the collected levies. As a matter of fact, in the parish farm
at Weikendorf in the Marchfeld, dungeons still exist
in the basement of the parsonage where, we learn,
peasants were chained as long as they could not pay
their tithes.

Along with the spiritual rulers, the knightly retainers also were successful, through their economic
potential, in achieving high renown. The most
important of these were the "knavish" Kuenrings
who contrary to all slander and libel were of royal
lineage being related to Bavarian and Saxon nobility.
Later, biased accounts describe them as "robber-
knights," who once waylaid merchants travelling
down the Danube to extort horrendous sums of
money from them. The truth is that the Kuenrings
merely exercised their chartered right along the toll-
gates of the Danube. After all, they were a prominent ministerial family, who held the honourable
office of Land Marshal of Austria, and subsequently
were even appointed to the Vicegerency of the country whenever the Duke was going abroad.

In 1192, the Kuenrings won a small niche in the
temple of European fame. The Babenberg Leopold
V was successful in capturing the King of England,
Richard I, nicknamed *Coeur de Lion* ('the Lion-
Hearted'), as he, suspecting trouble, attempted to
cross Austria disguised as a pilgrim. Richard was well
aware of the Austrian's desire for vengeance, for he
had humiliated him on a joint crusade and had also
defrauded him of the hard-earned spoils.

The guardianship of the valuable prisoner was
taken over by the trustworthy Kuenrings, who con-
fined the English monarch in their fortress at Dürnstein on the Danube. This is where, according to a
pretty legend, his loyal minstrel Blondel, wandering

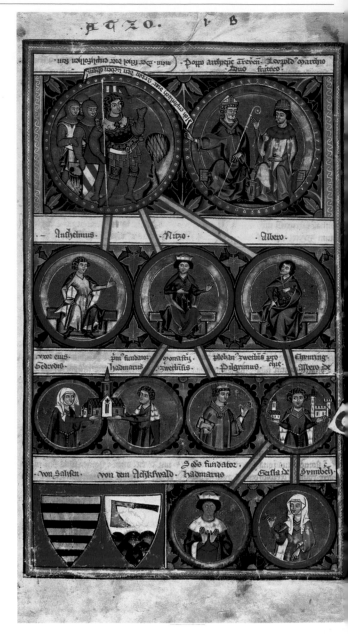

The Kuenring Family
Tree, a miniature in
the Roll of Endow-
ment of Zwettl Mon-
astery. Recorded on
bearskin, about
1311.

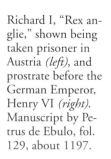

Richard I, "Rex an-
glie," shown being
taken prisoner in
Austria *(left)*, and
prostrate before the
German Emperor,
Henry VI *(right)*.
Manuscript by Pe-
trus de Ebulo, fol.
129, about 1197.

A sectional view of the terra-cotta statues in the arcaded courtyard of Schallaburg Castle. The figures were probably made elsewhere, and then assembled in a row in front of the residential premises.

down the river singing his lost master's favourite songs, suddenly heard the beloved voice take up the air through a slit in the grim walls of the castle. The historical truth is somewhat less romantic. Duke Leopold delivered Richard to the German Emperor, and together they divided a tremendous ransom. England was forced to melt down all her Church treasure in order to gain the monarch's release. The King declared afterwards that "Duke Leopold had sold him to the Emperor as he had been his steer or his ass," but he appears to have been treated throughout with courtesy and even deference.

Still, such disrespect for the immunity of a crusader quite naturally aroused the wrath of the Roman Curia. The Pope excommunicated Leopold, a sentence from which he was not able to free himself until, while lying on his deathbed, he promised to return the entire ransom. Unfortunately, the funds had long since been expended, and England might well be waiting in vain for payment to this day. The Austrian duke had put the money to extremely advantageous use. The capital city was enlarged and refortified. Indeed, there arose a 'New Vienna,' named *Wiener Neustadt* after the parent city, whose ancient walls still stand as reminders of the power politics occasionally entered into by the Babenbergs.

The period of Babenberg rule was, however, not solely one of political power-plays or brutal armed conflicts; it was also an epoch of impressive achievements in the arts and sciences. A brilliant example is the Verdun Altar in the monastic church of Klosterneuburg, a masterpiece of enamelling and a worthy setting for the sepulchre of St. Leopold. Legend tells us that the devoutly Christian duke caused the Pri-

Rueland Frueauf (active 1497-1545), "The Invention of the Veil," a scene from a set of panels depicting the life of St. Leopold.

The Verdun Altar of Klosterneuburg Priory, here seen as a triptych, is one of the finest works of art in the period between the early Gothic and the Romanesque. The enamel sheeting, done by Nicholas of Verdun in about 1181, was originally intended to panel the pulpit of the church.

ory to rise on the exact site where he rediscovered the veil of his newly-wedded bride, Agnes; while she was standing on the terrace of their hill-top castle, a sudden gust had snatched it away from her and thus brought about the famous search.

During the Babenberg period an architecture of bold defiance and a sturdy nature came into existence, such as the Vienna Gate at Hainburg on the Danube and Starhemberg Castle west of Wiener Neustadt; the latter was repeatedly used by the last Babenberg, Frederick the Quarrelsome, as a refuge during his turbulent life.

The minstrel Tanhûser (born ca. 1200), as depicted on the title-page of the Manesse Manuscript, which contains a number of his songs.

These imposing castles did duty not only for defence and protection but, as was the case with the courts of all the strong and wealthy, also served as scenes of intellectual and cultural life. The cliché of rugged and unsophisticated frontiersmen ill fits any of the Babenbergs. They were liberal and open-minded and, indeed, preferably chose their consorts from Byzantine ruling families. The noble households of these princesses invariably comprised a number of artists and artisans, scholars and diplomats from the East Roman Empire, whose cultural influence was variously felt.

Above all, much attention was paid to letters, for this was the heyday of minstrelsy. The minnesingers felt they owed allegiance and blind obedience to the high-born lady, a veneration which culminated in a veritable cult of the fair and noble sex; and it was not until the decades of Tannhäuser, or Tanhûser, with the matter-of-fact tone of his poetry, that the starry-eyed and languishing youth were brought down to earthly realities again. Tannhäuser had no patience with the exaggerated adoration of the troubadours, and his mind delighted rather in the sensuous charms of his *sumer töckel,* his 'little summer doll.'

This famous minstrel was made the title-hero of a monumental opera by Richard Wagner; however, only little of Tannhäuser's macabre, yet often delightful sense of humour has been preserved:

> *Some maidens fair, good wine to boot,*
> *With dainty morsels in the morning;*
> *And eke a bath ta'en twice a week -*
> *These cost a pretty penny.*
>
> *No worries shall becloud my mind*
> *While I have things for pawning;*
> *But when in time I'll have to pay,*
> *Then headaches I'll have many.*

What was he like in real life? The only authentic sources on this singer-poet are his own works. It is here that we learn what a financial burden he must at times have been for Duke Frederick of Babenberg to bear; moreover, he had depleted his own estates to the point of economic ruin.

> *They're landlords now who at my board*
> *Once feasted good and plenty;*
> *And yet I am the selfsame chap*
> *Though years have passed, near twenty!*

The Greed for Realm and Riches

The meteoric rise of the Babenberg dynasty on the political horizon was paralleled only by its sudden eclipse. Duke Frederick II, the last male descendant, died a hero's death in 1246 while defending the eastern borders against the Hungarians. Emperor Frederick II took immediate advantage of the opportunity to place Austria under his direct rule, and he awarded Albero of Kuenring the impressive title *Capitaneus Austriae.* The Emperor, however, had not reckoned with the ambition of the Roman Curia, which at that time saw its mission not only in pastoral activity but also, with little less enthusiasm, in the field of world affairs. Gertrude, the niece of Frederick the Quarrelsome, was married off to Margrave Hermann of Baden, and thus Austria had a new overlord. Unfortunately, he soon made himself thoroughly unpopular there, a problem which was readily solved by sending him on to his just rewards.

Frederick's elderly sister Margaret, nothing more than a helpless pawn in the political chess-game, was then given to the young Margrave Přemysl Otakar. This dynamic nobleman had speedily become King of Bohemia, and had now set his sights on a yet higher goal, the German Crown. The prospect was pleasing; at this juncture both the Babenbergs and the Hohenstaufens had died out, mourned by minstrels and the folk at large:

> *Our Lord and Sovereign is gone hence,*
> *Now stands the Realm withouten heir -*
> *Alas, what dire consequence!*

It did not take long for Otakar's overweening ambition to cast the German Electors into a state of alarm. With their usual regard for the balance of power, they chose a Swabian count, Rudolph of Habsburg, to succeed to the Imperial throne. What a striking contrast to Přemysl Otakar! Rudolph had nowhere near his power and possessions, and must indeed have looked a poor comparison.

Franz Grillparzer, the eminent Austrian poet and dramatist, conveyed the poignancy of the confrontation between two such radically different personalities. The final curtain dropped on "King Ottokar's Rise and Fall" with the Battle of Dürnkrut, on the River March, in 1278; and the insignificant Swabian count went on to sire one of the most powerful dynasties in Europe, one that was to shape the course of world events for almost six and a half centuries.

Historians of yore as well as minstrels tend to glorify great personages beyond recognition, and yet these rulers were not necessarily above the foibles and failings of normal mortal men. What is more, they seldom escaped an insatiable ambition and urge to dominate: the land, and those living upon it, were not only subjects, they were objects, mere chattels, to be divided, re-united, and mortgaged at will.

This was particularly evident in the way the Habsburgian possessions were partitioned in a series of legacies following the death of Rudolph I, for each scion of the family felt called upon to found a branch of his own. Brothers and cousins took up arms against each other, but the main victim was the common man, torn between opposing forces. Such violence did not end until 1439, when Duke Albrecht V, head of the so-called Albertinian branch of the Habsburgs, died of dysentery in Hungary.

But it was not only the "private wars" of this dynasty which brought death and destruction to the people and their land. At about the same time, John Huss (or Hus), a Bohemian religious reformer, had begun to preach his doctrines and quarrel with Rome, and his rabid followers believed that all "intractable" Catholics might best be enlightened by fire and sword. In 1425, the Hussites also invaded the northern parts of Lower Austria, putting towns to the torch and laying waste churches and cloisters. Again and again they crossed through the country, leaving a wake of charred ruins, a course of action little calculated to win ardent converts.

Such perils might possibly be coped with, but there are others against which mortal man is powerless - natural catastrophes. The ancient tale of the horse and rider who were reduced to bare skeletons by a swarm of locusts might even actually have occurred in Lower Austria during the year 1338. According to an entry in the old Chronicle of Zwettl, the plague of locusts was so great that year that it blotted out the sun. A scapegoat for the disaster was sought, and found - the unfortunate Jewish community of Pulkau.

It was an epoch when virulent anti-semitism flamed up in merciless pogroms, and justifications enough were quickly fabricated. The Jews were accused of desecrating the sacred Host, a crime which also figured quite frequently in the trials for witchcraft. It was considered tantamount to "killing Christ." Another popular crime for which non-believers were blamed was the murder of Christian infants, whose blood was supposedly a coveted ingredient for the unleavened matzo bread used in the Jewish Passover. Churches of the "Holy Blood" sprang up everywhere, and superstition and stupidity had their heyday.

Of course, it would be far too one-sided to regard this epoch merely as a series of random cruelties and blood-spilling wars. During the same period there were outstanding ruling personages, such as Emperor Frederick III and Duke Rudolph IV, "the Founder," who added sumptuous buildings to their palatial residences. These patrons of architecture wanted to be remembered for their magnanimity, however. In Wiener Neustadt, the "ever faithful," many buildings still carry Frederick's mysterious acronym, A.E.I.O.U. In spite of the more or less clever cogitations which these letters have given rise to, they could well mean little else than *Austria erit in orbe ultima*: Immortal Austria.

Ambition similar to that of Frederick III's had obsessed one of his ancestors, Rudolph IV. Duke Rudolph, probably the most peculiar of the more fa-

The Armorial Wall adorning St. George's Chapel (built in 1449-1460) of the former Castle in Wiener Neustadt. The Habsburg lands are duly represented by fourteen pictorial designs, but ninety-four fancy arms were added to fill the wide space.

mous Habsburgs, was all willing to improve his fortunes in any way possible, including forgery. Not content with the *Privilegium minus*, which had raised Austria to a duchy in 1156, Rudolph bestowed upon himself a *Privilegium maius* in 1359, granting Austria a great increase of both privileges and power. His "major" claim to power, proven by documents he himself had forged, received official confirmation one hundred years later under Frederick III.

The overwhelming competition of Rudolph's father-in-law, Charles IV, known as "the father of Bohemia and the indeed none-too-loving stepfather of the German Empire," constantly spurred Rudolph on to new deeds. When, for example, Charles opened the University of Prague, Rudolph was not content until Vienna had a university as well. Besides this achievement of great cultural importance, his pioneering economic measures most certainly assure him a place in history. He finally earned undying fame as the "Founder" responsible for the enlargement of the church of St. Stephen's in Vienna into a magnificent Gothic cathedral, into a "temple where Time has wed Eternity."

Those master-builders and masons of the lodge of St. Stephen's were sought after throughout the land; and we find that some of them, such as Masters Puchsbaum or Pilgram, directed a number of other, smaller projects.

Along with the stupendous religious monuments, the art of the Gothic period gave rise to many beau-

tiful dwellings. Among these was the Gozzo Castle, the house of the mayor of Krems. At the latest, most such buildings fell victim to the Baroque wave of the eighteenth century. We do, however, possess the means of reconstructing nearly perfect likenesses of Vienna, Krems or Dürnstein in the Late Middle Ages through the paintings of the panel artists of the Danubian School.

In considering the achievements of the architects of the Middle Ages, we should not, however, overlook the integral part played by Gothic glass-paintings, which, with their dazzling colours, steeped the cathedral interiors in a magic light. Nowhere in the old days was bare white glass, or even the ribbed grey or green or pink leaded lights which play substitute nowadays, to be seen in a cathedral; internally the great old houses of prayer and praise were bathed with "deepened glories, streaming from off the sun like seraph's wings"; the light which fell within them shone prismatic, in a rainbow of eternal hope. Quite often, too, medieval glass-stainers were at pains to picture entire lives of saints; such *libri idiotarum*, as St. Augustine had called them, were meant to tell a story, to teach and to edify.

One high point of the Gothic religious art were the elaborate folding altars, which blended all the various styles of architecture, sculpture and painting together in harmony. Unique works in this genre have come down to us, as for instance the altar in the Church of the Holy Blood at Pulkau, or the carved altar of Mauer, near Melk. The spirit of the Gothic period found consummate expression here: out of the misery of everyday life on earth, man was to be given a chance to catch a glimpse of Heaven.

But a time was coming when even the common people would not be satisfied with mere promises, however gilded. Feudalism, a system of hierarchy ostensibly ordained by God, suffered its first setbacks. With good reason the most important monarch of that era, Emperor Maximilian I, is called the "Last Knight." Even today it is difficult to resist the fascination of this dynamic ruler. Maximilian was the last great potentate of the medieval, absolutistic form; and yet he was also an open-minded supporter of the new concepts of Humanism.

How colourless by comparison is the life of Maximilian's grandson and eventual successor, as depicted by the historians! The crowns of Bohemia and Hungary, which Ferdinand I had managed to gain, meant at the same time war with Turkey. In 1529, for the first time, the Ottomans stood at the gates of Vienna with a powerful army. The Tartarian hordes burnt and murdered their way across the land. Whole villages, such as Perchtoldsdorf and Mödling, until then prospering wine-growing communities, were reduced to ashes and ruins. By 1532, this age-old enemy of the Christian Occident had advanced as far as Waidhofen on the River Ybbs, and was thrown back only due to the courageous resistance of the citizenry. The City Tower of Waidhofen stands today as an impressive monument to the bravery of the men of the local craftsmen's guild; it was erected by the armourers and blacksmiths following their victory over the Turks.

On the other hand, just outside of the territory invaded by the Turkish armies, many towns were beginning to flourish. The wine-growers were first to take advantage of the fact that the Turkish Wars had virtually eliminated Hungarian competition. Heightened prosperity was seen, not least, in a surge of building activity. The wonderful Renaissance mansions and townhouses, a distinctive feature of the Wachau wine-country, date from this period. The well-to-do vintners, in imitation of the upper classes, adorned their homes with elaborate furniture, paintings, figures and figurines, and even libraries. Sgraffito-decorated halls for dancing and game-playing invited men to pause awhile, but not without the admonition:

Be merry, eat and drink,
And yet on God and Heaven think!

The New Faith and the Counter-Reformation

The black-and-white sgraffito paintings, which followed Lutheranism into the land with their representations of Biblical scenes from the Old Testament, signalled a harsh contrast to the Catholic joy in vivid colours. These were the times of the great religious schism. The Lutheran faith spread rapidly and was soon embraced not only by the common people, but also by a majority of the Lower Austrian gentry. In villages and small towns there were often strident clashes between Catholics and Protestants; such sneers and taunts as "Popish, accursed, greasy, short-cropped pedlars of indulgences and murderers of souls" were not uncommon. Indeed, at the manorial seats of nobility, Luther's ideas had already taken deep roots. The famous Rosenburg Castle in the Kamp Valley can actually be regarded as the bulwark of Protestantism; here was the headquarters for the "League of Horn," which had called itself into being in 1608 to defy the Roman Catholic Emperor, Matthew. Was it in truth only a fascination with the teachings of Luther that induced the nobles into a conspiracy against the House of Habsburg? Or was it, as had so often happened before, an instance of a polit-

ical group advancing itself behind a religious façade? In any case, even the most pious man requires a little respite and distraction between his spells of penance, and so feast succeeded feast at Rosenburg, until the prodigal lord of the manor had squandered all his landed possessions. Eventually, the castle proper had to be offered for sale, and the Cardinal of Olmütz, Prince Francis of Dietrichstein, immediately seized this unique opportunity to establish a Roman Catholic observation post in the middle of Lutheran territory.

Luther's teachings were, for the common man, something other than a new path to Eternal Bliss. The reformer appeared, at least in the beginning of his career, to have pledged himself vehemently to the improvement of the abject conditions endured by the peasant class. In order to finance the extravagant

Gozzo Castle, at 12 Margaretenstrasse, high above the old quarter of Krems on the Danube, was a fortified mansion built by Mayor Gozzo for himself in 1258.

Richly decorated Sgraffito House, built in 1576 on the main square of Retz, also acts as an open book for pedestrians to read up on, and be visually impressed by, Greek fables and stories from the Bible.

life style they were accustomed to, the feudal lords had to raise their revenue through all the extortionate measures possible, and in doing so completely drained their bonded labour. In addition to the levies and manifold duties the bondsmen had to perform for the landowners, they were compelled to have their grain harvest ground in the estate mills - which probably contributed, among other factors, to the low opinion millers were held in among the peasantry. Moreover, bread had to be baked in communal ovens, and here too of course appropriate payment was due to the feudal lord. And last but not least, what meagre leisure time the peasant enjoyed was spent in an estate tavern, where only wine and beer produced by his lordship could be served.

The overcharged, overworked peasant class soon saw an open revolt as the only chance to free themselves from the yoke of the landowners. So it happened that towards the end of the sixteenth century Lower Austria became the scene of a peasant rebellion, which was centred in the woodlands of the Waldviertel and in the Alpine foothills. The State's internal strife led naturally to a continual deterioration of the economic situation, which in turn left the poor once again the regrettable victims. The majority of the masses lived in indescribable penury and distress. They suffered from starvation and disease, and were deprived of almost every right - an ideal breeding-ground indeed for revolutionary Lutheranism.

It is quite understandable that the Roman Catholic Church, faced with the swingeing success of the Reformation, took action of its own. Radically new religious orders like the Jesuits sprang into being, which would hardly have been possible had it not been for the effective public agitation of the Counter-Reformation. The leading man of the Catholic faction was Melchior Khlesl, son of a Protestant baker from Vienna. In 1590 he assumed the leadership of the Reform Commission.

The land was besieged by the unrest of religious controversy. The worst, though, was yet to come: the Thirty Years' War. With mounting anger the Protestant Estates in Bohemia resisted every attempt to revive Catholicism in the land. On 23 May 1618, pent-up emotions rose to the boiling-point - and two Royal commissioners and their clerk suffered the consequences: they made a sudden and unceremonious exit from a window of the Hradčany Palace above Prague. This unequivocal statement by the Protestants has gone down in world history as the "Defenestration of Prague."

The incident marked the beginning of a "horrendous destruction of life and land," as the Thirty Years' War has so aptly been characterized. The living conditions of the period could not have been more vividly recorded than by the chronicler Christoffel of Grimmelshausen. His Simplicissimus is the very embodiment of poor Common Man, tortured and humiliated. Every word of the biographical account that Grimmelshausen left to "dear posterity" reveals the depth of his worldly-wise and mellow detachment, but also the kind of irony which only cruel experience can teach a man - if it does not break him. Even in death and destruction, a true Simplicissimus sees God's Providence after all, for "such evils must often be meted out to us for our own benefit by the Grace of the Almighty." Indeed, to give one example, how would poor Simplicissimus have been able to encounter so many interesting people in his remote little village had not enemy soldiers laid waste to his father's house? In the course of this atrocious war, the eyes and ears of many a Simplicius or Simplicissimus were opened, who until then had been "human only in form and Christian only in name, while in all other respects little better than a dumb animal." Nevertheless, the conclusion of the peace treaty in 1648 was welcomed by the few remaining survivors.

Now every gate and gangway stood open to the Counter-Reformation, and court was paid to Simplicissimus as never before. The Church built him sumptuous temples, where he could communicate his needs and desires to God and the Saints, and erected Stations of the Cross for him. He was even allowed to pray at the traditional fountains, stone monuments, and trees with votive tablets - places of worship rooted in pure paganism.

In spite of all this, there were still some people who could not be convinced. For these, two alternatives remained: either to leave house and land and strike out for Protestant territory, or to be led back to the embrace of the Mother Church by force. It goes without saying that such "new converts" were required to demonstrate their beliefs in public, and pilgrimages offered them ample opportunity to do so. There were, of course, those who tended to exaggerate, carrying heavy crosses and stones or devising other means of doing penance on the way.

The Turkish Peril Banned forever

But the trials and hardships were not yet over. In 1683, the Turks stood once again before the gates of Vienna, and for the second time the inhabitants of the surrounding areas were just as harassed as the besieged city. Sultan Mohammed IV must have been absolutely certain of victory, for his declaration of

war on Emperor Leopold I is an epitome of Oriental theatricality: *"First We order you to await Us in Vienna, your city of residence, in order that We may behead you"*; and to King Sobieski, *"and you, you puny King of Poland, do the same!"* As it is, things were to turn out differently, however. The Turks were crushed on the field of battle, assistance from Poland playing a decisive rôle in their defeat. The commander of the Turkish forces, Kara Mustafa Pasha, was sentenced to death by his Sultan for cowardice in the face of the enemy. In their haste to depart, even the commander-in-chief's tent had to be left behind, and the sacred Green Banner of the Prophet was rescued only with difficulty. Along with news of the victory, King Sobieski presented the precious trophy to Pope Innocent XI: *"Veni, vidi,"* and more modestly than Julius Caesar, *"Deus vicit!"* God has conquered!

At last, that period of exuberant joy in life and intense piety which we call the Baroque could begin in earnest. Imposing houses of worship and luxurious residences for the nobility were created, and entire towns were transformed. At the princely courts, music and poetry were at their zenith. The composer Joseph Haydn, the architects Jakob Prandtauer, Johann Bernhard and Joseph Emanuel Fischer von Erlach, the sculptor Georg Raphael Donner, and the painters Daniel Gran and Martin Johann Schmidt, commonly known as Kremser Schmidt - all achieved world-wide fame.

Art had reached a point where further refinement in expression was not possible; and thus a return to simplicity of form began. Consequently, the early nineteenth century was a time when artists rediscovered the wonders of Nature and took a new joy in the smaller things of life. The paintings of men like Waldmüller and Gauermann present scenes of pastoral beauty; they show the peasants of the Vienna Forest at work, and depict popular dress and custom. Art drew its inspiration from the everyday experiences of landscape and Nature. It is a romantic and, at the same time, light-hearted music which Schubert gave to us, and the plays by Raimund are full of fairy magic.

However, the early nineteenth century was also the time when the idea of a "united" Europe once again became the pretext for ruthless genocide, this time at French instigation. And, as had so often been the case before, Austria rose to the occasion. At Aspern, an Austrian army was responsible for the first defeat of Napoleon's ever-victorious troops. Although the battle did not prove decisive, a huge stone lion in the local church square continues to bear mute testimony to the spectacular victory of Archduke Charles.

What followed is generally well known. Napoleon was defeated, and a costly Congress was convened in Vienna, where a great deal was discussed but very little was done.

Other Misfortunes Mastered by Austria

The nineteenth century still had many trials in store for the country. The widespread uprisings of 1848 brought about the abrupt end of the Biedermeier period, the so-called good old days. The Revolution did not originate in the capital, but at Pressburg (Bratislava), where Ludwig Kossuth raised a passionate protest against the Austrian system of government before the Hungarian Diet. Duly inspired, the three Provincial Estates of Lower Austria rallied together in Vienna and, in turn, demanded more freedom and reforms. The one and only result of these riotous protests worth mentioning proved to be the liberation of the Austrian peasantry from the oppression of the landowners; all other concessions promised to the people fell victim to the reactionary backlash.

It soon became apparent, however, that the landed nobility thus assailed had not been such a bad institution after all; they performed the same function in regard to their leaseholders as the farmers' co-operatives later would, guaranteeing their subjects a relatively secure existence. Actually, it was only under the manorial system that a good many smallholders were able to survive; and now they found themselves ever deeper in debt, eventually losing everything they had once owned.

The uprooted peasantry then swarmed into the factories, the very cheapest of labour; and history has shown us the glaring mistake made by the government and the employers of that period in that they failed to take steps to remedy the economic weaknesses in time - waiting, instead, until the situation had become dramatically strained. As a matter of fact, the craftsmen's guilds of the Middle Ages had early recognized the absolute necessity of a welfare plan for the sick, and material benefits for the disabled - needs to which modern industrial society was blind. In its sight, a worker existed insofar as he was capable of bringing profits. And in this situation lay the seeds of the great social and political changes to come.

But besides the social question, a second, nearly insoluble problem came to a head - the national one. From the end of the eighteenth century onwards, the Habsburg Monarchy found itself confronted with an awakening national consciousness in the peoples it comprised. Hungarians, Czechs, Serbians,

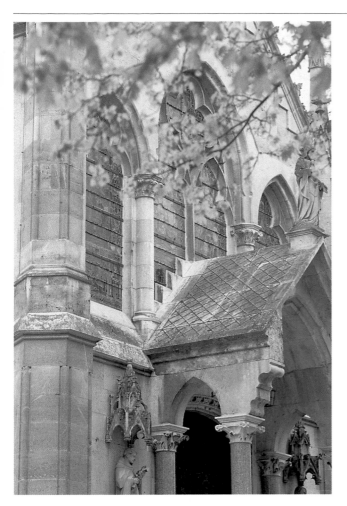

Croatians, and Slavs all demanded release from the supranational political confederation.

Like some awesome foreboding, the blows of fate rained down upon the Imperial family. In 1889, Crown Prince Rudolph, the only son of Emperor Francis Joseph I, committed suicide in his hunting-lodge near Mayerling in the Vienna Forest, taking his mistress, Mary Vetsera, with him. A tragedy of love? Hardly. Although the facts behind the actual event were carefully concealed, the man in the street was not content with the official version. Rather he suspected:

> *Prince Rudolph took the secret*
> *To his grave where lips are sealed;*
> *We have to bow in silence*
> *To Destiny unrevealed.*

The second great misfortune was the murder of Empress Elizabeth by an anarchist, Luccheni. This, in turn, was followed by the assassination of the new successor to the throne, Francis Ferdinand, which ignited the powder keg of the First World War.

As the coffins of the murdered heir and his wife were being brought home to Artstetten Castle north of Pöchlarn, a few miles from the left bank of the Danube, a fearful storm arose, tearing the ferry loose from its moorings. At just about the same time, Austria declared war on Serbia, which was the beginning of the end of the Habsburg Monarchy.

The War was lost, and the vast Empire disintegrated into the Succession States - and what was left of the Austrian homelands. This process of dissolution also affected some parts of Lower Austria, which had to cede territory near Gmünd and Lundenburg. On 12 November 1918, Austria was proclaimed a republic. In it, Karl Renner was to become the first Chancellor, Karl Seitz, President of the National Assembly; and Emperor Charles I, successor to the "Last Monarch of the Old School," went into exile with his ambitious wife, Zita.

The "new" Austria, of course, did not possess a fitting national anthem, and so a popular version made do at first by adapting the old Imperial Anthem to the present situation:

> *God preserve our good man Renner,*
> *God preserve our good man Seitz;*
> *God preserve - who knows what's coming? -*
> *Karl in faraway Swiss heights....*

As humorous as this may sound, the difficulties facing the country were enormous. The young republic lacked an economic system based on the country's specific needs. But radical change had created new needs for what was now the paltry remains of a great empire. Young Austria was thus cut off from her markets and sources of raw materials, and faced with the collapse of an economic system that had gradually developed over the centuries. Moreover, the world-wide crises of 1922 and 1929 brought in their wake mass unemployment and dire poverty.

As always occurs in such fated hours, there arose politicians who promised the people "a time of greatness"; the consequences proved to be even more disastrous than those of the First World War.

Still, the *Vae victis*, which Brennus, King of the Gauls, had once hurled at conquered Rome, was not necessarily to be repeated in this case. A segment of the victorious Powers demanded no war indemnity from the defeated. In fact, they made available considerable sums for the rebuilding of Germany and Austria. And thus began that period praised in Germany as the "Economic *Wunder*," but which the Austrians welcomed simply as a miracle.

So, many sources of income now enrich and vary business life in Lower Austria, the biggest federal province; and its inhabitants take pride in having, since 1986, a capital of their own, St. Pölten.

The hunting-lodge of Mayerling, in the Vienna Forest, was the scene of the suicide by Archduke Rudolph of Habsburg-Lothringen, the 30-year-old Crown Prince of Austria; Baroness Mary Vetsera, his teenage lover, died with him - a tragedy that continues to invite speculations to this day.

In 1890, barely a year later, an order of the Emperor transformed the hunting-lodge into a Carmelite convent, with the Archduke's bedroom turned into a chapel.

Upper Austria

Anyone looking at a map of Upper Austria for the first time is bound to notice the River Danube. A natural line of demarcation, it cuts across the land dividing it into two dissimilar halves - dissimilar in many respects. Below the Danube eternal Alpine glaciers form a natural borderline, while northwards the mountains recede into gently rolling hills.

Following an old tradition, however, people bisect these halves again, in accordance with the natural features and location of the area. The Traunviertel has for a long time been characterized by Alpine dairy farming, the Innviertel by the cultivation of grain, the Hausruckviertel by fruit-growing and the raising of livestock. Well into the nineteenth century the upper Mühlviertel was devoted to cottage industries, above all to the weaving of linen. The contrasting nature of these individual quarters is expressed not so much in their landscape or the structure of their economies as in the respective inhabitants themselves.

The Innviertel, for example, was incorporated into Upper Austria relatively late - 1779. This fertile region had previously belonged to Bavaria, and thus it comes as no great surprise that neighbourly differences of opinion in this part of Austria, which can at times be very extreme even from village to village, occasionally resulted in open violence between the people of the Innviertel and the *Landler*, or original Austrians. The exclusive collection of "brawling tools" in the Museum of Local History at Braunau speaks for itself.

A gnomic folk-rhyme expresses the distinctive feature of each of the four areas more vividly than simple prose might:

Innviertel, grain for foal and mare;
Mühlviertel, flax and things to wear;
Hausruckviertel, stores of fruit and fat;
Traunviertel, wood to build and salt to fill the vat.

Upper Austria is still a land full of discoveries for those capable of really seeing, and those whose hearts are sensitive to beauty. The widely branching mountain ranges, the romantic river valleys, the fertile countryside with its fields of waving grain are not merely a backdrop to that which enchants, but rather the very stuff that has nurtured the history and traditions of its people for thousands of years.

The history of Upper Austria is as varied as the land itself, a picture-book in which the early times have left their traces. The Traunviertel, which constituted the centre of Old Bavarian settlement in the Early Middle Ages, is a land of pristine culture, the beginnings of which extend back almost to the dawn of mankind. As early as 2000 B.C. a kind of settle-ment began here that still exists to this day outside of Europe: the lake dwelling. The present state of archaeological research has proved that lake dwellings were once built on the shores of Lakes Mondsee and Attersee and that these were probably places where copper and salt were stored and traded. "Bartering" was nothing unusual in prehistoric times. Like copper, amber and later iron were traded over great distances.

Salt, a product much in demand and traded for everywhere, has been mined in the area of present-day Hallstatt for more than 2,500 years. Even at that early date, salt-mining here was responsible for the growth of a European trade centre. Systematic excavations have uncovered evidence of this ancient and very advanced culture and have provided an insight into a fascinating, fabulous world, which had been buried and forgotten.

Flourishing cultures, however, have a tendency to disintegrate as soon as they reach their zenith and to become weak and susceptible. In the course of history, this basic theme has often been repeated. About 400 B.C., great disaster befell the wealthy salt lords of Hallstatt. Foreign warriors, the Celts, conquered their settlements and overran the whole country. That empire of the Celts was in its turn destroyed by a young, unspent people, the Romans; and when the Roman culture had reached its peak, the Germanic tribes stormed over them and brought the development of human history to a momentary standstill. This was in the fifth century A.D. The vast empire ceased to exist, but the intellectual and cultural values that Rome had left to her conquerors can hardly be enumerated. The crafts, stone constructions, architecture and, most important, the exemplary system of government and its bureaucracy are evidence of a new age.

The period of the Great Migration of the Peoples is estimated to have ended in about the year 600 A.D. At that time, the Bavarians, a tribe whose origin scholars have as yet been unable to determine, had settled in the area of what is today Upper Austria. They probably pushed forward out of Bohemia into the foothills of the Alps and the flat lands bordering the Danube. Linguists have been able to reconstruct the path they took almost exactly, for it is marked by those old place-names in *-ing*, a derivative suffix that has been identified as a verbal hallmark of Bavarian annexation. The region settled by the Old Bavarians encompassed the land between the rivers Aschach and Traun, extended northwards to the Danube, westwards to the Lech, southwards to the Inn and finally as far as the vicinity of Trient. In the period we are speaking of, a number of such "barbarian" kingdoms and dukedoms arose within the former boundaries of the Roman Empire. Of these, however, only one was to remain in the eighth century: the Frankish Empire. The hereditary duchy of Bavaria was able to maintain its autonomous position longest in the face of the Empire of the Franks. Not until the reign of Duke Tassilo III did a decisive political crisis occur. In the year 757, Tassilo swore fealty to the Frankish king Pepin the Short; yet at the same time, the Bavarian was clever enough to turn his overlord's temporary political weakness to the advantage of new efforts towards freedom. For two decades, Tassilo, using great diplomatic skill, managed to secure for his duchy prosperity and economic independence. The Bavarians were even able to take up peaceful trade relations with the Avars, then a daunting tribe. Yet it was this very pact of friendship - for that time a rather unorthodox one - which caused the new king of the Franks, Charlemagne, to remind Duke Tassilo of his fealty.

Orth Castle, with its venerable keep and chapel dating from 1138, is perched on a small rocky islet at the northern end of Lake Traun, just outside Gmunden.

Tassilo, however, disliked having to follow other people's advice, and he probably allied himself with the Avars in order to declare war on the Frankish king. But events were to take a completely different turn. Charlemagne's machinations against Tassilo, who henceforth seemed lacking in diplomacy, demanded no bloodshed. They were, rather, a masterpiece of political intrigue, with the result that the Bavarian nobility and clergy simply dropped their former lord and began paying homage to the ruler of the Franks. When Duke Tassilo saw himself deserted by all his followers, there was nothing for him to do but to bow as well to the sovereignty of the Carolingian. But that did not conclude the matter. During the Imperial Diet at Ingelheim in the year 788 Charlemagne had his "new" vassal arrested on the spot and condemned to death in a show trial. In the end, however, "pious King Charlemagne" pardoned the Duke, and "full of mercy and for the love of God" sentenced him to life imprisonment in a monastery instead.

At long last, the House of the Carolingians came into legitimate possession of the duchy of Bavaria. In 794, six years after the fall of Duke Tassilo, a totally broken man appeared before the Synod of Frankfurt. With a toneless voice he begged "to be considered worthy of forgiveness," just as he himself meant to forget "all anger and all tribulation." It was none other than "Brother Tassilo," who here in the

The Tassilo Chalice, at Kremsmünster, is still used today on the occasion of the election of a new abbot. It was given to the monks by Count Tassilo III of Bavaria, possibly when he founded the monastery in 1777. The chalice, made of gilded copper, is richly decorated with images and abstract ornamentation which, in a good many details, bears a resemblance to medieval Irish counterparts. It is the earliest and most magnificent relic of medieval German art. It is the earliest and most magnificent relic of medieval German art.

The Frankenburg Game of Dice. The linden-tree served as a gallows for the seventeen unfortunate leaders of the peasant revolt (1625).

name of all his descendants explicitly renounced his claim to the Agilolfing possessions in favour of the Carolingians.

Pro-Carolingian historians then did their best to convey to posterity a wholly distorted portrait of the last Agilolfing. More recent research has, however, been able to rehabilitate the unfortunate Tassilo in many respects and to explain his deeds adequately; for what else was this rebellious duke really than the victim of the dynastic policies of the Franks?

Now that the tribal dukedom of Bavaria had been subordinated to the Frankish crown, Charlemagne was able to devote himself at his leisure to the "pacification" of the Avars. The subsequent course of history is well-known. Out of the land they had conquered, the Carolingians formed the first Eastern March which in turn was to be devastated by the Hungarians. And when these wild people from the steppes finally recognized the merits of Christian civilization, the second Eastern March came into being. In 976, the Babenbergs duly set themselves up as margraves in the eastern Mühlviertel. From then on, what is today's Upper Austria shared under the name of *Land ob der Enns, Landl,* or *Austria superior* the same historical fate as that of most South German principalities.

It would be better, however, to consider Upper Austria as actually taking shape in the eighteenth century. At that time, when the last of the ruling line of the House of Wittelsbach had perished, the Habsburg Emperor Joseph II laid claims on hereditary grounds to the duchy of Bavaria, which of course immediately met with fierce resistance. Finally, King Frederick II of Prussia came to the conclusion that the Habsburgs should not be allowed to increase their power any further. The so-called War of the Bavarian Succession ensued, which, to be sure, was very soon brought to an end when France and Russia, then the major powers, took no steps to intervene and "disentangle" the conflict. Therefore, in 1779, the treaty of Teschen was negotiated, by which the Innviertel was deeded to the Habsburgs.

Although it was possible to end the War of the Bavarian Succession without any larger military engagements having taken place, the people suffered bitterly, as was so often their fate. To this day at Braunau, one can see the iron statue of a horse reminding people of that terrible period, during which the population were so starved that they were reduced to eating horsemeat. When one reflects upon recent history, this may not sound too dreadful; yet, an aversion towards horsemeat was rooted deeply in these people's minds and possibly had a religious background. The Ancient Germans had

sacrificed the "Holy Steed" to their gods, and its blood and flesh were solemnly consumed during cultic feasts. With the advent of Christianity, the eating of horsemeat was strictly forbidden as a "heathen custom." As a result of this, horsemeat might well have seemed as repulsive as the flesh of dead rats or snakes to a true Christian.

"It has to be!"

There must have been, all too often, times when even horsemeat was not available and the people were barely able to satisfy their most primitive

King Frederick II of Prussia, surnamed the Great, wearing the uniform of the First Life Guards Battalion. An oil painting on wood (Austrian National Library, Vienna).

needs. To be sure, there were occasionally short periods in which the peasants were well-off and thought they could live "like the great lords." The story of *Meier Helmbrecht*, written around 1250 by the native monk, Wernher the Gardener, shows what a dreadful end this kind of presumptuousness could lead to. Helmbrecht, the son of a peasant, set out to conquer the world and ended up as a vagabond on the gallows. The Monk of Ranshofen summed it up like this, "Perhaps Helmbrecht still has followers?" "They will be little Helmbrechts. I cannot protect you from them, but I assure you they will end as he did, on the gallows!" But Helmbrecht did find followers, hundreds and thousands of them. In 1525 all Germany was in flames. In loosely organized, undisciplined groups, formidably armed with sickles, scythes, and flails bristling with the nails that had been hammered into them, the peasants plundered the surrounding countryside haphazardly; they laid siege to smaller towns and put a few monasteries to the torch. But before this rebellion had met with any real success, the feudal lords struck back. By the end of the year 1525 the rebels were brought to trial at Vöcklabruck. In the original verdict, the guilty men were to have worn a noose around their necks for the rest of their lives. This sentence was, however, "graciously" converted, and those condemned ended up having only to pay their sovereign twelve additional farthings per year.

Yet, once awakened, the dream of human dignity, the lessening of oppression and exploitation, continued to exert its influence. A whole series of uprisings failed and each time the result was a bloody tribunal, which nevertheless was unable to quash the revolutionary fervour.

In 1594, trouble broke out repeatedly in Upper Austria, triggered by the famine and continual oppression by those in power. The consequence was - at least temporarily - wholesale arrests and executions once again. Only Stephan Schwärzl, the town judge of Ischl, considered himself equal to the problems and, in 1601, he organized a rebellion against the Catholic overlords, which finally led to the compulsory conversion of the inhabitants of the Salzkammergut. Under such duress, the doctrines of Protestantism meant probably not so much a new path to a distant God, but rather offered a chance to lead a decent human life here on earth. Schwärzl's idea that the Protestant peasants should therefore fight against their Catholic oppressors persisted, and the revolutionary spirit in Upper Austria lived on.

The peasant uprisings then spread to the lower classes in the towns. Beginning in March 1621, the citizens of Steyr had had to supply provisions to a Bavarian garrison which at the time was occupying the land above the River Enns. Before long there were loud objections raised against the Bavarians who were *"filling themselves up with wine and brandy, mead, beer and every excess of food and drink, blaspheming God, fornicating, offending and ruining honest people's children, and devouring most of their property."*

Yet, the final motivation to take drastic steps against a political power hundreds of years old was still lacking. Taken as a whole, all the revolts up to that time had been of local significance only. But then the peasants suddenly arose in masses, after Count Herberstorff had forced thirty-six highly respected men to cast dice for their lives on the Haushamerfeld near Frankenburg. To this day, the performance of *The Frankenburg Game of Dice* commemorates this cynical and gruesome instance of perverted justice.

The upheaval now spread more rapidly, but the rebelling peasants were not equal to the forces of the feudal lords this time either, and they were beaten in decisive confrontation. Stephan Fadinger, one of the intellectual leaders of the Upper Austrian peasant revolts, was killed during the siege of Linz on 28 June 1626, while on reconnaissance. Wolf Madlseder, the town judge of Steyr, was captured, beheaded, and drawn and quartered by his executioners. His disfigured head was exhibited at the pillory in his home town for months as a warning to all rioters.

It was the goal of those in authority to so intimidate the people that they would never again rise up against them. The fire of open rebellion appeared quenched and the embers stamped out. But under the ashes there glowed a spark. Soon a new leader of the people arose: Martin Eichinger, *der Laimbauer*, a man who was also capable of ensnaring the superstitious people with all sorts of trickery.

Tragically, Eichinger also lost his life on the block on 20 June 1636. From this point on, there were no more bloody peasant revolts, although the situation of the rural populace had in no respect improved. Horrified, the parish priest of Ternberg reported at the time, "A peasant together with his household eats in three months less than a pound of meat; he drinks with the geese, dresses in coarse *loden*, 'walks on German leather' (i.e., goes barefoot) and uses wooden torches for candles."

"For seldom does he have good fortune who rebels against his station, and your station is behind the plough!" exhorted Wernher the Gardener, and as it turned out, the much desired economic and social changes did not come about for centuries.

The victory of feudalism was documented nowhere as clearly as in the field of architecture. A

new style, the Baroque, was meant to express the triumph of the Counter-Reformation. In almost every village, churches and convents were restored, and bishops' palaces and residences for the nobility were built.

Clearly bearing witness to this period are shrines of pilgrimage like Christkindl near Steyr. According to legend, the gracious child Jesus is said to have converted even a Protestant soldier to a pious hermit. Carlo Antonio Carlone and Jakob Prandtauer erected the famous church, where to this day the Christ-Child is said to stop by the post office each Advent season to collect the Christmas wishes.

It is said that in all Austria there was no blossoming of the Baroque more profuse than that in the area above the River Enns. Wherever we may go, we encounter here the works of long forgotten artists - in old village churches, on lonely crossroads or at the edge of a field. And it was this same spirit, which enabled simple man to find prayer and comfort in art, that also filled Master Prandtauer; that leading architect gave form and expression to the new style from his own emotional experiences following the death of Carlone.

Small Towns - Meaningful Names

The well-to-do upper middle classes of the larger cities, the merchants and wealthy master craftsmen, were all eager to follow the example set by the rich nobles. Linz, nowadays the political and cultural centre of Upper Austria, was, at that time, unlike Vienna, Graz or Salzburg, not the residence of an art-loving prince, but instead owes the historical character of its streets and squares and houses solely to its citizens' appreciation of art. Renaissance and Baroque architecture can be seen everwhere, and of course there are also examples of the *Empire* and more modern styles.

The Linz of today is not just an important port on the Danube; it also serves as the junction of an extensive railway system. It may underline the economic significance of this town to note that the first horse-drawn railway on the European continent, carrying salt freight to Bohemia, was opened here on 21 July 1832; in the opposite direction, the line was extended as far as Gmunden four years later. Nevertheless, Linz became only gradually the capital of Upper Austria. For a long while the population of Enns or of Steyr, for example, was far larger than that of Linz. What is more, Enns had proudly owned its own mint since the Middle Ages, which, however, acquired a sorry reputation when Albrecht VI had the infamous *Schinderlinge* coined there.

One might well have spoken of a contest between Archduke Albrecht and his brother, Emperor Frederick III, to see who could put into circulation the worst and most low-grade coin. A contemporary chronicler said this of the *Schinderling* Period: "And such a lot of these farthings and pennies were brought to Vienna that in the end the children played tossing games with them in the alleys."

Nowadays War, Famine and Dearth are forgotten; Enns is a quiet little town in the country, in whose narrow lanes the past dreams on. An active economy and good trade have given this city near the Danube its individual character. Navigation along that big river was early to join the peoples along its banks to their hinterland. "And before the onslaught of men and their steeds, the water ceased to sparkle, as if it were dark earth, as far as one might see...," sang the poet of *The Lay of the Nibelungs*. Indeed, the Raffelstetten Customs Regulations, an extensive toll record dating back to the year 906, bears witness to the fact that trade and business dealings were quite active even then.

During the Crusades, one trading settlement after another lined the river and collected market dues and tolls. When, in 1189, the citizens of Mauthausen insisted upon having their privileges honoured even by an army of Crusaders, violence broke out. At last Emperor Barbarossa, the leader of the pious band of pilgrims, simply ordered the homes of the obstinate citizens of Mauthausen to be burnt down.

Normally though, trade seems to have gone on peacefully. Actually, the voyage on the Danube itself held many hazards in store for "Christian navigation"; before the relieved boatsmen could jubilate, "Saint Nicholas, Saint Nicholas, for glee! Of whirlpools and of rapids we are free!" there was many a danger to overcome. At Grein, in the face of the swirling maelstrom, the most valuable goods were loaded into waggons and taken to St. Nikola by the land route, and it was said, "The Devil wanted to place a stone wall in the middle of the Danube one night in order to bring about the ruin of the pious Christian folk of Grein. But when the cock greeted the new day a little too soon, Satan flew into such a rage that he smashed his work with one mighty blow of his clawed hand..." And from that time on the Strudengau is said to have become a watery "cemetery" for rivermen. In this connection, an ordinance of 1770 issued to captains navigating the Danube sounds rather inhuman; it ruled that no sailor should be hired unless he was a non-swimmer, lest he desert his ship to rescue himself in case of danger. *[See p. 36 offering a reference to two contemporary accounts featuring the horrors of the deep between St. Nikola and*

Grein; one is a legend-embroidered episode in the life of an Austrian journeyman, and the other a page from the chronicle of an early English traveller.]

But not only the cities and markets on the Danube display their own unique characters. Even an old industrial town like Steyr, through its provincial surroundings and quaint old buildings, can well be considered one of the most charming places in Austria. As early as the tenth century the *Stirapurch* stood upon a steep hill here at the junction of the Enns and the Steyr. Like the Ennsburg, it served as a bulwark of the Christian Occident against the rapacious Magyars. It did not take long for the first traders in military supplies to settle near the castle of the Otakars of Steyr. In the course of time, palisades and earthen walls were built around the huts of the craftsmen; a fortified settlement was established. With the flourishing of trade in Styrian ore, the once humble beginnings grew into one of the richest and most active towns in the country, producing steel and iron goods that have been exported to ports on the North and Baltic Seas, to Bohemia and Moravia, to Poland, Russia, Hungary, and Italy since at least the sixteenth century.

Venerable patrician houses speak eloquently of its citizens' prosperity to this day. The *Bummerlhaus*, the former Golden Lion Inn, enjoys almost international fame. In the vernacular, the rather strangely shaped lion on the sign of the house was quickly dubbed a *Bummerl*, or a poodle. Occasionally such house signs even led to the creation of whole myths and legends. The *Innerberger Stadel*, a former warehouse that now accommodates the Museum of Local History with its rich exhibits of folklore, including a mobile nativity scene dating from the Baroque age, enjoys a fame similar to that of the *Bummerlhaus*.

Upper Austria, and above all the Traunviertel, is well-known for its wealth of medicinal springs. The spas at Bad Ischl, Hall, and Goisern draw their clientele from all over the world.

Certainly the peace and majesty of nature, which provides the setting for these charming health resorts, contributes to the success of their treatments. Ischl lies on the banks of the River Traun, protected on all sides by mountain ranges. The bracing climate of this woodland area is ideal for recovery and recuperation. The radioactive saline springs are said to work veritable wonders for a variety of illnesses; drinking the water can be successful in treating bronchitis and asthma, and is even said to have good results in cases of unfulfilled desires for children. Rumour has it that the Austrian Archduke Francis Charles and his wife Sophia did not have

their "Salt-Prince," later to become Emperor Francis Joseph I, until after a lengthy stay in the spa town.

Bad Ischl soon became the spa which set the fashion, where not only crowned heads, but also many prominent personalities from politics and cultural life were seen. Next to the Imperial residence there grew up sanatoriums, villas and exclusive hotels. The world-famous Elisabeth Hotel played a not insignificant part in the love-story of Emperor Francis

The "Bummerlhaus," a venerable patrician residence erected in 1497.

The richly ornate heraldic arms on Wels Castle, the last halt on the tragic path through life of Emperor Maximilian I.

"White Gold"

This same Emperor Maximilian, who even in death wanted to cry out his abysmal contempt for mankind and his spiritual anguish, was one of the most capable statesmen of his day. As a result of his circumspection the extraction of salt became a monopoly of the state.

Even then, of course, salt-works had been in existence for more than 2,000 years. Indeed, eight centuries before the birth of Christ the salt-mines at Hallstatt had been a flourishing centre of European trade. The wealth thus opened up to the original inhabitants of that locality is exemplified most clearly in their graves. A scholar of prehistorical studies, Friedrich Behn, compares the splendour and appointments of the burial grounds of Hallstatt with those of Etruscan and Scythian princes. The riches deposited in the graves is indeed astonishing: decorative objects, weapons, bronze cauldrons, and vases arrived at Hallstatt from afar, perhaps from Italy, Southern Germany, and Hungary; while others, like amber, may have come from even farther away. These objects were most probably used as currency in payment for the salt, which was so much in demand.

For nearly four hundred years this wealthy and powerful people had been actively mining salt when from among the Alpine foothills a strange tribe, the Celts, invaded their territory and assumed power. The Celts also took possession of the salt-pits above Hallein, in the Dürrnberg. Ultimately, it was in the sphere of Celtic influence that the salt deposits achieved particular significance.

The economic and political organization of the new rulers rested upon castles and other fortified centres of power. These hill forts, or *oppida*, were not merely defensive settlements extending their influence over smaller or larger areas; they also served as the nodal points in an extensive trade network and were thus established with great forethought on the vital traffic routes and at road junctions. Only recently has research at last been able to provide us with a clearer picture of the configuration and development of this culture. The remains of Celtic fortifications are being examined meticulously and offer important evidence of the early history. In the Upper Austrian valley of the Krems, archaeologists excavating on the Georgenberg near Micheldorf have even uncovered the relics of a Celtic temple dedicated to Tutates and containing a circular gallery for religious processions. According to the writings of the Bavarian chronicler Aventinus, the little community of Braunau on the River Inn is said to have developed from the Celtic Brundunum. In Linz, Celtic

Joseph and Elizabeth of Bavaria. It was here that the young monarch met his beloved Sisi for the first time when he came to escort his aunt Ludovica and her two marriageable daughters to a court ball.

Just as there is much more suffering and sorrow in men's lives than there is good fortune and joy, so are most of the stories handed down to us in the chronicles of ancient houses full of woe and misery. The last act in the tragic life of Emperor Maximilian I also took place in the Castle of Wels. It was here that he died on 12 January 1519. The "Weisskunig" was no longer the skilful politician, the "Last Knight" described to us in history books. Instead, he had become a bitter old man, whose contempt for the world is nowhere more apparent than in his last will and testament. In glaring contrast to normal practices the Emperor had ordered that his corpse be neither disembowelled nor embalmed, but rather be scourged and then covered with quicklime and ashes. And if that were not enough, his servants were to cut off his hair and pull out his teeth and bury them in red-hot coals. It appears as if the Emperor, through his martyred body, intended to remind his fellow beings one last time of the fact that "since Jesus Christ no one had suffered as much as he."

The Emperor's Villa, set in a spacious park on the outskirts of Bad Ischl, a wedding present from the Emperor's mother to Francis Joseph and Elizabeth (1853). Here the monarch came every summer to stay and live the simple life he liked best, sometimes hunting the deer and chamois on the neighbouring mountains. High-level diplomacy, of course, also duly filled his rural agenda. King Edward VI, for instance, came two or three times from England, and was heartily welcome; even when Francis Joseph had to make at Ischl his famous refusal to King Edward's appeal that Austria should be cut loose from the German alliance, there was no breach in their mutual affection.

Hallstatt, a picturesque place, used to be the centre of the salt trade and of the so-called Hallstatt Culture. Crammed in between the lake and the mountain slopes, the houses nestle against the rocks.

settlements have also been discovered in the hills of Freinberg and Grünberg. The intersection of the old Salt Road from the Traunviertel, both with the River Danube and with the important east-west line of communication from Salzburg, constantly attracted merchants here even since prehistoric times, which duly resulted in a concentration of trade in the area.

When the Romans pressed forward into the Celtic Kingdom of Noricum, they already found a number of important trading depôts connected by a fairly well developed network of roads. However, the epochal turning-point in the political and economic development of this region was not reached until the influence of the Roman civilization had made itself felt. It was not the Celts, but the Romans who laid the foundations of the European municipal system, a solid basis for commerce and trade, and for a state religion as well.

Roman Noricum

The findings of archaeologists have sufficiently documented the fact that around the time of Christ's birth Roman auxiliary citadels were being built on the southern bank of the Danube, following the Norician *limes*. These were primitive constructions of timber and earth, made in order to maintain control of the sparsely settled and almost impassable no man's land on the other side of the river. It was only after the bitter experiences of the wars with the Marcomanni that those strongly fortified military camps were set up whose names have come down to us in the *Notitia Dignitatum*. During Roman times Wels was called Ovilava, Linz was Lentia, and Lorch near Enns, Lauriacum; presumably, Eferding is the ancient Marinianum, and Aschach, Joviacum.

There has never been a lack of archaeological evidence dating from Roman times in the southern part of Upper Austria. From the workmanship of the objects found it may be concluded, however, that, as for example in Carnuntum, there was a clearly established frontier culture, in which Germanic influence had an active share.

Obviously, the Romans also knew how to put the rich salt deposits in the Traunviertel to effective use. This staple commodity was at that time shipped along the old trade-routes through the Traun valley into the countries along the Danube, or carted over the Pötschen Pass into Styria, and on to the South.

Likewise the cultural development continued hand in hand with the flourishing of economic life. Christianity had probably been accepted by the Roman inhabitants of Noricum by the third century. Legend has it that as early as the year 303 A.D.

Christians were being persecuted at Lauriacum, and that Florianus, now the patron saint of Upper Austria, was one of those martyred. Florianus, an important Roman official, was condemned to death for his forbidden religious convictions and drowned in the River Enns. But the river refused to accept its victim and put the corpse ashore upon a rock. For the first time we have here a phenomenon that is found everywhere in the history of German Christianization: the Germanic peoples accepted Christianity, altering, at the same time, the teachings to fit their own conceptions of religion. From their point of view the river, which returned Florian's body, was nothing other than a deity that refuses a sacrifice, for to these people the death penalty was essentially of an expiatory nature.

Similarly, the legend which followed the founding of St. Florian Monastery reflects the traditions of classical antiquity far more than Christian ones. In order to find the grave that God had chosen, the martyr's corpse was bound to an ox-cart and the animals were given free run. According to the legend, the place where they came to a halt is the site of today's famous Abbey of St. Florian. The motif involved probably belongs to the most original myths in the field of Indo-European civilization. The solar deity drawn by sacred cattle or horses is found in Greek myths and in Celtic and Germanic sagas alike. In the Sun-Carriage of Trundholm and in the Cult Chariot of Strettweg (see p. 129) we possess graphic representations of this sacred act.

Ten years after Florian's martyrdom, in about 313 A.D., Christianity became the official state religion following the so-called Edict of Tolerance issued by Emperor Constantine. It is quite possible that the famous St. Lawrence Church at Lorch goes back to this period. The temple, dedicated to Capitoline deities, was probably transformed into a Christian basilica around the year 340 A.D. The architectural history of St. Martin's Church near Linz can also be traced back to the Early Christian era. It must be stressed that research in this area has by no means been completed. The chain of discoveries, as various findings allow us to suspect, is likely to continue for some time to come.

Towards the middle of the fourth century Christianity already had a strong hold in the province of Noricum. To be sure, the new religion had developed distinctive features of its own on this side of the Alps, a cultural phenomenon paralleled by the Christian forms which European missionaries have introduced to Africa and South America in modern times. In the Roman Empire of that period, two views of Christianity faced one another implacably,

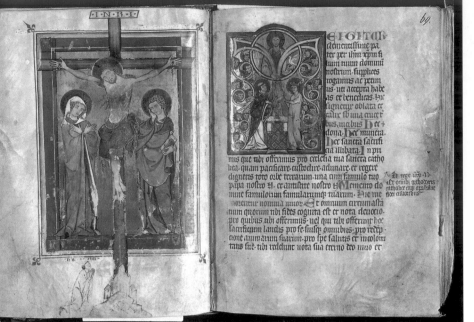

St. Florian Monastic Library comprises some 130,000 volumes and 800 old manuscripts.

The Bruckner Organ is one of the largest in size and best in sound quality. "The Organist of God" often used it *ad majorem Dei gloriam*, and recitals are still being given there every year.

On the death of his father, in 1837, Anton Bruckner was received into St. Florian Monastery; and that ingenious composer of symphonies and church music also found his last resting-place there, right beneath the magnificent pipe organ named in his honour.

as represented by the adherents to the teachings of Arius and those of Athanasius. The Germans were largely Arian, whereas the Romanic inhabitants of the provinces were Athanasian, or Roman Catholic. Unfortunately, little has come down to us of the Germanic Christian theology, but at least we know that, to the Germans, Christ was a sort of 'Lord Christ' *(Herre Krist)*, who demanded feudal loyalty. This concept neatly corresponded to the tradition of Germanic fealty among true warriors. *Herre Krist* was the one to bring salvation to mankind not as the Saviour and Son of God, but solely to act as a moral exemplar to be guided by.

The universal empire of the Romans was not threatened as seriously by religious schism and battles over intellectual viewpoints as it was by danger outside its borders. The frontiers of the Empire, torn by spiritual, social and economic crises, presented tempting possibilities to the Germanic tribes. In 405 A.D., the armies of the Ostrogoth King Radagais marched through Noricum; two years later, the Visigoth Alaric occupied large portions of the country. The provinces, bled by taxes, rose up in arms in the years 430 and 431, but they were cruelly defeated by the West Roman general Aetius. During the following decades, the Huns were a constant menace. The final act in the decline of Roman rule on the Danube is described to us by the historiographer Eugippius in his *Vita Sancti Severini:* "Under Severinus' circumspect leadership it was possible to evacuate a large part of the Romanic inhabitants along the Danube and to move them from those frontier areas threatened by invasion to the relative safety of Favianis. Finally Odoaker, the commander-in-chief

of the German army and the man who overthrew the last West Roman Emperor Romulus Augustulus in 476, decreed that the Romans living in the provinces be resettled in Italy." That, then, was the end of Roman rule in this country.

The Heritage of Rome

When the Germanic tribes had come to rest, it became apparent that the spiritual as well as material

Pagan beliefs dictated the site on which the Christian Monastery of St. Florian was to be founded in the eighth century. Close by, the holy martyr of that name is said to have been drowned in the River Enns, with a millstone around his neck.

heritage of Rome was still alive. We know today that the civilization of the Early Middle Ages owes a great deal to the preceding epochs. The best example of continuity in development is to be gathered from the trading activity that sprang up in the immediate vicinity of Roman military bases. Admittedly, this was limited to a few commodities like wine, grain, textiles and spices. The famous inventory of the customhouse Raffelstetten on the River Enns from the year 906 deals in detail with the salt trade between Bavarian Reichenhall and Bohemia and Austria. To be sure, this source offers us no information on domestic production, but it is relatively safe to assume that the precious crystalline compound was also being mined in the Salzkammergut at about this time, for in 777 the Bavarian Duke Tassilo assigned to his monastery, Kremsmünster, rights to the use of a *salina*, or 'salt-mine.'

On the whole, the Church indeed served a very important economic function during this period. Whether it was a matter of peacefully reclaiming uncultivated land, or one of engaging in campaigns of conquest under the pretext of Christianization, or one of taking in hand the administration of trading settlements, the Church was always at the forefront of events.

In present-day Upper Austria, which until the time of Charlemagne was still a part of the Bavarian tribal duchy, the Agilolfing dynasty had already founded two important religious houses in the eighth century. About 739, Duke Odilo had established the Monastery of Mondsee; and in 777, Duke Tassilo called the Benedictines to Kremsmünster. And since no ancient building can exist without being entwined with sagas and legends, it is recounted that Duke Odilo had the Mondsee Monastery built in gratitude for having had his life miraculously saved in an extremely dangerous situation. Kremsmünster, we learn, was erected on the spot where Gunther, Duke Tassilo's son, was killed in a tragic hunting accident.

It is a fact that these abbeys and priories prepared the way for the civilization of the Christian Occident. They were places where the sciences and the arts flourished, where the monks did pioneering work in medicine and in the care of the diseased. For these purposes, they planted their own herb gardens, furnished sick bays and even had special rooms for blood-letting. We know, for example, that at St. Florian there was a well-administered infirmary around the year 1100, and its Augustinian canons were expressly encouraged to provide the inmates with a "cheerful and comfortable life" - even the daily glass of wine was not lacking.

Besides, the monks maintained their own schools, which were not only the focal point of scientific studies but also centres for a field of art intimately connected with religion, that of painting. It was desired that every piece of writing meant to edify the reader be provided with precious ornamentation. In the *scriptoria* of the monasteries books were illuminated with delicately wrought initials and miniatures. It is legitimate to assume the existence of such a workshop for the illumination of manuscripts at St. Florian's under the Carolingians, since we are informed that in about the year 819 a Bavarian chaplain had compiled a collection of legends there.

At this time the foundation was also being laid for the famed monastic libraries in which, besides theological disquisitions, classical Christian works and those of antiquity were to be found. Soon, the monasteries even had their own "agents," who were under contract to locate new treasures for the libraries on the "international" book market.

Opposite:
One of the lakes in the upper Gosau Valley, with the majestic Mt. Dachstein (9,830 ft.) rising in the background - a sight not to be missed in Upper Austria.

Kremsmünster Monastic Library, built in 1675, is a partitioned hall extending for 74 yards. Its ceiling has splendid frescoes in stucco frames. The library houses some 100,000 tomes, 418 old manuscripts and 792 incunabula.

St. Wolfgang

It cannot be denied that the monasteries were the homes of art, science and literature for centuries. Beyond that, however, the religious orders left their mark on the countenance of the Church and were themselves distinguished above all by their desire to approach the masses of the faithful. The Church always took into account the consideration that although simple man felt bound to the Catholic faith, he nevertheless persisted in keeping the ancient customs, legal practices, and concepts of religion. Thus many pilgrimages reach their destination in places where "Paganism and Christianity have wondrously joined hands."

One such place is St. Thomas am Blasenstein. The so-called *Buckelwehlucken* in the Sacred Stone is considered by those in the know to be an ideal cure for backache even today. A bit of old folk medicine is alive here, namely the belief that an illness can be "brushed off" by crawling under rocks or trees. The Church frequently carried these ideas over to the elevated graves of prominent saints, like St. Hemma at Gurk or St. Nonius in Freising. Certainly the "Barrel Slide" on Leopold's Day is a reminder of the healing magic once associated with the grave of St. Leopold at Klosterneuburg.

Numerous ancient cultic sites in Upper Austria have been connected with the most popular regional saint, St. Wolfgang. In many places he is said to have left "sacred traces" while in prayer or seeking his legendary axe as, for example, at the Headache Stone in the chapel of St. Anne at Kirchschlag or on the Repentance Stone in the shrine on the lake then known as Abersee. It is certain that all these "trace stones" are relics of an old natural religion; yet for centuries pious pilgrims came to St. Wolfgang in order to lie "for the length of a Lord's Prayer" on the sacred stone, and thus to become immune from foot disease. To this day the stone is displayed in the church; it is enclosed in a marble shrine done in High Baroque style with the late Gothic figure of the saint, axe in hand, enthroned upon it.

The picture of a hermit detached from the world does not necessarily fit the portrayal of the progressive and dynamic man that the chronicles describe. Bishop Wolfgang was not only an important statesman, adviser to Otto the Great and missionary in Hungary, he also earned special merit for the Bavarian colonization of the Eastern March. The progressive economic policies of the Ottonians would certainly have achieved only limited success had not men like Bishop Wolfgang functioned as "administrative officials," who had to vouch for the peace, as well as trade and traffic, within the confines of their diocese.

Beyond this, the Church had the even more important task of representing the dominant might of the German Empire, and the Clergy was able to appreciate the value of a representative gesture, of prestige and symbolism. Soon there arose on Lake Abersee a splendid church, which today contains one of the gems of Gothic workmanship, the famed triptych by Michael Pacher. Noted art historians, like Wilhelm Pinder, place the Pacher Altar on the same level with that of Veit Stoss in Cracow. Gothic art, "the art of light," reaches its culmination here in the shrine with the Coronation of St. Mary. Yet it is striking how much the saints, the angels and the madonna resemble the young women in the villages, as though they had stepped down to us from their consoles, sublime in their pure beauty, admirable in their wholesome simplicity.

Michael Pacher created a work of art that is worthy of this beautiful country, whose praise no one could express better than Franz Stelzhamer, a peasant-poet from the Innviertel:

> *Sweet home's always home!*
> *Stay as long as you can,*
> *For homeland has e'er been*
> *A mother to man.*

Opposite:
The Altar at St. Wolfgang (1471-1481) is a splendid work by Michael Pacher, a painter and sculptor from South Tyrol. Indeed, it is one of the few that came down to us untouched - a dazzling array of Gothic framework, tracery, finials, canopies, and the carved Coronation of the Virgin in the centre shrine; the panels, brilliantly coloured, narrate legends from the life of St. Wolfgang and the Passion of Christ.

"Get me Salzburg, or get you gone!"

This ungracious alternative is said to have been posed by Emperor Francis I to Prince Metternich, then Chancellor of Austria; it was 1815, at the Congress of Vienna, when Europe was to be carved up along new lines after the downfall of Napoleon. Actually, there are no records of whether the monarch spoke these words, but the story does remind us of the fact that Salzburg, until then, had never been a permanent part of the inherited territories of the Habsburgs. Instead, it was an archiepiscopal principality, independent of Austria but a constituent of the Holy Roman Empire.

As it turned out, Metternich's skilful negotiations won the land for Austria in May, 1816, although some major portions of it remained Bavarian.

The province now covers an area of 2,762 square miles, and the population figure is now at 500,000, of which approximately one third live in the capital. Geographically, Salzburg is situated for the most part on the northern slopes of the Alps; accordingly, the two main rivers, the Salzach and the Saalach, flow out into the Alpine foothills. The Rivers Enns and Mur, on the other hand, of which only the upper reaches lie within Salzburg territory, face east towards the interior of Austria; and so does the remotest part of the province, the Lungau.

Precious Mineral Deposits

This natural division of the land was taken for granted, and in earlier times the natives had a simple way of giving this geological dichotomy its due: they spoke of the "mountain land" and of the "land beyond." To this day, the Lueg Pass is clearly a gateway to the interior. There are two other lines of approach across the mountain border, somewhat less apparent: one leads along the Saalach and through the German Salient of Bad Reichenhall to Unken and Lofer, re-entering Austria at the Stein Pass; and the other starts at Golling, skirting the Lammer upriver from its mouth, and then follows the Salzburg Dolomite Road into the Fritz and Enns valleys towards Radstadt and beyond.

The range of the Hohe Tauern is crowned by the highest elevation in the province, Mt. Grossvenediger (12,058 ft.). Salzburg does not share any part of Mt. Grossglockner (12,460 ft.), the highest elevation of Austria, which rises on a southerly spur of the "herring-bone" structure of the Tauern Range, and can thus be claimed in full by Carinthia. The situation is reversed in the case of majestic Mt. Kitzsteinhorn (10,512 ft.), which lies on a northerly slope. It

provides a commanding view in the Kaprun and Zell-am-See areas, and its possession by Salzburg goes unchallenged.

The headwaters of the Salzach are fed by a number of mountain streams cascading from the Hohe Tauern, or rushing down romantic gorges towards the main valley. The most famous of these are the Krimml Falls, plunging in three giant steps some 1,250 ft. into the valley below, and Liechtenstein Gorge, near St. Johann im Pongau, the last stretch of a local torrent forcing its way through from the Grossarl Valley.

The volume of water carried by the glacial streams is utilized by power stations, especially by those of the Tauernkraftwerke, whose scenic storage lakes are situated in the Kaprun Valley. In other parts of the Hohe Tauern there are nature reserves. But what used to be a storehouse of gold is now long depleted. Even during the times of the Romans, some high-yielding veins of ore are said to have been close to the surface of the ground, only a few inches down; by the beginning of the Modern Age, the Gastein and the close-by Rauris Valley were teeming with more than 2,000 miners. But, by present-day standards, further mining would be economically infeasible in view of the high costs of production. Still, there have been several attempts to get the mines going again. Such an attempt was made in the 1880s by Ignaz Rojacher, a local peasant-genius from the Rauris Valley. In fact *Kolm Naz*, as people were wont to call him, was also the mind behind the project of building the weather station on Mt. Sonnblick (10,191 ft.). Gold-mining continued for some time in the Gastein Valley during the decades of the First Republic and through the Second World War.

For many centuries, these lonely valleys leading up to passes and mountain gaps of more than 8,200 ft. above sea level were well-travelled by carriers and pack-animals; after all, *Tauern* means 'mountain pass' in the original Celtic. This inland traffic was arduous and often fraught with danger. Today, however, road transport has found a way to negotiate such formidable barriers.

In the rock zone lying between the Central and the Limestone Alps, known as the greywacke, various ores are to be found which were earlier mined in numerous small diggings. The most famous of these on Salzburg soil was the Mühlbach Mine, located on Mt. Hochkönig. This, in prehistoric times, was the most important copper mining area of the Eastern Alps. Far and wide the routes of trade led out from Mitterberg, carrying the essential raw material for bronze production. But in the Iron Age, the deposit at Mühlbach, due to unascertaina-

The Krimml Water-
falls, their crest at an
altitude of 4,760 ft.,
plunge down in
three thunderous
stages, with a total
drop of 1,250 ft.

The "World of the Ice Giants," in the Tennengebirge massif high above Werfen, is one of the biggest cave systems in the world; so far some thirty miles of passages and caverns have been explored. A conducted tour takes one hour and a half, leading to those arcana of rock and ice formations over wooden planks and staircases, all made safe for the inexperienced visitor.

ble causes, had already fallen into obscurity. More than 2,500 years passed before it was accidentally rediscovered in 1827 by a farmer who had lost a loaf of bread from his cart. While searching for the loaf, which had rolled into a ditch, the farmer strayed upon the outcrop of an old copper vein. From that point on the mine at Mühlbach developed into Austria's largest domestic copper source. Eventually, however, due to the low grade of the ore, it degenerated into a deficit-ridden operation and had to be shut down in 1976. The same was true of the ore from the "mountain of eternal snow," as the Hochkönig was earlier called, lending truth to the saying which a hundred years before had already correctly assessed the possibilities, "Salzburg is rich in poor ores"... The rich salt deposit in the vicinity of Hal-

lein, which will be discussed later, is the sole exception. It raises the question of when man first made his appearance in those parts, and when the beginning of cultural development can be established.

Fearing Heights and Mountain Streams

Although the first signs of man's presence in the Danube valley in Austria can be traced back 150,000 years, the mountains were generally avoided. After the end of the last Great Ice Age, some 20,000 years before recorded time, there was a longish period before the melting waters assumed the configuration of present-day streams and rivers out of the glaciers gradually receding into the interior. The vegetation advanced through masses of rubble and debris, and the forests began to develop. Such areas would not invite settlement, although intrepid hunters of the Old Stone Age did occasionally pass through them.

In the following New Stone Age (about 4000-1800 B.C.), however, man began to settle, to cultivate the land, and to breed livestock. The successive stages of development can thus be traced: use of natural caves led to the more advanced dug-out, which in turn gave way to the rectangular, one-room hut with stone foundations and horizontal rafters, the archetype of the Alpine hut as we know it. From Rainberg, inside the modern city limits of Salzburg, to far out in the Upper Pinzgau district, evidence of such dwellings is to be found. As a rule, they sat on higher ledges, which were safe as well as sunny, and overlooked the largely impassable valleys with their deep river gorges.

The Seidlwinkel Gorge, if only threaded by a narrow footpath, must for ages have been known to function as a long-distance link with the South; it is actually a lateral offshoot of the Rauris Valley leading up to the Hochtor on the Grossglockner, and to Carinthia beyond. Along this route, quite a number of ancient coins have been found, and so has been the fragment of a golden neckband, the only one discovered on Austrian soil.

As has been mentioned before, the Mitterberg was a major economic and cultural centre during the Bronze Age.

Then, towards the end of the ninth century, iron began to oust bronze as a material to make tools from, and the Earlier Iron Age (or Hallstatt Age) began. During that period of time, the isolated elevation of the so-called Hellbrunn Hill developed into a significant trading post; it in fact became even more important than the Rainberg, which also had its rôle to play in the history of Salzburg.

The construction of the Grossglockner Alpine Highway was a masterpiece of high-altitude road-building. Its creator, Franz Wallack, is buried in Salzburg.

Male head with detailed facial features, made of embossed bronze; a fine example of Celtic art from the fifth century B.C. (Celtic Museum, Hallein).

ly speaking, it was a somewhat loose union of different tribes, with no particular pretensions to power or central authority.

The Celtic Museum at Hallein offers us invaluable information on this period, which is of extraordinary cultural interest, although politically uneventful. It has an extensive selection of artifacts such as tools, household utensils, weapons, and jewellery, discovered on burial sites and largely connected with salt mining at Dürrnberg above Hallein (now conducted on an industrial basis). In the mines, too, because of the preservative nature of the salt, parts of the miners' clothing and, at Hallein as well as at Hallstatt, even their bodies have come to light.

Juvavum

Steel from the Norician Alps and gold from the Tauern were sought-after commodities in Rome, and other articles were actively traded as well. But in 16 B.C., when the Romans set out to change the basic relationship from one of protection to one of subordination, the neighbouring Raeti in the west took up a bitter fight for freedom. In Noricum, however, there was no extensive fighting. Thus began the approximately 450 years of Roman rule in Salzburg, during which Juvavum developed into the seat of government for a district which extended from the Radstädter Tauernpass to the vicinity of Wels.

In the period of the so-called Great Migration of the Peoples which followed, Juvavum was probably destroyed; but the Roman inhabitants had already left the overrun province. According to legend, St. Severinus (died in A.D. 482) repeatedly visited Salzburg during those tempestuous times. As the "Apostle" or "Comforter of Noricum," he was said to have interceded courageously on behalf of the afflicted and downtrodden everywhere.

For two hundred years or so there was little peace throughout the wide Alpine and Danube regions. Then, from the sixth century onwards, after the passage of numerous and different peoples and powers, the Bavarians finally settled permanently in the area.

Here and there, a few large groups of the Roman population lived on in the area. They have given us the modern *Walch* names (derived from the Roman term for a Celtic tribe), cp. Tyrolean *Walsch, Welsch* for 'Italian'; names like *Wals, Seewalchen, Strasswalchen, Walchen* in the Pinzgau district; and, for that matter, many English place-names such as *Walden, Wallasey, Walmer*, not least in *Wales, Welsh* and *Cornwall.* Only little by little did the remaining Romans, who had stayed behind voluntarily, begin to intermingle with the new ruling class.

Those identified with the culture of the age were the Illyrians. It should, however, be pointed out that recent research has questioned the traditional use of the word *Illyrian*, and only accepts it as a comprehensive term for a variety of tribes whose names are unknown. They mined salt around the Hallein area, and dug for iron ore in many parts of Austria. They also panned gold in the rivers and streams, and were probably already mining it. The use of the word Hall for the names of areas with salt deposits stems from this period, as does the word iron, *isaron*. The River Salzach, however, had a different name, the Igonta. The Early Iron Age (also called the La Tène Culture, after the major area of archaeological excavation in Switzerland) lasted from about 400 B.C. until the beginning of the Roman Empire, and was marked by the appearance of the Celts, who spread throughout Europe. As far as Austria goes, it is often referred to as the "Kingdom" of Noricum; but strict-

In the meantime something else had occurred: Christianity had begun to assert itself. Already introduced during Roman rule and taught secretly at that time, the new faith eventually came to be tolerated and was later adopted as the state religion.

Very little is known about the rise of Christianity in the Salzburg area; bits and pieces, as for instance the apocryphal story of how Maximus and his companions were thrown to their deaths from the catacombs in the cliffside of Mt. Mönchsberg by the invading Germanic hordes. But today it is nearly impossible to distinguish fact from fiction. It is certain at any rate that the Great Migration did not extinguish these early enclaves of Christianity everywhere in Austria.

Hardly had these wide expanses been thinly colonized by the Bavarians than another event of consequence occurred at the end of the sixth century. The Slavic peoples, who were at first subservient to the Avars, advanced upon the land from the south.

During the sixth to eighth centuries the empire of the Franks gradually developed into a focus of ever expanding power. Nor were the Bavarian dukes able to resist such a strong centre of influence for long.

St. Rupert, St. Boniface, and St. Virgilius

Out of the north-west came the second, more encompassing surge of Christianity. It was borne in the south primarily by missionaries in the Iro-Scottish spirit of their predecessor, St. Columban. In their teachings, the liturgy of the Mass, the baptismal rite, and the celebration of Easter took on partic-

ular forms. As the "Apostles of Bavaria," three of their number are prominent: St. Emmeram in Regensburg, St. Corbinian in Freising, and St. Rupert in the Salzburg area.

A second major epoch of Salzburg's history opens with the appearance of Rupert (Hruodpert), towards the end of the seventh century, for his initiative paved the way for developments that were to make the area a leading centre of culture for more than 1,100 years. Rupert is the patron saint of the country, and his feast is celebrated on September 24. He became a bishop in later life, and was a Frankish nobleman (legend claims he was the son of a king). But the question of why he left his native country remains something of a mystery.

At any rate, the course of his missionary work in the south took him to Regensburg, where he stayed at the court of Duke Theodo, preaching and baptizing. His hagiography states that "he converted the Bavarians to the true faith," a formulation which might be taken as an indication that at least some of his converts were Christians already, possibly of another sect, such as Arianism.

Rupert and his companions were resolved to carry Christianity further southwards, and they had the

The ancient and venerable Graveyard of St. Peter's, with the "catacombs" in the cliffs directly overhead. These caves served as a secret meeting-place for Christians as early as the period of Roman *Juvavum* in the third century.

St. Rupert, the patron saint of Salzburg and of saltminers; he was born in about A.D. 640, and he died in Salzburg.

The Benedictine St. Peter's Archabbey, with school and church attached, was founded by Bishop Rupert in A.D. 696. The town which grew up around the Abbey became an archbishopric under Charlemagne; and Rudolph of Habsburg raised its archbishops to the dignity and powers of Imperial princes.

full support of the Duke in their endeavour. Around 700, Rupert set foot on the territory of Salzburg for the first time. Legend has it that he built a chapel on the present-day site of Seekirchen. Then he heard of a former Roman settlement somewhat nearer the mountains. Whether or not Juvavum had been completely abandoned is open to question; it is certain, however, that Bavarian farmers did settle the surrounding area throughout the Salzburg Basin. Beneath the sheltering cliffside of Mt. Mönchsberg, right next to what had centuries earlier been Roman catacombs, Rupert founded the Monastery of St. Peter, which still stands today. Some years later, on a magnificent site halfway up the southern slope of the mountain, a convent was built for Rupert's niece, St. Erentrudis. Today Nonnberg is the oldest Catholic convent in the German-speaking countries that has loyally continued to serve its original purpose from the very beginning.

The Duke of Bavaria provided Rupert with economic security for his foundations by presenting him with land from what is now the modern city of Salzburg, as well as a number of dairy farms in the area and some twenty salt wells in the vicinity of Reichenhall. Theodo's successors and the Bavarian aristocracy added further land grants to the original territory.

The Venerable Basilica of St. Peter's was erected in 1130-1143; its interior, which holds the grave of St. Rupert, is now in the High Baroque style.

Opposite:
Salzburg, Innerer Stein, 1846. Oil painting on canvas. The scenery shown clearly reflects the placid spirit of the Biedermeier Age,

Hunters and fishermen, merchants and tradesmen began to settle around St. Peter's, and a village was recorded under the name of Salzpurch in 755 for the first time. Although not explicitly designated as such, Salzburg must have been a town in all but name, for it became an episcopal see in 739, a status accorded to towns only. An official town charter, however, is not documented until 1368.

The name *Salzpurch* is a contraction of *Salzachburg*, 'walled town on the salt river,' but does not refer to the Hohensalzburg fortress, which did not exist before 1077. On the contrary, the fortification referred to is a smaller Bavarian one, once situated halfway up to Nonnberg Convent and last mentioned in about 1000. In later times, too, a feudal manor house is known to have stood for a considerable time on the present site of the archbishop's palace.

The following may be considered the oldest parts of the city: the Waagplatz, the Kaiviertel, and the quarter of the Gold-, Brod- and Judengasse. Also the section on the opposite riverbank called *Am Stein* (now the Steingasse) was settled at a very early period. But the townspeople of Salzburg were limited in space from the outset. On the one side, they were confronted by the natural boundary of the unregulated wild waters; on the other side, they were hemmed in by the "religious quarter" around St. Peter's, multiplied by further churches, piazzas, fountains, and palaces. For a time this "finer" precinct was even separated from the rest of Salzburg by a wall (the approximate western border of today's Residenzplatz), and at night the gates were locked. It amounted to a town within a town, one in which a commoner was forbidden to build or even to reside.

but also offers visual proof of the former existence, since the early seventeenth century, of a turreted wall encircling Mt. Kapuzinerberg. We owe this masterpiece to Friedrich Loos (1797-1890), who was one of the greatest landscape artists of his period; he lived in Salzburg from 1826 to 1835, and produced a great many drawings and paintings of the surrounding countryside.

As early as the era of Pope Gregory II (715-731) there was a plan to draw the scattered Christian missions in the realm of the Franks closer to Roman jurisdiction. The idea was to form a Bavarian episcopal see, in which an archbishop would be placed over a number of subordinate bishoprics in much the same way as the Duke ruled over the Bavarian duchies. In this manner the Iro-Scottish influence could be counteracted, and the entire administration of the Church be given a Roman character.

It is a well-known fact that it was Boniface (whose Latin name reflects the character of the original Anglo-Saxon *Wynfrid*, literally meaning 'Goodwill') who shouldered the enormous and largely unpopular burden of setting up such an organisation. Rupert's successor was a highly educated Iro-Scottish monk from the British Isles, Virgilius by his Latin name, actually an Irishman called O'Farrell. Among other accomplishments, Virgil advocated the idea that the earth was round, and saw himself impeached because of it by Boniface in Rome. Under his leadership the young Church in Salzburg began to flourish. He had the Cathedral of Salzburg built in Early Romanesque style in 774 and introduced Christianity to Carinthia.

Afterwards Salzburg set about on an intensive mission to convert wide areas from heathendom. To be true, the River Drau (Drava) checked the onward zeal in the south, its right bank and beyond being the domain of the Patriarch of Aquileia. However, there were no boundaries to be observed in the east, and cultural betterment, as well as Germanization (but not ethnic repression), followed in the wake of these early Christians. Somewhat later, Passau on the Danube took on similar tasks downriver in Upper Pannonia, whereas Salzburg became active in the geographical angle formed by the Mur and the Drau. In fact, it is possible to trace no fewer than 125 St. Rupert's churches in what is now Carinthia, Styria, Western Hungary, Slovenia, and Croatia, which had all been founded under the auspices of Salzburg. And it was not until the two missionaries of the Slavs, Cyrillus and Methodius, set out to stride across history during the second half of the ninth century that these glorious chapters of religious and cultural expansion initiated by distant Salzburg came to a close.

Charlemagne

At the behest of Emperor Charlemagne the province was raised to an archbishopric in 798, and duly became the metropolitan see of Bavaria. This was the first church domain east of the Rhine to be given that distinction. The bishops of Augsburg, Regensburg, Eichstätt, Würzburg, and other places were thus subject to Salzburg, and as a consequence relations with Passau were strained for a long time. The latter see even resorted to the shady expedient of forgeries, albeit without success, to prove its seniority over the unloved rival on the shores of the Salzach.

During the reign of Charlemagne, "Earn the Eagle," better known as Arno, held the see of Salzburg. This archbishop, said to have been born in the Bavarian Isengau county, was a personal friend of the Emperor, who came to visit on several occasions. Once, so the story goes, that august scion of the sunny Rhineland received a welcome-gift he had not encountered before - a canvas umbrella! Arno was a highly educated man and never lost touch with the Academy, a circle of illustrious scholars established by Charles; he was particularly intimate with Alcuin, the great Anglo-Saxon and intellectual leader of the continental Church.

In order to safeguard the Salzburg possessions of the Church when Tassilo, the Duke of Bavaria, was deposed, the archbishop ordered a comprehensive record of ownership to be made, not unlike the Domesday Book in England; and today it is one of the oldest and most significant documents on the cultural and economic history of Austria. The Emperor was highly regarded by the people at large; it is natural, therefore, that legend makes "Grandfather Charles" a native of Reismühle, near Gauting in Bavaria. After his death he is supposed to have been removed into the depths of Untersberg, where he sleeps among his faithful liegemen "until called back by the Empire when the need is greatest."

Charlemagne's Successors

But let us return to historical facts. Under Charlemagne's successors the great realm disintegrated, and the tribal dukes were in the ascendancy. The large empire was divided, and as a result every summer "when the roads were dry again," savage hordes of Magyar horsemen arose from the east to murder and pillage in the west. In those times of decay, however, the Church of Salzburg experienced a considerable increase in territory: King Louis the German made a generous gift of lands along the Mur and the Drau, in the Danube valley of the Wachau and also on Lake Neusiedl.

Along with the best of the Bavarian troops, Archbishop Theotmar fell in battle against the Magyars near Bratislava. This event also had repercussions for the development of Carinthia and Styria, two main strongholds of the Salzburg Church. It was not until fifty years later, after Otto the Great had destroyed the Hungarians on the Lechfeld, near Augsburg, that the settlers returned to the hilly lands surrounding the Mur, Raab and Drau river valleys.

In Carinthia, which became a duchy in 976, and in Styria, the Salzburg Church established subordinate dioceses at Gurk, Seckau and Lavant; in these, the right of appointment was reserved by the archbishops. Eventually, in 996, Archbishop Hartwig also obtained the prerogative of minting coins. Consequently he was able to strike the "Regensburg Penny," which was in wide circulation at that time. But the very first minting on Salzburg soil probably occurred during the rule of the Bavarian Duke Arnulf (909-937). This independent mint in Salzburg specialized in producing gold and silver coins which are highly prized in collectors' circles, for example, the silver "Rübentaler" struck under Leonhard von Keutschach. The Salzburg mint in the Griesgasse was not closed until 1810, during the period of Bavarian rule.

Let us turn the wheel of Salzburg history back to where we left off. A fundamental change within the Church took place around the year 1000. Originally, the presiding abbot of St. Peter's was also the bishop. In line with the extensive church reforms of the period, these two posts were separated. Henceforth, the abbots administered St. Peter's Monastery; the bishop, who had to be confirmed in office by the Pope, selected the higher clergy of the diocese. In this way

Opposite:
Richly domed Salzburg as brilliantly illuminated by night. "Walking about at midnight, if you can, especially if there's moonlight," Clara E. Laughlin, the famous travel writer, enthuses, "is almost a rite with Salzburg-lovers."

The "Regensburg Penny," the basic currency in Bavaria during the tenth and eleventh centuries, was also highly regarded as legal tender abroad.

The reverse of the coin carries the effigy of Emperor Henry II. On the side shown, the central ornament is distinctive both of that monarch and the period, 1009-1024; the legend tells the name of the mint (*RIN CI VS* [<*Regina civitas*, 'City of Regensburg']) and that of the moneyer, *ECCHO.*

Portrait of the Baroness von Waldberg, about 1876. Oil on mahogany, by Hans Makart. This native of Salzburg (1840-1884) did not find his models in the regional Baroque tradition, but rather turned to Rubens and Delacroix for decorative representation of colours and forms.

The tiled stove in the "Golden Room" of the Fortress of Hohensalzburg. It is one of the most beautifully ornate, and completely intact, works of late Gothic handicraft to be found in Austria.

the Cathedral Chapter gradually came into great power. It repeatedly played an important rôle in the political decisions of the ecclesiastical principality and later became a highly exclusive religious body, requiring strict proof of noble ancestry. A province of Salzburg as such, with sovereign rights, did not yet exist in the year 1000.

The land once occupied by castles, now largely fallen to ruin or completely lost to sight, was only administered by counts; it still belonged for the most part to the duke, who had given it in fief to his retainers. It was but in the course of the following centuries that the Salzburg archbishops managed to increase their property systematically through purchase, exchange, donation, and inheritance, and to appropriate the old rights of the counts.

In 1077 Archbishop Gebhard began constructing the Hohensalzburg fortress which looms so large today; and he was likewise responsible for building the Castle of Werfen, meant to guard the Lueg Pass. But Gebhard's successors continued working on the Hohensalzburg fortress off and on for nearly six hundred years, and it was not struck from the list of Imperial Austrian military objects until 1860.

From 1184 onwards the Archbishops of Salzburg also carried the title of Papal Legate, and therewith the right to make decisions with papal authority in certain cases. Later this was augmented by the title of Primate of Germany. At the same time, a class of lesser nobles in ministerial positions subservient to the head of state arose, one which later was to form the basis for a system of paid civil servants.

Beginning in the fifteenth or sixteenth century, the country was divided into territories under a regional lord or governor. He was often responsible not only for the executive administration, but quite often for the judiciary administration of his area as well. He was even expected to organize military conscription and to place a levy of troops at the disposal of his superior. Even after the dissolution of church government, the system was retained in a slightly modified form until 1854, when it was replaced by county divisions.

Centuries ago, however, Salzburg was far larger than it is today. For a time it also included the district of Berchtesgaden. More important - above all for agricultural reasons - was its possession of the Rupertiwinkel ('St. Rupert's Corner') previous to 1816. This was the area west of the Salzach, with the old jurisdictional centres of Laufen, Tittmoning, Teisendorf, Waging, and, as an enclave in Bavarian country, the manor of Mühldorf. In addition, the Church Principality owned land in North and East Tyrol, as well as scattered territory in Carinthia, Styr-

Salzburg faithful and fortified: A nocturnal pageant of domes and spires, and sturdy battlemented walls.

ia and Lower Austria. There was even an isolated Salzburg possession as far south as the edge of the North Italian Plain, near Pordenone - the dominion of Naunzel, on the road to Treviso. In the eleventh and twelfth centuries settlement of the land was intensified - a process precipitated by a corresponding increase in population.

This second wave of "colonisation," as well as settlement of the country in general, was severely hampered in Salzburg and throughout Austria by the plague. In the plague year 1348-49 entire valleys died out, and the fiefholders recalled peasants from the upper mountains, reducing their Alpine farms to seasonal pastures and holdings. It took hundreds of years, particularly for the mountainous parts, to recover from the great losses due to epidemics during the fourteenth century. Specialists on population growth and settlement even claim that some areas never again regained the agricultural strength they had once enjoyed.

Later on, two further historical events amounted to severe crises for Salzburg. The first was caused by peasant revolts in 1525 and 1526. The Pongau area suffered the most; there were terrible losses of lives and material goods, and for many years afterwards fiscal affairs were a disaster. The last desperate struggle for freedom of Salzburg's peasants in the summer of 1526, between Altenmarkt and Radstadt, is aptly characterized by the words of the poet:

... here lie the peasant masses,
void of name or even cross.

The second tragic occurrence had little to do with war, it is true, but was every bit as devastating as far as the population was concerned: it was the Great Emigration, the Expulsion of the Protestants.

Just a few years after Luther's appearance in the first half of the sixteenth century, Protestantism had found a foothold in the city and province of Salzburg, and had spread particularly in the Pongau and Pinzgau districts. As much as 75 per cent. of the local population in several valleys had become Protestant; this applied, for example, to Werfen and Radstadt, Goldegg, Gastein, as well as the Greater and Lesser Arl valleys.

The individual spiritual sovereigns fought back with varying force. Archbishop Wolf Dietrich, for instance, had the Lutherans banished from the capital at the start of his period in office. A similar edict, however, intended for the rural areas, was never put into practice.

At other times the Protestants were quietly tolerated, as was the case under Archbishop Paris Lodron, in whose time external difficulties outweighed all other concerns. Eventually, in 1731-32, Archbishop Leopold Anton Count Firmian attempted a radical solution to the problem. Over 23,000 Salzburgers, the majority of them peasants from the mountain regions mentioned, were then exiled on account of their religious beliefs. This amounted to one seventh of the inhabitants of the Province at that time. As a result, over 1,800 farms stood empty awaiting new owners - a situation which did not always invite the best elements into the land.

Exodus of the Salzburg emigrants in 1732. Lithographed by an unknown master.

A small group of the emigrants settled temporarily on the island of Kadsand in Holland. Others continued on to America in 1734, where they set up a new town called Ebenezer ('The Rock of Help'), in Georgia, and became known as the "Salzburgers." Most of the migrants, however, were allowed by Frederick the Great's father to settle in East Prussia, which had been partly depopulated by the plague. After initial difficulties in adjustment, they were able to adapt exceptionally well to their new homes. Their internal unity was borne out through a "Salzburg Club," which single-handedly founded important charitable organizations, and had its headquarters in Gumbinnen up to 1945. As a result of the Second World War, descendants of the original emigrants again suffered the fate of losing their homes. The majority moved to Western Germany where the "Salzburg Club" continues to function, with its new headquarters at Bielefeld. For many years now, the Salzburg provincial government has annually invited children from these families to spend the summers in their former homeland; and for many decades, other descendants of the Salzburg emigrants have repeatedly come to visit the valleys and farms of their forefathers.

Cultural Landmarks

After this glimpse into the most recent past, let us return once again to the Middle Ages. It was the age of the great conflict between empire and papacy; even to an emperor like Barbarossa, Salzburg seemed so strategic within the political constellation that he paid several visits to the town, in an attempt to win the Prince-Archbishop over to his side. Since the outcome of his efforts did not quite meet his expectations, he had the Count of Plain, a loyal follower, burn the city to the ground in 1167. Plain Castle is

The Horse Pond beside the Neutor ('Newgate'). Prince Eugene of Savoy is said to have offered 7,000 guilders for the commanding statuary, but to no avail; the remarkable piece of sculpture remained in town, and Salzburgers have indeed become very fond of the rearing horse.

impressive even in our days, and the people call the mighty ruins that stand beside Grossgmain the "Salt Cellar." It is, however, not to be confused with the famous Maria Plain pilgrimage shrine.

Despite this and many other grievous incidents, and sometimes even heinous atrocities, in the latter

Left:
Archbishop Marcus Sitticus of Hohenems (1612-1619), the sponsor of Hellbrunn, an amazing Manneristic country villa south of Salzburg, with an elaborate park of grottos and trick waterworks: Unsuspecting guests sitting at a carved stone table in a baroque arbour are suddenly fenced in by rows of jets spurting six or seven feet high from unseen holes in the ground; and in the porch at the back of the house they may be cut off by a curtain of water and sprays from the antlers of two innocent-looking stags' heads.

Right:
Archbishop Paris Count of Lodron, a wise diplomat and father figure.

days of chivalry, Salzburg managed to produce cultural landmarks of lasting importance. For example, construction of the Cathedral, known as Conradin's Cathedral, was begun in 1181. It was a late Romanesque edifice of huge dimensions. Its true size was not discovered until this century, when the original foundations of the church came to light during the ten years of reconstruction after extensive bomb damage caused by the Second World War. In the centuries after, the Principality was able to strengthen its position further; indeed, among the prince-archbishops of the time there were some whose lives and achievements are still well remembered today. Leonhard von Keutschach, who enlarged the Fortress and suppressed the people's desire for direct rule under

the Emperor; Matthäus Lang, who before his appointment was secretary and confidant to Emperor Maximilian I, the "Last Knight"; and Wolf Dietrich von Raitenau and Marcus Sitticus - both of whom had Italian architects convert the city into a "German Rome" under the influence of the Renaissance and Early Baroque.

The charm of Salzburg was decisively influenced by these changes in the sixteenth and seventeenth centuries, and has formed a major attraction for foreign visitors ever since. In 1779, it caused Alexander von Humboldt, the great globetrotter, to make the famous remark:

I consider Naples, Constantinople and Salzburg the most beautiful places on earth.

The Thirty Years' War, and After

During the seventeenth century, Salzburg was unique in its position as an "island of peace," while the rest of Central Europe suffered the untold terrors of the Thirty Years' War. In these decades Salzburg was ruled by Archbishop Paris Lodron (1619-1653), originally from the area around Trento. He was successful in keeping both forces, the Protestant

Union as well as the Catholic League, outside his country. At a time when it was difficult to provide sufficient supplies for the armies, this was absolutely essential; for "the War had to provide for War," and friend and foe were regarded with equal trepidation by the civilian population.

Thus it once happened that on the march through Salzburg an Imperial officer of noble birth shot and killed a peasant at Lofer. The man had resisted a wild band of soldiers as they were preparing to enter and plunder his farm. The young nobleman was brought before the sovereign in Salzburg. He clearly felt quite comfortable being surrounded, as he thought, by his equals, for when queried about the reasons and outcome of his deed he replied, "As an Imperial officer, what should I care about a mere peasant?" Paris Lodron answered, "If an Imperial officer does not care about a mere peasant, what should I care about a mere Imperial officer?" - and thus saying had him publicly executed on the river bank at Gries three days later.

Along with the political measures, extensive military ones were taken in the Principality. Everywhere fortifications were enlarged and new ones built; Mt. Kapuzinerberg, for instance, was then completely enclosed with a wall. Not only were the old territorial "colours" and troops gathered into the city, but through a constant exchange of veteran soldiers and new recruits a strong reserve army was built up. While this is standard modern military procedure, it was a surprising innovation for an age in which the mercenary system predominated. Simultaneously,

A Mozartian Family Idyll, painted by Johann Nepomuk della Croce. The father, Leopold, resting his arm on the grand piano, is an eager listener to his children, Wolfgang Amadeus and Nannerl, playing a duett; the mother, Maria Anna, is no longer alive, but her likeness on the wall nevertheless makes the family quartet complete.

the regiments stationed in Salzburg were assigned to peaceful duties. Paris Lodron had them drain the large swamps, Schallmoos and Langmoos, where the Central Railway Station is to be found today.

These measures ensured that Salzburg stayed the only part of the Empire to be spared battle within its borders throughout the war. Indeed, for a long while the Elector of Bavaria stored his entire treasure away in the fortress vaults at Werfen and Hohensalzburg; he himself repeatedly spent several months in the capital. In spite of all the financial burdens involved, Paris Lodron was also a managerial wizard over two major cultural landmarks. He finished construction of the present Cathedral, which had been planned and begun by his predecessors, Wolf Dietrich and Marcus Sitticus. In 1623 he also founded a university, one which was to become, in its time, the second largest in German-speaking countries. Of those who succeeded Rupert, this illustrious prince of the Church lives on in the minds of the people of Salzburg as the "Father of his Country."

But in spite of such outstanding individuals, one cannot overlook the fact that the height of Salzburg's historical greatness was long past. The period of Absolute Rule was drawing to a close: the world stood on the eve of the French Revolution.

At the beginning of the second half of the eighteenth century, in the year 1756, Wolfgang Amadeus Mozart was born in a substantial townhouse in Salzburg's Getreidegasse. His genius came into inevitable conflict with his employer, Hieronymus Colloredo, the last Prince-Archbishop, who, while of an enlightened and liberal political bent, remained none the less a narrow-minded bureaucrat. As we know, Mozart turned to Vienna and died there at an early age.

But to consider Colloredo only in this light would be thoroughly misleading. Among other things, with the appointment of Franz Michael Vierthaler, he laid the basis for an educational system which was well in advance of those in other countries. He gathered around him a number of exceptional administrators and brought into town some of the best scholars who, through their geographical and historical writings, contributed a great deal to the rise of research into the many facets of the Province's past.

But other, more important events were already casting their shadows upon Europe's kingdoms and principalities. Napoleon's troops were marching victoriously forward on all fronts, and entered Salzburg territory several times.

The old German Empire began to disintegrate, and in 1803 Hieronymus Colloredo was forced to flee to Vienna before the advancing enemy. He never returned to Salzburg, and died in 1812 in the Austrian capital. The archbishopric was now subjected to the fate which it had so often narrowly escaped: secularization. Therewith the Province had ceased to exist as a separate governmental entity. It meant the end of more than eleven hundred years of religious leadership and control, during six centuries of which Salzburg had been the largest ecclesiastical principality in the Southern German area.

Thus began the third great epoch in the history of the country. In the period between 1803 and 1816 Salzburg changed hands several times. To begin with, it was an electoral principality under Duke Ferdinand of Toscana, a brother of Emperor Francis I. He soon bartered the Province for the domain of Würzburg, which meant that Salzburg became Austrian and lost the independence it had zealously preserved until then. In 1809 it was occupied by Napoleonic troops as well as Bavarian contingents of the Rhenish Confederation, which was allied with the Corsican.

The inhabitants of the mountainous regions, however, fought stubbornly on the Lueg Pass and in the Saalach valley to bar enemy penetration of innermost Salzburg. The men of the Pongau and Pinzgau districts were duly reinforced by peasant riflemen from Tyrol; for the effort as a whole was connected with the uprising in that province, led by Andreas Hofer, a heroic patriot, and also with the Alpine Confederation, which had been ably brought about by Archduke John.

In this defence of the country, great leadership was shown by simple men such as Struber, Sieberer, Wagner and Strucker. The victory of the Austrian regular army on the battlefield of Aspern, at Whitsuntide of 1809, was followed shortly afterwards by the defeat at Wagram, and with the end of the rebellion in Tyrol, Salzburg's fate was sealed. Salzburg was then annexed by the Kingdom of Bavaria, which ordered the closing of the university as one of its first rulings. Concern over the possibility of competition with the old Bavarian institute of higher learning at Ingolstadt may well have been the principal reason. Until 1816, the Province remained under the Bavarian crown, which incidentally did not govern Salzburg badly in a number of respects.

For this reason the repossession of Salzburg by Austria in May 1816, this time for good, by no means met with the undivided approval of the civilian population.

Metternich was given the Province in exchange for that of the distant Rhenish Palatinate. Though the tragic state of unrest of so many years had come

to an end, an unprecedented stagnation set in in its place. After the loss of the Rupertiwinkel, and that of the small territory of Berchtesgaden, which had at least temporarily belonged to Salzburg, the Province assumed its present-day borders. But in general the people were bitterly disappointed when Salzburg was attached to Upper Austria and governed from Linz, which at that time was still no more than a staid little country town .

The city and province of Salzburg were impoverished; a good many respected commercial trade-centres were closed down. Palaces and mansions were abandoned, and the large squares which for centuries had witnessed the splendour of the princely court and its visitors were literally overgrown with grass. In 1823, the Archbishopric was reinstated by Rome, but only for purposes of church organization. The population of Salzburg, which had reached 16,000 inhabitants as early as Mozart's time, had now dropped to 12,000. The city developed so slowly that by 1870 there were still only somewhat more than 20,000 residents. As a result of the Revolution, Salzburg finally became an independent crownland in 1848. However, it was another thirteen years until a parliamentary assembly, and therewith central government for Salzburg, could be established. But the real impulse for change came from another direction. As early as 1820, painters, poets, and "Alpine explorers" had begun to discover this sleepy little city in the wake of the Romantic Movement, and now even some of the smaller parts of the Province were receiving more and more attention.

Among these were, for instance, Gastein, long famed for its medicinal springs, Zell-am-See with its magnificent countryside, and Krimml with the imposing scenery of its waterfalls, the finest in the Eastern Alps; there were also the lakes to the north-east of the capital, and the larger lake district of the Salzkammergut (to this day, as the name implies, Nature's own storehouse of salt); and many others. Tourism, which began in these areas, increased markedly when the Great Western Railway reached Salzburg in 1860. In the same year the route to Munich was opened, and finally in 1874 the connection with Innsbruck was completed.

To be true, it was not always to the advantage of the city's appearance that the many gates and walls fell, but Salzburg was expanding. Nonetheless, the population increased but slowly; as a matter of fact, there were only 36,000 in 1920. Today the figure approaches 140,000.

Around Salzburg lie a number of former archiepiscopal palaces, now within the actual city limits. Certainly the layout and setting of Hellbrunn, about three-and-a-half miles from the centre of town, make it the most beautiful of them all. An aviary, a deer park, and a fish-pond had long been part of the grounds before it became a princely summer residence from 1613 to 1619, when Archbishop Marcus Sitticus commissioned his cathedral architect, Santino Solari, to build him a pleasure palace in the Italian style. It was intended for daytime diversion, and that is why the famous waterworks, with its grottoes, statues and mechanical devices set in motion by running water, were created. An attraction all its own is the quaint Stone Theatre, a natural cave and one of the oldest open-air stages in Europe. In addition, Waldems was built on a wooded hill within the park grounds; called by the people the Single-Month Château, it was completed in accordance with the Prince's wishes in a very short time, though not really in one month.

Left:
The Grotto of Orpheus, a detail from the Hellbrunn Waterworks Follies; the animals are enchantedly listening to the singer trying to spirit Eurydice, his wife, back from the netherworld.

Right:
Archbishop Marcus Sitticus ordered Hellbrunn Palace to function as a château de plaisance, complete with waterworks - and the shrieks of terror by those caught unawares, as well as the peals of laughter managing to stay dry, have not ceased to this day.

Pigeonholing a musical genius like Wolfgang Amadeus Mozart is a sheer impossibility. He was a past master in every field of composition, and ranged supreme over all the genres.

The Salzburg Marionette Theatre, too, is known all over the world, and its members are just wizards at making life flow through their fingers' ends into those puppets and make them seem part of humanity.

From *Everyman: A Morality Play on the Death of a Rich Man*, by Hugo von Hofmannsthal, presented outside the portal of Salzburg Cathedral.

This central piece of stagecraft opened the Salzburg Festival in 1920; and theatre-lovers from over seventy countries have since been attending a wide range of plays, operas, concerts, and other performances in July and August every year.

Salzburg, a Festival Town

The idea of arranging festivals first arose in the 1880s, and in 1917 the "Festival Hall Committee of Salzburg" came into existence. Three years afterwards, the first performance featuring *Everyman* took place under the most adverse circumstances. The original Festival Hall was built in 1925, and the Salzburg Festivals rapidly gained international status between the two World Wars. The huge theatre of today dates from the second half of the 1950s.

The growth of the Salzburg Festivals is inextricably linked with the figure of Max Reinhardt (1873-1943). As a founding member, he rather uniquely merged the talents of an actor, producer and stage-manager; and anybody having had the privilege of witnessing *Everyman* under his direction in the Cathedral Square will hardly have seen a more impressive spectacle, in the true sense of the word.

In the second half of our century, musical life was galvanized by the personality and magic wand of Herbert von Karajan, who as a native of the town felt called upon to further Salzburg's international reputation.

Among other attributes, such as "The German Rome" and "The Festival City," the sobriquet "The City of Mozart" is one of the oldest and most venerable. The name of that composer carries a mystique all its own, and no one can really hope to do justice to the phenomenon. So let us, at least in our imagination, mingle with the crowd of sightseers from home and abroad who, with varying intensity and reverence, visit the respective memorial sites, such as the birthplace of the young genius in the Getreidegasse or his parental home on Makartplatz. We stand bemused in front of the Mozart monument erected in 1842, still in time for Mozart's widow to have looked down at the ceremony from her residence at No. 8 close by; and then we move across the river into New Town, where the world-famous musical academy bearing the name of the composer now stands near Mirabell Gardens.

A World-famous Christmas Song

In 1817 the paths of Franz Xaver Gruber, a teacher, and Joseph Mohr, a young Catholic priest, converged. The latter was worried by the fact that the little organ of his parish church had temporarily been silenced by mice, which had gnawed a hole in the leather bellows. He suggested writing a choral piece for a Christmas Eve performance to be held in the local St. Nicholas Church. Mohr had already done the text, and in the darkling afternoon of 24 December 1818 he handed Gruber the sheet, asking him to set it to music; provision should be made for two solo voices and a chorus with guitar accompaniment:

"Silent Night! Holy Night!
All is calm, all is bright..."

The teacher busily set to work and indeed finished the song on that very evening. His friend, as a cleric trained in the art, is likely to have added some corrective touches to the composition; in any case, the new tune was pleasing to both, and promptly had its world premiere in that midnight mass.

It was not until many years later that the song was taken by Tyrolean singing groups through German countries and beyond. In 1873 it was sung as the "Chorale of Salzburg" in the United States, where waves of Central European émigrés doubtless helped to carry it from coast to coast. Today that carol belongs to the entire world, yet its authorship and the story of its origin have been all but forgotten.

This is the score of a Christmas carol that was first intoned on 24 December 1818 in St. Nicholas Church at Oberndorf, near Salzburg, but that has since won the hearts of pious singers the world over... Who would not know, and love to lend his voice to, "Silent Night! Holy Night!"?

Green Styria, astonishingly rich in its many areas of natural beauty, is the sparkling emerald in the diadem of the Austrian Alpine region. The highland area of the beautiful province of "Lady Styria" encompasses parts of the Northern Limestone Alps and the Central Alps. Charmingly enclosed within this high Alpine region is the Styrian Salzkammergut, which owes its world-wide reputation not so much to its richness in salt as to its blue lakes and delightful health resorts. In attractive contrast to the majesty of the mountains is the Central Styrian hill country with its multitude of magnificent fruit trees and grassland, which lend the countryside the appearance of one huge garden. Further contrast is offered by the sun-kissed lowland area, the broadness of which gives one an inkling of the Pannonian Plain; delicious grapes and sundry other fruits here ripen in great abundance.

It seems only natural that man should have settled in such splendid surroundings at an early stage in history. Even in prehistoric times the valleys and mountains were inhabited by a race of men classified by science today as "Neanderthal." *Homo sapiens neanderthalensis King* had clearly discovered fire, lived by hunting, and fed on wild fruits. Following his hunting instinct he even ventured into the high mountains. Legends are told about the Dragon's Cave near Mixnitz, the Repolust Cave near Peggau, the Ligl Hole in the Enns valley, and the Salt Ovens near Aussee. After the passing of these first "highland tourists," untold centuries were to go by before man again ventured into the upland regions.

In the meantime, important chapters had been written in the history of mankind. Much had taken place in Noricum and the Carantanian March, which were the names the earliest settlers here gave to today's Styria, Carinthia, Carniola, parts of Lower Austria, and the land around Pitten, in order to distinguish their territory from that of other tribes.

The first inhabitants of Styria who considered themselves important enough to possess a name were the Celts. It was in this region that they founded their Kingdom of Noricum, the first "state" on Austrian soil.

There is hardly another race in early European history which is as bizarre and yet so shrouded in mystery as the Celts. Their kingdom was governed on the strength of specific laws; and they are known to have traded and mined extensively. According to notes made by Julius Caesar they were even divided into three classes: the "common people" composed of peasant farmers, the middle class of "knights" and landowners, and the upper class of "druids" - priests who performed animal and human sacrifices and had the power to see into the future. Tacitus added more detail to Caesar's reports when he wrote that the Celts, in contrast to the Germanic tribes, built *oppida* which were similar to Roman towns, and gave as an example the Romano-Celtic settlement of Mt. Magdalen.

The findings of later excavations were to substantiate the evidence of the two Romans. In his writings Tacitus described the local cult of the goddess Nerthus or Hertha, a "great mother goddess," believed by the Germanic peoples to have come to them riding in a chariot. For this purpose a consecrated vehicle always awaited the divinity in a grove sacred to the goddess, supposedly situated on either Sjælland (Zealand) or Als, two islands east of the Danish mainland. The chariot, covered with a cloth, was watched over by specially chosen priests. When Nerthus wished to come down to earth and go among men, she veiled herself, mounted the chariot, and let herself be drawn along by the holy men in great solemnity. As long as the faithful believed that Nerthus was on earth, weapons were all laid down and peace reigned, until the Divinity, tiring of mankind, returned to her sanctuary. "Then the chariot, the veil, and the goddess herself were cleansed in the waters of a hidden lake. Such service was carried out by slaves, who were swallowed up immediately afterwards by the lake. Hence there was a secret terror, a sacred darkness surrounding a divine being who could be looked at only on pain of death..." So much for Tacitus' report.

There is, in fact, evidence that this cult dated back much further. At Strettweg, a place near Judenburg, a finely wrought chariot was found on which a tall female figure dominates the scene, surrounded by a group of warriors and hunters, as well as some stags. These features seem to point back to some mysterious prehistoric period when such creations were not really "art" in the modern sense, but rather myth given visual form.

The Romans, who first came into contact with Celtic and Germanic tribes on the eve of Christianity, could only make judgements on the basis of their own religion, where people worshipped bronze and marble idols but no longer knew any real piety. The "natural religion" of these primitive peoples must therefore have been incomprehensible to the Romans. The same might be said of their vitality, which enabled them to stand up unflinchingly to the much-feared Roman legions when they saw their independence and freedom threatened. Life meant little to these fierce Germanic "barbarians," for only those who fought heroically in battle had the prospect of being permitted to join in the carousing in Valhalla.

The increasingly decadent Roman Empire could not match the robust strength of the barbarians for any length of time, and yet Rome did in a way manage to conquer and bring peace to the Germanic tribes. The historical development of Germany would not have been possible without the confrontation with Roman order. From the Romans the barbarians learnt the necessity of using their forces sparingly, of fighting wars not only with valour but also with tactics.

The "heritage of Rome" lived on in the tribes uprooted through the Great Migration of the Peoples, brought about their eventual resettlement and even facilitated the founding of new states, which were finally incorporated into one great empire - the Kingdom of the Franks. Rome formed the cultural and political model for this state. An example of this was the way in which newly conquered regions were immediately made secure against the neighbouring barbarians. Though not on the same scale as the earlier Roman *limes*, or fortified border, there was a comparatively well organized series of border provinces (*Marken*, or marches), which the Empire, along with its spiritual dignitaries, was perfectly competent in governing.

The Realm of the Silver Panther

As we have heard, the Carantanian March covered the area of present-day Carinthia, Styria, Carniola, parts of Lower Austria, and the land around Pitten. Only after Charlemagne's campaigns against the Avars and after the terrible Hungarian Wars was it reconstructed in about 960. The centre of the margraviate was at that time Hengistburg Castle near Wildon.

We know little more than the names of the rich and powerful men of those days; for instance, the margraves belonged to the Eppenstein family.

Preceding double page: Lake Grundlsee in the eastern Salzkammergut, 2,330 ft. above sea level, is a paradise for hikers and mountaineers.

Opposite: The Tauplitzalm plateau is a favourite with holidaymakers in summer and winter alike.

The Cult Chariot of Strettweg, from the sixth century B.C. On its four-wheeled platform, a tall naked goddess, holding a wide sacrificial bowl over her head, is seen attended by priests, and warriors, and servants; they are all in procession to her sanctuary.

Wealthy, and therefore also of significance, were the Sponheim family and the Counts of Wels-Lambach. The Traungau family, who in 1122 inherited the riches of the Eppensteins, managed to attain the most prominent status. Alone the fact that they gave Styria its name shows their historical importance; for their hereditary place of residence was the estate of Steyr in Traungau, which is today part of Upper Austria. The Traungaus are, therefore, more commonly known as the Otakars of Steyr, or Styra.

It is a confusing puzzle trying to piece together the nature of the relationships between individual estates; one generation inherited property from another; marriage took place exclusively within the family circle - and so did murder, on occasion. Such an event occurred in the year 1140, when Adalram von Waldegg slew his powerful cousin, Adalbero von Feistritz. Two years after the murder Adalram von Waldegg founded the monastery of Seckau as a penance and richly furnished it with family possessions. The reasoning behind this "good deed" is enlightening - "so that his brothers and relatives would not quarrel over the inheritance"!

During this period other noble families also distinguished themselves by their generous donations to the Church. Around 1074 in *valle Ademundi*, 'the Valley of Edmund,' the first Styrian monastery was founded by Archbishop Gebhard of Salzburg, and endowed with large amounts of landed property in the surrounding area by the Carinthian Countess Hemma. In the twelfth and thirteenth centuries this monastery was already considered to be one of the wealthiest and most powerful in all "Austria."

The year 1096 saw the foundation of St. Lambrecht by Count Marquard of Carinthia; and 1163, that of Vorau by Otakar III. Otakar was known as the *princeps de Styra*, and flattering reports of his countrymen make him to be "of exceptionally noble birth, bearing and status;" it was also said that he seemed to "exude" power and wealth. He himself was well aware of his outstanding qualities, for he said in praise of himself (modesty not being his strongest suit) that "it was by the grace of God, who had granted him his life, his looks, his rank and fame, did he attain a higher position than that of his parents and his ancestors." This statement seems to have had more than a grain of truth in it, for under Margrave Otakar III the literal creation of the province of Styria took place. Around 1160 Otakar III self-confidently chose the well-known heraldic panther for his coat of arms as a symbol of the independence of his estates.

Twenty years later, even more ambitious dreams were to be fulfilled. At that time the continuous feud

The Georgenberg Contract of Inheritance is one of the most important documents not only of Styrian but also of Austrian history: it provided the legal basis for the unification of Austria and Styria, which materialized on the death of Duke Otakar in 1192.

between Emperor Frederick Barbarossa and his rival, Henry the Lion, had reached its climax, the Hohenstaufen having deprived the Guelph of his duchies of Bavaria and Saxony. At this juncture, the flexibility and political flair of a *princeps de Styra* were to make themselves apparent for the last time. In the Diet of Regensburg Otakar IV was made a duke, thus ensuring that his whole territory became part of the Empire. Historical ties such as the ones with the Dukes of Bavaria and Carinthia were duly severed. 1180 can, therefore, be seen historically as the year of Styria's birth. However, young Otakar was not able to enjoy his success for very long. He contracted incurable leprosy and had to find a worthy successor for his duchy. As he had no immediate heirs, the nearest relatives were the next in line, and these turned out to be the Babenbergs. On 17 August 1186, Leopold V and Otakar IV met at Georgenberg on the River Enns, the border of

Ostarrîchi and *Styra*. The famous Contract of Inheritance made the Babenbergs heirs to Otakar's estates. In return for this, Leopold V explicitly agreed that the Styrian ministerial knights would in no way be deprived of their due.

When Otakar IV at last succumbed in 1192, the Babenbergs inherited an estate which stretched roughly from the Mühlviertel and Traungau to Friaul (Friuli) and the land of Pitten. From this time onwards the Babenbergs proudly displayed the heraldic panther on their banner.

The Babenberg Interlude

The new ruler, however, had no decisive political or economic changes in store for Styria. Above all, the ministerial knights were allowed to keep their privileges according to the Georgenberg Treaty and were themselves rich and powerful enough to stand up effectively to the Duke, a state of affairs which was to provide the Habsburgs with many a headache in the following period.

But let us stay awhile with the Babenbergs, the Crusades and the knightly minnesingers. One of the

most prominent of these poets of the nobility was Sir Ulrich von Liechtenstein, described in history as a man who, apart from carrying out his noble office as Chamberlain of Styria, also found time to unsettle opponents on the jousting-field, first as "King May," then as the mythical British "King Arthur," and finally in the guise of "Lady Venus." Although it is true that there were a large number of potentially worthy opponents fighting in the Holy Land at the time, Sir Ulrich is reported to have defeated approximately two hundred and seventy-one knights in duels, and all this just to win the favour of a prudish beauty he worshipped from afar.

When the object of his worship continued to refuse his advances, Ulrich was forced to take desperate measures. He cut off his finger, which he had injured in a tournament, and sent it as a gift to his beloved, perhaps one of the most macabre pieces of wooing in history. The noble lady's reaction to this ultimate proof of the knight's affection was, unfortunately, not recorded for us by the chroniclers.

How much greater must have been the success of the knight known as "the Kürnberger," whose intuition told him that

Left:
A beautifully carved wooden door in Strechau Castle, a major stronghold of sixteenth-century Protestantism near Liezen in the Enns Valley.

Right:
"Death," a wood carving by Joseph Thaddäus Stammel, in the library of Admont Abbey (1760) - from a group of allegorical figures showing man's last four encounters, Death, The Last Judgement, Heaven and Hell.

A woman and a birdie soon
Can well be snared by charms;
For one who can but sing the tune
Both fly into his arms.

Sir Ulrich's mentality was completely different:

…When two loving hearts are plighted
Faithfully without deceit,
When two loves are so united
That their love must be complete,
They are joined by God to capture
All that life can hold of rapture.

And in order not to arouse false hopes in the beloved, he concludes this *May Song of Minne* with a basic declaration:

Constant love is minne truly.
Love and minne are the same.
I can not distinguish duly
Aught between them but the name.
Nor can I tell the two apart.
Love is minne in my heart.

Whatever else a minnesinger might have been, he was first and foremost a gentleman of principles:

…Only God alone knows,
And no one else, which woman I love!

It is because of such discretion that we are better informed of Sir Ulrich's jousting deeds than of his successes in the bedchamber. The gentle knight belonged to a distinguished noble family, the Styrian line of the Liechtensteins. This family owned numerous fiefs which were strung out along the upper reaches of the River Mur. Chief among their residences were the castles of Obermurau, Frauenburg, and Liechtenstein, the ruins of which can still be seen today. At Murau near Judenburg they had their ancestral seat. Sir Ulrich lived up to the nobility of his birth. He was Chamberlain of Styria and commander of the Styrian nobility in the battles against the Carinthians and the Hungarians. It is certain that he fought in the fateful battle on the Leitha alongside Frederick the Quarrelsome and witnessed the latter's heroic death:

When he was dead (God send him speed!),
The land sank into darkest need.
In Styria and in Austria eke
The rich and strong were left poor and weak.
Forsooth I tell you all anon

What came to pass when he was gone:
They robbed the land both night and day,
The villages in ruins lay.

The Liechtensteins, at least, emerged from this general collapse relatively unscathed. When the Austrian and Styrian nobility called in the King of Bohemia, Otakar II, to be a "saviour in distress," Ulrich von Liechtenstein's offices and titles were confirmed; and even when the King of Bohemia's great rival, Rudolph of Habsburg, came to power, the Liechtensteins were in no way made to suffer.

The real reason for this was that Herrand von Wildon, Sir Ulrich's opportunist son-in-law and brother-in-song, had sized up the situation in good time, and along with several other Styrian noblemen had sworn allegiance to Rudolph I in the monastery of Rein near Graz. Thus it was inevitable that Herrand von Wildon should also inherit the office of Chamberlain of Styria upon his father-in-law's death.

The "ever faithful" opponents of the Habsburgs

In spite of all their oaths of allegiance, the Styrian nobility was soon numbered among the most steadfast enemies of the Habsburgs. By the time Rudolph came to the throne, the balance of power in their country had undergone radical changes. The Habsburgs, unlike the Babenbergs, were not bound by the conditions of the Georgenberg Treaty, and thus they now set about procuring territory for obvious strategic reasons. This dynastic power policy soon gave occasion to the worst of the Styrians' fears. The grim struggle against the "immigrants from Swabia" caused the knights, for once, to present a rarely unified front.

The anti-Habsburg inclinations of the nobility received the most circumspect support from Bavaria and Salzburg; occasionally, actual revolts broke out, which the Habsburgs could only put down by confirming and asserting inherited privileges.

It was dangerous for a member of the House of Habsburg to venture into Styria. Indeed, if he did so, it was said that he already had one foot in the grave. The tale is told of a tournament in Graz, at which the Austrian and Styrian warriors reached an agreement whereby their strength should be reserved entirely for one of the Habsburgs who had done them the honour of measuring himself against them in knightly combat. This may sound like a harmless "prank," but worse was to come. On one occasion Duke Albrecht, a son of Emperor Rudolph I, was a guest at the castle of a Styrian knight. All of a sudden, half-way through a sumptuous banquet, the Duke felt violently ill. Strangely enough, a murder-attempt was at once suspected and the physicians who were hurriedly assembled at first seemed at a loss as to how to treat the poor wretch. Their solution consisted in suspending the half-dead man by his legs from the ceiling in order to let the poison "run out of the body through mouth, nose, eyes and ears." In the general confusion the pitiable Duke also lost one of his eyes. But this fact in itself was acclaimed as proof of the efficacy of the cure, for "the poison must have gathered there whilst flowing out of the body and thus destroyed the eye." Nevertheless, the stubborn determination of the Habsburg guest to stay alive triumphed over medical science; and the Styrian knights, who were already arming themselves in anticipation, were forced to postpone their planned revolt indefinitely.

Even generations later, when the Habsburgs had long become "genuine Austrians," they remained unpopular intruders for the Styrian nobility - intruders who in 1379 even had the audacity to settle in Grätz (Graz), the present-day capital of Styria.

However, it would be unjust to claim that the status of Graz as the residential seat of the Habsburgs was to its disadvantage. With their feudal standard of living, the Duke and his court revitalized economic life. And thus like all cities where the Habsburgs maintained a castle or palace, Graz became an important trade and industrial centre.

The best known personality among the Habsburgs who resided here was Emperor Frederick III. But who would remember this rather unfortunate monarch if he had not coined the most ingenious phrase after *Tu, felix Austria, nube*? His somewhat cryptic, though of course definitely patriotic motto, A.E.I.O.U., variously interpreted as an acronym of *Austriae est imperare orbi universo* or *Austria erit in orbe ultima*, is to be found all over Graz, where the Emperor devoted himself to improving the city - for example, on the sovereign's castle and the cathedral. Next to the southern entrance of the parish church the remains of an impressive fresco from the year 1485 can still be seen. The famous picture of the plagues afflicting the country at that time, shows the "scourges of God" which decimated the population - pestilence, locusts, and Turks.

For the Habsburgs, moreover, there was a fourth plague - the Styrian nobility - who were given an opportunity to make trouble for their enemies by certain turns of events. By the start of the sixteenth century Luther's teachings had already begun their triumphal march through Germany. At first it was only the "hornless cattle," as the landowners liked to

Ulrich von Liechtenstein, a poet-knight of the mid-thirteenth century, held several high offices in his country, e.g. that of Chamberlain of Styria (1241), but also fought bravely in battles.

Here he is seen entering the tilting-ground to challenge his opponents under the guise of Lady Venus.

Herrand von Wildon, Sir Ulrich's son-in-law and comrade-in-song, was also a noted verse novelist. In our picture, he has slipped into the rôle of minnesinger, offering a poetic message from his pen to the high-born lady whom he (let us assume) so much reveres.

The Palace of Eggenberg, west of Graz, was built in the seventeenth century; it once served as the spiritual centre of East Austrian Protestantism.

A fresco, richly detailed, contrasting the Beatitudes of Heaven with the Miseries of Life on Earth (1485): sinful mankind down here is subject, above all, to three scourges wreaking havoc - The Plagues, Swarms of Locusts, and the Turkish Scare.

call their peasants, who joyfully embraced the new ideas of the dignity of man and brotherhood. As early as 1515, there had been a revolt in Carniola against the feudal overlords, and this revolt soon swept over wide areas of Carinthia and Styria. Although the flame of rebellion was quenched just as quickly as it had flared up, Lutheranism had already rooted itself firmly in people's souls; and when in 1525 another bloody uprising occurred, the fighting spread like wildfire from Tyrol via Salzburg as far as the Enns valley. It was inevitable that the miners who dug for copper and silver there should support the cause of the peasant mobs. However, after several initial successes, the people of the Enns valley were quickly beaten by the well-armed mercenaries of the feudal overlords. Not content with this, the victors even deprived Schladming, considered to be the centre of the revolt, of its traditional freedom. This might not sound a very harsh punishment today, but at that time the freedom of a city was a privilege that provided the inhabitants with important sources of income from trade and industry.

Despite all attempts to punish them the inhabitants of the Enns valley clung to their Protestant faith. Later, during the Counter-Reformation, the Ramsau region, in the shadow of the Dachstein mountain range, and the Gosau valley became a last refuge for many Protestants.

However, it was the Styrian nobility, as usual, who caused more problems for the Habsburgs than the despised "shorn heads" (the peasants were forced to wear their hair cut very short as opposed to freemen). The nobility had also announced their allegiance to the Protestant cause, and the staunchly Catholic ruling dynasty was forced to meet many of their demands because in the so-called Inner Austrian dukedoms of Styria, Carniola and Carinthia the Turks were continually threatening invasion and could only be kept at bay with the support of the Estates. Of course, attempts were frequently made to limit the power of the nobility but these, because of the circumstances, did not meet with the desired

The arcaded courtyard of the Landhaus ('Regional Parliament') in Graz was designed in a lavish Renaissance style.

The Clock Tower, built in 1561, a landmark of the City of Graz, is one of the remaining parts of a mighty fortress.

In its vicinity, the soul can be on the wing like a bright bird of paradise - at least that is what the natives there claim, and they ought to know.

success. One such attempt was made by Ferdinand I, who in his will decreed that among other things the Habsburg lands should be divided up between his sons. His main consideration for action was the wishful thought that the nobility might be easier to keep under control in smaller provinces. Around 1554, then, this Division of the Habsburg Inheritance took place.

But the unfortunate heir of Inner Austria, Archduke Charles, troubled by his conscience, quickly granted the Styrian lords and knights freedom of worship. This Religious Settlement of Graz of 1572 was later redrafted in the *Brucker Libell* and was in fact the last great success of the Protestant Estates. Emperor Maximilian II had always been anxious to reach an agreement with the Protestants, but at his death a dedicated supporter of the Counter-Reformation, his son, Rudolph II, came to power. Archduke Charles was seriously criticized for his leniency to the Protestant Estates, although the pious man had really only looked upon the concessions as a way of rallying support against the Turks. His son, later to become Emperor Ferdinand II, was to make up completely for his father's softness. Commissions on Religious Reform soon began to sweep through the country, often accompanied by a small army of mercenaries who destroyed and burnt everything even slightly connected with Lutheranism. Because of these exploits Ferdinand proudly dubbed himself *Advocatus ecclesiae.*

Such a gallant "Defender of the Church" naturally had to make a fitting show of power. As his father had done before him, Ferdinand invited some prominent architects to his Inner Austrian city of residence - which at that time (and indeed until well into the nineteenth century) was still called Grätz, in memory of the fortified place of refuge, *gradec*, the Slovenes had built for themselves around the year 800 on what is now the Castle Hill. The nobility and the wealthy bourgeoisie did not want to be outdone in any way by their rulers, and thus Grätz became "a magic ring which married the lively appeal of Upper Styria with the more gentle charm of Lower Styria."

After Emperor Ferdinand transferred his court to Vienna in 1619, Grätz gradually sank into a sleeping-beauty slumber, from which it only awoke for a short while when Emperor Charles VI betook himself and his resplendent entourage to the Inner Austrian capital to receive homage from the Styrian nobility. Once again Grätz found itself in the midst of Baroque ceremonies and pageants, and celebrated as only the feudal society knew how. Even the common people felt something of the joy and magnificence of such occasions, for when the high lords celebrated they were allowed to watch and rejoice with them.

Art to the greater glory of God

The common man could enjoy a similar spectacle whenever the Church celebrated the Kingdom of God in a manner just as impressive as that in which the nobility manifested its abundant wealth.

Even the most insignificant village churches and chapels were built with Baroque pomp, and the venerable monasteries endowed by the Styrian margraves saw themselves transformed into monumental palaces; their greatest treasures, the collections of medieval manuscripts, were given a worthy new setting. Thus, for example, the library of the Benedictine Abbey of Admont in the Enns valley was rapturously referred to as the "eighth wonder of the world." As it is, this library may indeed have been the scene of a miracle, because in the year 1865 the whole monastery was destroyed by fire - except for the library.

Exquisite works of art, rather similar to those at Admont, are to be found in the library of Vorau.

The Augustinian Priory houses such precious items as the oldest collection of early medieval German poetry and the famous *Imperial Chronicle*.

As can readily be understood, these libraries were never open to the public who, in any case, would have derived little benefit from them - the common people then could neither read nor write. Unlike the learned monks they did not seek God in disputations and treatises, but purely in their own hearts. And after the cruel religious wars and the pillaging by the Turks, the people had completely returned to the God and saints of the Catholic Church.

"The Great Mother of Austria"

Above all, the worship of the Blessed Virgin, who seemed to spread her protective mantle equally over all believers whether rich or poor, found a place in the hearts of the common people. Hosts of pilgrims visited the ancient sanctuary of the *Magna Mater Austriae* at Mariazell. Legend has it that pilgrimages to the Blessed Virgin Mary had begun as early as

1157 by a monk of the St. Lambrecht monastery. In a miraculous way a simple statue of the Madonna directed him to the very spot where today the monumental Pilgrims' Church stands on a wide open space. The first shrine of the Blessed Queen of Heaven was a mere cell; but when miracle after miracle took place, it is said that about the year 1200 a pious margrave, Henry of Moravia, felt the

Emperor Charles VI (1711-1740), in Hungarian uniform draped with fleece, the St. Stephen's Crown and Imperial Orb beside him (cp. pp. 27 and 203). He is succeeded by Maria Theresa, his twenty-three-year-old daughter.

divine inspiration to endow the first chapel. These facts are somewhat uncertain, but the earliest verifiable evidence of the name dates from the year 1243.

During the Middle Ages a large number of pilgrims from many different countries visited Mariazell. Mariolatry reached its high point during the Baroque period. From every end of the Danube kingdom hosts of people wended their way to the "Great Mother of Austria." Such a pilgrimage was not just an ordinary journey all lightly undertaken. The faithful had to take as many penances as pos-

sible upon themselves in order even to hope for the forgiveness of their sins.

As was the case with other prominent places of pilgrimage, Mariazell had its own pilgrims' roads leading to it, of which the Via sacra was the most important. The 'holy way' linked the throne of the *Pater Patriae* in Vienna with the throne of the *Magna Mater Austriae* at Mariazell. As centuries went by, monasteries and churches were built along this devotional route, where the pilgrims regularly paused on their journey in order to rest and prepare themselves, step by step, for the great moment when they were permitted to stand before the throne of the Blessed Virgin.

The "black counts"

Styria is frequently referred to as "The Iron Province." Indeed as early as the Middle Ages, Styrian iron and Styrian ore dominated the European market. The iron craftsmen in the town of Leoben, today the main industrial centre of Styria, were given exclusive trading rights for the Vordernberg iron by the Babenberg, Frederick the Fair. Later, in the year 1360, the whole of the iron-workers' guild of Mürzzuschlag was granted similar privileges.

The first iron-forges grew up around the ore deposits along the rivers. Their owners were astute

The Riegersburg on the Styrian-Hungarian border, first mentioned around 1130, proved an impregnable fortress to the approaching Turks.

The Benedictine Abbey of Admont, in the Enns Valley, treasures some 130,000 volumes and about 1,100 manuscripts. This library, by Bartolomeo Altomonte (1702-1783), is a splendid example of how to create intimacy of space and human proportions.

Mariazell, in eastern Styria, has been a place of pilgrimage since the fourteenth century. The faithful flock to the pilgrimage church - the finest of its kind in this federal state - as do masses of art-lovers. The altar in the Chapel of Grace, reputed to work miracles, was designed by Johann Bernhard Fischer von Erlach (1656-1723).

enough to make use of Austria's water power to supply their factories. These iron-forges were later to become the backbone of Austrian heavy industry, but in the beginning industry and businesses were run on a small scale, although even then their products were exported to many different countries. Scythes, sickles and knives from native workshops were a well-known commodity not only in Germany but also in Poland, Russia, Bohemia and England.

With full justification the affluent "iron-lords" referred to themselves proudly as the "black counts," until at a later date a different way of thinking demanded the reform of the industry. The achievements of the Industrial Revolution made the older, smaller businesses unprofitable, but their owners succeeded in making the transition. Nowadays, the names of a long line of factories and businesses in Styria have a good reputation throughout the world. As early as the end of the 1880s the Alpine Mining Company, today amalgamated with the VOEST-Linz Company, was the dominant force in the country's economy. At Donawitz and in Linz a new type of blast-furnace that reduced the need for imported scrap iron was developed. Then, the name Puch is well known in the vehicle industry. An inhabitant of

Graz, the railway-carriage builder Johann Weitzer, was one of the co-founders of the Simmering-Graz-Pauker Joint-Stock Company, which today manufactures not only railway-carriages but also diesel cars and diesel engines.

Agriculture is prevalent and profitable among the East Styrian Hills as well as on the Graz and Leibnitz Plains, and livestock rearing in the Mürz Valley; the native soil, though, yields brown coal at Köflach, Voitsberg, and elsewhere, magnesite near Grossveitsch and St. Michael, and graphite especially at Trieben.

Coal and ore (with iron ore from the Erzberg, or 'Ore Mountain') have long laid the foundation for a flourishing iron industry; other mineral deposits also spell out wealth galore, and make for a sound national economy, offering work and income to ten thousands of people. A mining college was established at Vordernberg as early as 1840, which was later on moved to Leoben; now renamed "Montanistische Hochschule," it counts among the best specialist institutes of higher learning for budding mining engineers.

Both in the economic and technical developments of the past century and a half, and also in cultural achievements, a name that often seems to be linked with pioneering deeds is Archduke John. In Styria people continue to relate the moving romance of this august scion of the Habsburg family with the Aussee postmaster's daughter, Anna Plochl, whom the Archduke later even married.

Around 1813 the Archduke, along with Baron Joseph von Hormayr and Dr. Alois Schuster, had taken part in a plot by the Tyrolean Alpine Confederation. The essence of this plot was that the Tyrolese should rise in a heroic struggle for independence against Napoleon, as they had once done before under Andreas Hofer. The plan, however, was thwarted by Prince Metternich. The prudent statesman saw clearly that as Napoleon was arming himself for war with Russia, this was an opportunity for Austria to remobilize her forces. An uprising in Tyrol might readily have ruined Metternich's plans and, over and above, would in all probability also have caused Bavaria, neutral at the time, to ally herself with the French: the Austrian Alpine inhabitants would then have been in danger of a pincers attack from Italy and Southern Germany.

Metternich did not hesitate to have the Baron von Hormayr and Dr. Schuster arrested. Archduke John was taken into custody by the police. Because of this political miscalculation, the capable Habsburg found a normal career closed to him; and so it came about that he discovered his great love for Styria.

Archduke Johann is to the Styrians what King Ludwig is to the Bavarians. The Province indeed has reason to be most grateful to the son of the Grand Duke Leopold (who in 1790 was duly crowned after the death of Emperor Joseph II). Archduke Johann did a lot for the living conditions of people by giving planned assistance both in agriculture and trade. His love for a postmaster's daughter, Anna Plochl, even affected national politics, but the common people admired the Archduke the more for it.

This country is certainly worthy of such love, that love of one's native land which the Styrian poet Peter Rosegger acknowledges in these moving words:

> *Of all great lands*
> *That in the world are found,*
> *Beloved Homeland,*
> *You wear the Crown.*

The Styrian's love of nature, his delight in silence and solitude most certainly came from the splendour of the countryside about him. It is well known that evergreen Styria is one of the most richly wooded regions in Europe, a fact that is indeed of great importance for the Styrian economy. The possession of a piece of timberland often allows the owners of small-scale farms to survive, and forestry as well as wood-manufacturing industries above all mean jobs for thousands of people.

Yet despite its economic value we must not forget that the forest can also be a "friend," who leads us to peace and contemplation. This notion may in turn lead us to an understanding of the lines of Peter Rosegger: "Only the solitary person can discover the forest. When sought after by several people, it flees, and only the trees remain!"

More and more visitors now come to Styria to enjoy its special magic. There are regions of fairy-tale beauty to be found. The much-praised king of the Northern Limestone Alps, the Dachstein, is one such area. The mountain itself towers nearly 10,000 feet high, its heights crowned with glaciers. It offers recreation both to the serious rock-climber and the more modest hiker, who only wishes to enjoy the view from grassy hill-tops and from Alpine dairy pastures; a good many summits can be reached by cable-car in any case. Well-appointed tourist-centres cater to the needs of even the most demanding visitor; idyllic mountain villages offer solitude and a relaxing break from the bustle of modern technological life.

Not quite as famous as the Dachstein is the limestone range which stretches away eastwards. As far as imposing grandeur and the sheer rugged drama of their scenery is concerned, these mountains can compete with the Dolomites. The "roaring" Gesäuse (hence the name), where the River Enns breaches the massif of the Northern Limestone Alps, is world-famous. The mighty mountain block of the Hoch-

Opposite:
Altausee nestles idyllically on the shores of the lake of the same name. In good weather, the glaciers from the Hohe Dachstein are reflected in its waters.

schwab, moreover, has a rare claim to fame - it is one of the homes of the chamois, the most noble species of highland game.

But it is not only the imposing mountain scenery which gives "Green Styria" its charm. In the south, romantic vineyards and wine-cellars often persuade visitors to tarry there a little longer. Since Southern Styria was lost to the then Yugoslavia, the region of the Lower Mur south of the Graz Plain has acquired increasing importance as a wine-growing district. More is the pity that the delightful produce of the Styrian vineyards is still little known abroad. Such delights are yet another reason for experiencing at first hand that "Styria is the land of warmth and geniality."

Mt. Dachstein (9,830 ft.) plunges into the Enns valley. The snowfields and rock faces are lit up by the midday sun when the valley still lies in the shade of the Radstädter Tauern mountains.

For other views of that majestic massif, whose rugged grandeur can be seen for miles around, see pp. 84-85, 100, and 137.

The romantic Gesäuse, a ten-mile-long gorge between Admont and Hieflau, where the River Enns breaches the Alps. The wild ravine is filled with the roaring of the rapid stream past a turmoil of huge boulders in its bed.

Maximilian I - a born ruler

"This land is like a horseman's cloak - rough, but warm!"

These words are attributed to the Emperor Maximilian I, the "Last Knight," who not only loved Tyrol more than any of the other Habsburg lands but also appreciated its geopolitical significance and understood the special qualities of its people. And thus it is easy to understand another statement supposedly made by the same sovereign, who was himself a rather headstrong character, "Tyrol is the heart and the shield of the Empire."

Maximilian died in 1519. Since then nearly five hundred years have passed and, outwardly, everything is different. Yet the nature of the country and the essential characteristics of its population have not altered at all. The Tyrolese constitute a type of their own, they are a true reflection, to all appearances immutable, of what used to be referred to simply as the "Land in the Mountains."

It is seldom wise to form an opinion of a whole country on the basis of a fleeting acquaintance with its cities, and one should certainly not pass judgement on a popular holiday area like Tyrol after merely watching some of the displays of Tyrolean music and dancing performed for the visiting tourists. There is much more to it than meets the eye.

Today, the delightful capital beside the green waters of the River Inn has more than 120,000 inhabitants. Innsbruck, or *Sprugg* (in the vernacular form of endearment), has become "a city in the mountains," through which passes a never-ending stream of people and goods of all kinds: the paths of goods traffic and holidaymakers travelling in every direction of the compass cross there; and, what is more, it is one of the places which all these people

A view of Innsbruck, the delightful "city in the mountains." Receiving its civic charter in 1239, it was made the capital of the land in 1420. Emperor Maximilian I dearly loved this town and made it his preferred place of residence.

from Central Europe with their unslaked thirst for sunshine and sea are often simply *bound to* pass through on their long journey south.

Tyrol has been a destination for travellers for a long time, however - it was well-known as such since before the days of the Romantics and, nowadays, with increasing mechanization and the expansion of winter sports into a coveted pastime, the native population, not excluding some of those in the remotest of valleys, have adjusted their way of life accordingly.

And yet even the modern Tyrolean manages to keep one corner of his heart hidden from the prying gaze of strangers. An outsider who wants to settle permanently in the area will find it harder than elsewhere to make real contact with his new neighbours. Once he has succeeded in doing so, however, all his friends will surely stand by him through thick and thin, although they will not hesitate to let him know a few home truths if ever they consider this to be necessary.

We can find plenty of examples in the history of Tyrol to confirm the truth of what has been said, but probably no one can bear a better witness to this trait in the Tyrolean character - since, we must presume, he was occasionally a victim of it - than the Last Knight himself. He, the strangest and, in spite of all his weaknesses, the most lovable of rulers, had

plenty of problems with his Tyrolese, but in times of real need they never failed him.

On one occasion, for instance, the peasants complained bitterly because of the excessive zeal of the Imperial huntsmen and the consequent damage to the crops. Conversely, they were inordinately proud of their ruler, who, like them, had the courage to go up into the wildest regions of the mountains. It was a peasant, too (or was it an angel, as people tended to say later on?), who in the year 1493 rescued Maximilian from a cliff above Zirl (ever since then) called "Martin's Cliff" after the Emperor had got trapped on a ledge while hunting chamois. And, whenever Maximilian, who was perpetually in financial straits, had to turn for help to Tyrol's four estates - the clergy, the nobles, the burghers, and the peasants - , the Tyrolese always gave him generous assistance, albeit not without some grumbling.

Yes, even the peasants. For it was a peculiarity of the area that the peasant population, too, had a say in the regional parliaments. Ground rents, services, tithes, and arrangements for the vassal's obligatory workday were less oppressive than in the neighbouring countries, and most of these people of the soil had for generations been the proud owners of their freehold property anyway.

By granting numerous favours, the Emperor in his turn gave repeated proof of how very much this

The marble cenotaph of Emperor Maximilian I, as part of Europe's largest memorial shrine. The tomb was designed by the monarch himself; his kneeling effigy and the lavish reliefs, done between 1561 and 1583, are the work of Alexander Colin, a sculptor of fame from Mechlin (Malines), Belgium.

The cenotaph is flanked, right up to the high altar, by twenty-eight bronze statues, larger than life-size, of the Emperor's ancestors and relatives and also of figures from heroic tales, among them King Arthur and Theodoric the Great (Dietrich of Berne).

On the *left*, Elizabeth of Luxembourg, Maximilian's great-grandmother; and on the *right*, Mary of Burgundy, Maximilian's first wife, who died young.

Four other members of the cortège.

Cymburga of Masovia, grandmother of the "Last Knight." She was famed for her almost masculine strength and for the protruding lower lip, which henceforth marked the Habsburg dynasty.

country had grown on him. He reconfirmed the ancient right of Tyroleans to bear arms, and in 1511 he decreed that local contingents would be levied for armed conflict only that directly concerned the borders of the land.

Maximilian saw to it that gun foundries (where he, a nobleman who never lost "the common touch," himself often lent a hand with the work) as well as the best-equipped armoury were set up in the Tyrol, the latter at Innsbruck. On other occasions, too, the sovereign did not remain aloof and, as at Augsburg, he danced many a night away with the fair daughters of Hall and Innsbruck.

Notwithstanding their great affection for the Emperor and the respect due to him, the Tyrolese were quick to point out the limits of their hospitality, if necessary. Thus, when the Emperor in November 1518, only few weeks before his death, came to visit his beloved Innsbruck, a delegation of the local innkeepers informed him that he himself was very welcome, but that the members of his entourage would have to find lodgings outside the city since some sizeable bills run up during his last visit were still outstanding. Full of angry bitterness, the Emperor thereupon left the city, only to die at Wels, on 12 January 1519. And yet such sporadic differences (the last one admittedly a tragic one in the outcome) could not, however, destroy the esteem which the Emperor and the people of Innsbruck had

for each other; and for this reason Maximilian went ahead with his plans of having his monumental tomb erected there before he died.

Ever since that time the Court Church has been popularly known as the "Black Men's Church," and indeed this is a very apt name for the unique building. At the back end of the nave, the elevated tomb immediately catches the eye. Its sides are decorated with some alabaster reliefs showing scenes from the Emperor's life; a bronze statue of Maximilian himself kneels on the lid of the coffin, his head bowed in reverence. On either side of the nave, right up to the high altar stand twenty-eight bronze statues, larger than lifesize, of the Emperor's ancestors and relatives and also of figures from heroic tales, among them King Arthur and Theodoric the Great. Their hands are still outstretched, waiting to hold the torches which were to have burnt during Maximilian's funeral rites. Indeed, the place is in many ways typical of a sovereign who planned and began many projects, and yet accomplished so few of them. Although there were to have been forty bronze figures, thirty-four busts of emperors and one hundred statues of saints, work on the memorial was never completed and the tomb is - empty. Maximilian, as laid down in his last will, was buried beside his mother in St. George's Chapel of what is now the Military Academy of Wiener Neustadt. In spite of this, his memory still lives on in many stories and legends in Tyrol today.

Rustics of Mettle and French Troops in Battle

The fact that scarcely four years after Maximilian's death the very same Tyrol could bring forth the revolutionary pronouncements and decrees of a man like Michael Gaismair is once again proof of the pervading sense of liberty felt by the Tyrolese, who were always able to make a clear distinction between fighting for an individual ruler they loved and fighting for a system. The system, in this case, was embodied in two men, Archduke Ferdinand I, the uncongenial brother of Emperor Charles V, and Gabriel Salamanca, his money-grabbing treasurer-general, who made a point of grossly disregarding the vested rights and liberties of this country.

Their adversary, the said Michael Gaismair, was born at Tschöfs, near Sterzing, round about 1490, at a time when even in Catholic Tyrol radical anabaptists were proclaiming their religious and social message and when also Luther's doctrines were soon beginning to spread. For many years Gaismair acted as confidential secretary to the Bishop of Brixen (Bressanone); being so well informed about the "masters'" ways of thinking and doing, he naturally presented a very real danger for the authorities. In twenty-two Articles he laid down the guide-lines for the establishment of a

St. Christopher, an ancient relief in Weiherburg Castle (above Innsbruck), carved out of cembra-pine wood.

A detail from an entire cycle of Gothic frescoes in the parish church of Obermauern, East Tyrol. This magnificent series portraying the Sufferings of Christ was painted about 1488 by Simon von Taisten.

kind of democratic "Peasants' and Miners' Republic" on decidedly religious and totalitarian principles.

The foremost principle was *"to strive in all matters not after selfish advantage, but to add to the glory of God, and then to the common weal."* Gaismair peremptorily called for the abolition of the prerogatives enjoyed by the nobility; the creation of new arable land by draining the swamps along the River Etsch; the provision of social institutions like hospitals and poorhouses; the establishment of a state trading monopoly rigorously excluding "foreign" concerns, the nationalization of mines, etc. On some other issues he was obviously carried away by his imagination and made demands which could never be translated into practice; as for example, when he pontificated about "the elimination of every bit of legal hocus-pocus," the razing of city walls, and the demolition of all castles.

Andreas Hofer, the stalwart innkeeper from the Passer Valley, ably led the Tyrolean rising against the French and Bavarians who had occupied his country. After some brilliant engagements and battles, the freedom fighters found themselves outnumbered in early 1810; the revolt collapsed, and Andreas Hofer was shot in Mantua on Napoleon's personal orders.

Gaismair met a tragic end. When the Tyrolean riots had been suppressed, he became one of the key men in the peasant riots of Salzburg, in 1526. After losing the final skirmish near Zell am See, in the Pinzgau, he led his insurgent mob to safety on Venetian territory, conducting a strategically brilliant retreat. Eventually, however, he was murdered in 1532 in Padua, where he owned a country estate.

Gaismair was one of the few really important leaders of the peasantry up-in-arms, and he proved a very capable military commander as well. Even today his rôle is underestimated, or altogether ignored; most history books dismiss the matter with a few lines.

And yet, surely, in their loyalty to their ideals and their willingness to risk their lives, there is a close resemblance between the headstrong Gaismair and Andreas Hofer, the stalwart innkeeper near the bank of the Passer, outside St. Leonhard, at the southern end of the Jaufen Pass, who remained true to his Emperor even when the latter had long since given him up. Hofer's enthusiasm, guided as it was by a deep religious conviction, quickly rallied his countrymen behind him. In engagements and battles which were masterpieces of strategy, he drove Napoleon's troops, as well as the allied Bavarians, out of the country in 1809, entered Innsbruck as the Imperial governor - but in the end lost both Tyrol and his own life. His dead body was solemnly laid to rest in the Imperial Court Church of the capital in 1823.

Song of the Meran Riflemen, anno 1809

The Emperor's foe is in the land,
Which sorely needs defending;
In vineyards now our women stand
Alone to do the tending.
But we must leave house, home, and all,
For Vintner Death has us on call;
Since other means are lacking
The foe we must send packing!

Though some of us will sink to dust,
To Death his sickle bending,
The best of wines to lesser must
Quite oft give ground in blending.
Red Eagle, fly triumphantly!
And grant us, Lord, that victory
Should stop those rascals messing -
And give our wine Thy blessing!

The Tyrolean rising of 1809 was able to draw on the skill of another fighter, also Tyrolean by birth, with a real talent for strategy: Josef Speckbacher, who stemmed from Gnadenwald near Hall. Curiously enough, most accounts speak only of the other side of Speckbacher's character, of his devil-may-care audacity and his bravery.

It is general knowledge that the revolt collapsed, and on 20 February 1810 Andreas Hofer was shot in Mantua on Napoleon's personal orders. Many years have passed since then, but even in our days of party politics the Tyrolese are united on one point: none of them wants a new Tyrolean anthem! On all ceremonial occasions, the rousing strains of the old song are to be heard, 'Enchained in distant Mantua, our loyal Hofer lay...'; with the breezy marching tune of the Tyrolean Rangers as a fitting sequel:

Our song to you is swelling, from heart to throat and mouth,
Where'er you may be dwelling, in lands both north and south,
Both east and west where lusty our banner proud does wave:
We Rangers are the trusty, the loyal and the brave ....

Here is another intriguing point. The song of the Imperial Rangers dates from the First World War, but a later verse has been added; and in a country in which faith, patriotism and fighting spirit have always been closely interwoven, it does not come as a surprise that these moving lines should have been written by a priest, Brother Willram (Anton Müller, 1870-1939), from the venerably old Praemonstratensian Monastery of Wilten, placed at the foot of Mt. Isel, the scene of much bitter fighting in 1809. There, close to the memorial to Hofer, we find his verse inscribed in a bronze book of honour:

They struggled, grim and gory, and man by man they fell;
Their deeds of mountain glory but lays and songs will tell.
If found some day by strangers, their graves will bear no name:
Here lie th' Imperial Rangers, a regiment of fame!

Austria Loses All of South Tyrol

And what happened in 1915, when Austro-Hungary's southern neighbour took up arms on the side of the Entente Powers while the Imperial Army was desperately staving off the Russians on the eastern front? The old defence system of the militia came to life again, and the very youngest of men and the few old men who had not been mobilized held the passes and the approaches to the valleys for several weeks. Commanded by officers they had themselves elected, and reinforced by only a few regular units, they contained battle-fresh Italian contingents until sufficient Austrian troops could be brought into the Dolomites and to the glaciers around the Ortler to continue the fight. And there, high up in the mountains, the enemy forces, vastly superior in number, became enmeshed in an unprecedented battle which dragged on for years. At last, in autumn 1917, Austrian troops fighting alongside the German Alpine Corps succeeded in breaching the enemy lines at Flitsch-Tolmein and in driving their opponents down to the North Italian Plain, behind the River Piave.

A remark made by the distinguished old Emperor Francis Joseph I must also be seen against the background of these events. In the negotiations preceding Italy's declaration of war, when it still appeared as if she would allow her neutrality to be bought in return for certain concessions, the discussion eventually turned to the subject of yielding territory. At that point Francis Joseph declared, *"I would rather perish with my house than sacrifice a single acre of this land!"*

Things turned out differently, however. A good many years later it was in fact revealed that it had then been too late for negotiations, anyway. In a secret London agreement signed in 1915, the Allies had already promised Italy, among other things, the Brenner frontier. Certain Italian nationalist groups had been demanding this ever since 1866, but in 1915 Italy was officially promised something that no one had ever really dared to consider.

In the Peace Treaty of Saint-Germain, concluded in 1919, Austria lost the whole of South Tyrol, not just the southern, mainly Italian-speaking part of the territory (which extended as far as Lake Garda, and of which Trento was the centre) but also the traditionally German-speaking area reaching from the Brenner Pass to the language boundary at the Gap of Salurn (Salorno), some twenty miles south of Bozen (Bolzano), and including historic towns such as Bozen itself and Meran (Merano), long a part of the German settlement area. In addition, Italy was given the ancient cathedral city of Brixen, the religious nucleus from which the whole region had been

Kaspar Wallnhöfer from the Schlanders Militia Battalion, a veteran of the 1859 and 1866 Wars, on the Southern front in 1915.

Matzen Castle near Brixlegg (rising over an ancient Roman encampment, Masciacum) had its first mention in a document in 1176; its Romanesque keep also dates back to this time. The castle was renovated in our century by Fanny Read of Mount Heaton.

Christianized, as well as several other districts and villages of Old Austria. Over the centuries, the German linguistic islands further south, like the Seven Parishes and the Thirteen Parishes (which lie close to where the Southern Alps descend to the lowlands), had already lost most of their cultural links with Germany as a result of the influx of non-German speakers. In the German-speaking region of South Tyrol, a process of Italianization was begun in 1918; and although people the world over became aware of what was happening, no international body did ever anything to stop it. By means of industrialization and

immigration from Southern Italy, an attempt was made to alter the structure of the population: such measures had little impact in rural areas, but were quite horrifyingly successful in urban ones.

When Europe's frontiers were re-drawn after the Second World War nothing was done to remedy the obvious injustices committed in 1919, in spite of the fact that in 1946 an overwhelming majority of the South Tyrolean people demanded the return of their region to Austria. So, with regard to Italy's new international partnership rôle, the Allies, in the 1946 Paris Peace Treaty, decreed that South Tyrol

The Innergschlöss glacial stream, at the head of the Matreier Tauern Valley in East Tyrol, with regal Mt. Grossvenediger (12,058 ft.) shining in the background.

should remain Italian, and granted her merely an autonomy (under the misnomer "Alto Adige").

Even so, the geographical position of North Tyrol and South Tyrol alone would seem to demand that the two should be seen as a unit, as a single piece of territory linking Central and Southern Europe. When seen topographically, Tyrol is a gigantic natural fortress which cannot be ignored by anyone wanting to wield influence in the Alpine region or in the countries on either side of the mountains. This was already common knowledge to the Romans, and much later also to the German kings who crossed the Brenner no fewer than sixty-six times on their progress to Rome, to be crowned Emperor by the Pope. More recently, too, Napoleon, the strategist, was well aware of the potential danger inherent in Tyrol, and so concerned himself more about the outbreak of the Tyrolean struggle for liberation in 1809 than about the Spanish rebellion, which had already been smouldering for some time.

into the Frankish Empire, Tyrol also became part of it; and in the end, after various interludes, formed a territory of the Holy Roman Empire of the German Nation.

The Christianization of the country was begun by monks from the monastery of Säben, above Klausen (Chiusa). Records show that this was the seat of a bishop as early as 559 A.D. The bishop's residence was transferred in 992 A.D. to Brixen, the oldest city in Tyrol, and it remained the seat of the ecclesiastical administration for all Tyrol right up to 1925. In fact, not until 1964 did the present-day Austrian province of Tyrol become a diocese in its own right, with a bishop residing at Innsbruck.

Although, in the Middle Ages, the country nominally belonged to the Dukes of Bavaria, various counts continued to hold virtual dominion over the Inn, Eisack, Puster, and Etsch valleys. In 1004 and 1027, however, the Emperors Henry II and Conrad II, respectively, bestowed the counties on the bish-

The former Imperial Palace of Innsbruck is one of the most imposing pieces of architecture. It was built in late Viennese rococo style.

The Beginnings of Tyrolean History proper

In the sixth century, the Great Migration of the Peoples brought the Germanic Bavarians to Tyrol. As a result, the country was annexed to the great Duchy of Bavaria, but its rulers then had their residence in faraway Regensburg. When Bavaria was incorporated

ops of Brixen and Trient, while raising them to the rank of Imperial Princes. This marks the real beginning of Tyrolean history.

In the course of the next three centuries, the counts of Vinschgau, who may originally have come from the area of Freising in Bavaria, finally won the upper hand, mainly as a result of their political skill, but also by fighting against their own ecclesiastical overlords and their mundane competitors among the nobility. From then on they called themselves the Counts of Tyrol, taking this title from their family seat, a castle built above Meran in the eleventh century. Tyrol Castle safeguarded not only the approaches to the upper Etsch and Passer valleys (in the latter case, thus to the Jaufen Pass [Passo del Giovo]), but also, indirectly, to the Brenner. This was due to the fact that, for a considerable length of time, there was no more than a bridle-path through the Eisack Gorge above Bozen, and in order to bypass this narrow section it was necessary to make the arduous ascent of Mt. Ritten (Renòn). In consequence, many travellers preferred to cross by the Jaufen Pass instead.

The Counts of Tyrol practically never allowed themselves to be carried away by visions of territorial aggrandizement, even at periods when they would certainly have been in a position to materialize them: their Land in the Mountains formed a natural fortress as it was, and served indeed in the office of "the heart and the shield of the Empire."

Under the protection of Tyrol Castle, the present-day town of Meran grew up *auf der Meran*, as the alluvial cone was called, and until 1420 this was the capital of the whole territory on both sides of the Brenner.

A cavalryman's helmet, one of the many exhibits of shiny medieval armour at Ambras Castle, near Innsbruck.

The Festive Hall at Ambras Castle which Archduke Ferdinand II had ordered reconstructed for himself and his wife Philippine Welser, a commoner, in the second half of the sixteenth century.

The elaborately decorated oriel in the Old City is due to an order placed by Emperor Maximilian I in 1497, who was intensely fond of watching with his court the tournaments and games on the city square below. The roof was to be of gold-plated copper - hence the name, "Golden Roof" -, and visitors will be delighted even today to single out a multiplicity of mural paintings, dancing figures, and armorial shields in high relief.

Maria Theresa Street, facing the towering range of the North Tyrolean Limestone Alps. The St. Anna Column, in front, was erected in 1706 to commemorate the withdrawal of the Bavarian troops.

By 1258 Meinhard II of Görz-Tyrol, the "Architect" or "Smith" of his country, as history calls him, had forged the northern and the southern half together; this is clearly evidenced in the territorial designation, used from 1271 onwards, of the "County of Tyrol on the Rivers Etsch and Inn." Only the Puster Valley remained temporarily in the possession of Meinhard's brother Albert of Görz and his heirs. Then, in 1363, Tyrol was handed over to the Habsburgs by Meinhard's granddaughter, Margarete Maultasch ('Satchel-mouthed Meg') of Carinthia, after the untimely death of her only son and heir. The countess herself died in Vienna, where the district of Margareten is named after her.

In 1500, the Puster Valley and the dominion of Lienz were incorporated into Tyrol; and four years later, Rattenberg, Kufstein, and Kitzbühel, which had previously been in Bavarian hands, were also added. In 1516, Maximilian also won Cortina from Venice, the Lager Valley including Rovereto, as well as parts on the northern end of Lake Garda, with Riva. At that point Tyrol had reached its maximum extent, apart from some minor possessions that still belonged to the ecclesiastical principality of Salzburg, namely the Ziller Valley and East Tyrol, Brixen (some sections of the Puster Valley, the Basin of Brixen), and Trient (a few districts). The final additions were made in 1803, when the archbishopric of Salzburg was dissolved. From 1805 until 1809, Tyrol was ruled by Bavaria, after which it returned to Austria again for a brief spell, under Andreas Hofer.

Following the suppression of the Tyrolean uprising in 1809, the land was ruthlessly broken up. The northern and central regions, together with Meran and Brixen, were given to Bavaria; Bozen and the surrounding area as well as the whole of the Italian-speaking region became part of the Kingdom of Italy; and East Tyrol was attached to France's Illyrian provinces.

In 1814, however, Tyrol came back into Austrian hands. As a crownland during the Monarchy, and later, considerably shrunk in circumference, as a federal province in both the First and the Second Republic, it has retained its identity up to the present day.

For the unique cultural and political identity of Tyrol, one other factor was no doubt of great consequence. Between 1379 and 1490, and (if intermittently) again between 1564 and 1665, Tyrol was ruled by a separate branch of the House of Habsburg. This is why, strange as it may seem, Innsbruck, which became the capital of the country in 1420, possesses an Imperial palace, the Hofburg. Besides a good many other precious objects, the palace houses

The Parliament
Conference Room
in the Old Diet.

The twelve-sided Münzerturm ('Mint Tower') at Solbad Hall, in the Inn Valley, is a venerable landmark visible from afar; however, it is a symbol also of the significant rôle played by the Tyrolean economy in the Middle Ages. It faithfully served the Counts of Tyrol in the function its name reveals; and was last used when Andreas Hofer, as Regent of Tyrol, struck his famous Zwanzigers.

The motorway over the Brenner Pass from North to South Tyrol: The 875-yard long *Europa Bridge* is a feat of modern road building; its construction rests on the highest concrete piers in the world - a twenty-storey house would fit underneath it.

the "Silver Chapel", which is of particular interest to art historians. The castle at Ambras near Innsbruck dates from the same period, 1564-89. With its collections of paintings, armoury, coins, and manuscripts, it is still one of Austria's most important museums, despite the fact that many of its valuable exhibits were transferred to Vienna in 1806. Famous in the world of literature is the *Ambras Book of Heroes* (originally, the *Book of Heroes from the Etsch*). In this richly illuminated manuscript, Hans Ried, Bozen's town clerk at the time of Maximilian, recorded twenty-five heroic lays, among them the *Lay of Gudrun.* Since this poem is not extant anywhere else, it might otherwise have been lost to posterity.

After being replaced by Innsbruck as the capital, Meran nevertheless retains a place of honour among Tyrolean cities. Tyrol Castle, since the times of Meinhard II, long saw a "Burgrave" in residence, and the expression *Burggrafenamt* 'Burgraviate', to mark the area around Meran, continues to be common. In this part of South Tyrol, one finds particularly fine examples of the traditional Tyrolean costume.

Innsbruck's International Standing

Innsbruck, one southern district of which, at the foot of Mt. Isel, was a Roman settlement (Wilten *[Veldidena]*), rapidly increased in significance as a result of its situation on major trade routes. The city lay at the junction of the highway skirting the River Inn and the road winding its way southwards through the narrow Sill valley up and beyond the Brenner, while to the north it had easy access to the

A view of Kufstein and its fortress bearing the same name; the walls of that stronghold are extremely solid, in its "Kaiserturm" ('Emperor's Tower') indeed up to 23 feet.

The *Wilde Kaiser* massif (its name actually means 'mountain dairy hut among the wild heights'), majestic and rugged as can be, has the finest mountain scenery Tyrol and possibly even the Alps at large can offer.

Alpine foreland of Bavaria and, more important, to Augsburg, in those days one of the Continent's leading trading centres. However, the major portion of Old Innsbruck dates from the High Middle Ages. Walking along its streets and lanes, with their Gothic and Renaissance buildings, the splendid houses with arcades and bay windows built by wealthy patricians and nobles, one frequently catches glimpses of the Northern Limestone Chain, the nearby mountains so typical of Innsbruck - all in all, a unique city and quite different from Salzburg, Graz or the other ancient Austrian cities. Innsbruck soon attracted attention in the realms of the humanities and medicine as a result of the presence of the Habsburg court and the foundation of the University in 1669. Over the centuries, artists and scholars have chosen to settle there. Conversely, the Tyrolean soil has itself brought forth many talented men, only a few of whom can be singled out for mention here: Jakob Prandtauer (1660-1726), from Stanz near Landeck, whose crowning achievement as a Baroque

Der Brenner, in 1910 became a Catholic forum for the leading writers of the day.

Other figures that immediately spring to mind in this context are Ludwig Purtscheller, who played a major rôle in making the Alps and other high-level ranges accessible, and many of the impressive guides from the Dolomites, as well as the skiing pioneers. One should not forget, however - strains of heroic lays! - the countless Tyrolean peasants from the Austrian Alps who emigrated to the state of Santa Catarina, in Southern Brazil, during the lean years of the thirties and who founded the Tyrolean village of Dreizehnlinden (Treze Tilias).

Tyrolean summits spell pure and varied joys for rock climbers and mountain walkers alike from all over the world.

architect was the splendid monastery at Melk on the Danube; Jakob Stainer (1621-1683), the violin-maker from Absam, whose instruments stand comparison with famous Italian violins; and Peter Anich (1723-1766), from Oberperfuss near Innsbruck, who produced the first orographical map of the country, an admirable feat of accuracy. Painters like Franz von Defregger and Albin Egger-Lienz successfully portrayed the Tyrolean character in their work, which is of a highly individual genre; and a sophisticated journal for the arts and letters, Innsbruck's

Here is a *Zottler* ('Shaggy Man'), a masked figure from a Tyrolean Shrovetide procession in the Innsbruck area. His coat sports many-coloured linen ornaments sewn on in spirals, and his hat is stuck with peacock feathers and artificial flowers arranged like a fan.

Tyrolean Shrovetide (Carnival)

Even today, many villages and market towns of Tyrol are the scene of peculiar and mysterious customs during Shrovetide. Anybody fortunate enough to be in Imst "on call" to witness the procession of masked groups (*Schemenlauf*) will remember the do for the rest of their lives. Just as in centuries gone by, crowds of masked figures (*Maschgerer*) run and hop and leap through the streets: first come the *Scheller* and *Roller* with their headdresses; and then, in order to parody these beautiful and solemn masks, come the *Laggescheller* and the *Laggeroller* figures impersonating wizened old men and women, to remind radiant youth of the fleeting nature of all things earthly.

Traditions of this kind have very deep roots, and there are bound to be divergent theories concerning their origin, the majority of them however being chiefly based on guesswork. There is not even an entirely satisfactory explanation for the words *Schemen, Larve,* and *Maske* all three of which, rather indiscriminately, refer to the disguises used. To the Arabs, a *maschera* was merely a clown or buffoon, while the Lombards, whose culture had a major influence in this region, gave the name *masca* to the netted shroud in which the dead were swathed. Similarly, the ancient Romans employed the word *larvae* for the shades of the departed who roamed around at night; and, in much the same way, the masked figures at Imst regard themselves as emissaries from a world beyond.

On the morning of Shrove Tuesday, all the mummers attend a mass for the souls of their dead. And then, as the noontide bells fall silent, suddenly pandemonium breaks out. In all the streets and alleys, on every corner, the fools' bells ring, and there is a sound of howling and wailing as if a thousand devils had been let loose; frequently indeed the capers and gambols develop into real dancing and jigging, culminating in ecstasies of movement reminiscent of the ritual dances known among pagan peoples.

Of course, Tyrolean Shrovetide practices, like all carnival customs, have undergone many changes as the years flow past. For instance, a mock trial once used to be a traditional feature in country areas. At such "court hearings," infringements of the unwritten social and civic codes, especially sexual offences, were dealt with, often in a highly drastic fashion. On occasion, this kind of popular justice even went so far as to have a waggon-load of dung piled up on the roof of a farmhouse whose owner was suspected of using his maid in an unmaidenly way.

The bear is another staple feature of Shrovetide in the country. In fact, this ursine symbol seems to be one of the most important characters of all; it is the embodiment of fertility and of re-awakening life.

Vorarlberg may well be second to the last among the federal provinces of Austria, as far as size and population are concerned, but one should be careful not to draw wrong conclusions. The people from the *'Ländle'* (as it is endearingly called) are renowned for their distinctive and abiding sense of independence, and the politicians in Vienna cannot afford to treat the most western part of their country as some kind of *quantité négligeable.* The Vorarlbergers jealously guard their position and rights within the advantageous federal system, and want to see them respected at all costs. In the past they repeatedly shied away from a union with Tyrol, and yet they have always been good neighbours. After the First World War, for example, when Vienna was in a state of seething unrest and the powerful Danubian Monarchy had been whittled down to a German-speaking Austria, Vorarlberg felt it was not receiving its due care and attention from the Viennese government; indeed some powerful circles started toying with the idea of a political union with neighbouring Switzerland, the "Blessed Isle." Perhaps this idea, which found a considerable amount of public support, was never meant to be taken seriously, but it did cause Vienna to prick up its ears and oblige the Vorarlbergers with the required respect and more impressive demonstrations of good will.

This "stepchild" complex is still ingrained in the people - whom Emperor Joseph II once allegedly referred to as the "impossible" ones -, as evidenced by an eruption of public opinion a decade or two ago. The Viennese Minister of Transport had insisted upon christening a ferry-boat intended for Lake Constance, the *Dr. Karl Renner*, after the first President of the Austrian Republic. However, there was such a wave of protest that the Minister was forced to abandon the scheme; and in the shipyard at Fussach the boat was given the name *Vorarlberg* instead, which it has proudly displayed upon the "Swabian Sea" ever since.

This event may have increased the caution and consideration with which the Viennese government handles Vorarlberg, but there are also other well-founded reasons. The 310,000 inhabitants of the province, which occupies an area of 1,000 square miles, are rooted deeply in their native soil and have always remained loyal to Austria, to be relied upon in times of trouble. After both World Wars, for instance, they contributed a great deal of effort towards the reconstruction of the nation, within the limits of the modest means at their disposal. In the turbulence of history, Vorarlberg was seldom left in peace, and the Romanic and Alemannic elements of the population became one people with one com-

1. Skikurs Zürs 1908

Herr Ikle
St. Gallen

Bergführer Schallert
Bludenz

Franz Josef Mathies
„Lawinen-Franz-Josef"

Engelbert Strolz
Zürs

Hannes Schneider
Stuben

Albert Mathies
Zürs

Theresia Sohm
Bregenz

mon destiny, capable of standing up under any adversity. Indeed the extreme seclusion of the area favoured such a development, and played a decisive rôle when it came to resisting the repeated assaults upon their independence or to regaining it when it had been lost, no matter how stubborn a struggle was necessary.

The geography of the land, with its 5,905 foot high Mt. Arlberg as a mighty barrier, precludes the easy construction of traffic links with the rest of Austria; it was, in fact, not until late in 1978 that an eight-and-a-half mile toll tunnel was completed, providing an alternative connection to the mountain route, which in any case was often impassable in heavy snows.

The province is relatively poor in mineral wealth and other natural resources; so there is no mining industry of any great import, and agriculture seldom proves profitable, especially since it often demands an unusual amount of labour and is always at the mercy of the weather. Even in earlier times, these considerations made Vorarlbergers leave the old home in order to earn a living elsewhere. Many sought seasonal employment abroad, and some of these never returned. At the turn of the nineteenth century, when traditional handicrafts were gradually being developed into a modest cottage industry the basis for a small and medium-scale textile production was provided, which was furthered and intensified by the use of natural water-power.

The Pioneer Land of Skiing

The necessity of depending on the natural environment for a living eventually led to the cultivation of a tourist trade. It took on sizeable proportions as time went by, contributing greatly to the economic growth of this province endowed with scenic beauty. Skiing soon played a decisive rôle in attracting holidaymakers from near and far. It was a sport that was already gaining popularity in Vorarlberg at the beginning of this century, and was to spread like wildfire from there throughout the rest of the world. Georg Bilgeri (1873-1934) from Bregenz, and Hannes Schneider (1890-1955) from Stuben are two of the pioneers of this newly dominant winter sport, and Vorarlberg can boast of the first skiing course, which took place at Zürs in the Arlberg mountains. Although only a very small minority of people was drawn to the snowy romance of the lonely heights before and after the First World War, nowadays myriads of people descend on the winter sports centres of Austria. This influx has had its effect both in private and in public spheres. Many owners of Alpine farmhouses in idyllic surroundings were quick to respond to the rising demand for accommodation. Tourism had finally begun to be a major economic factor, as it still is today of course.

inhabitants; it is both the industrial and economic centre of the land, and has grown considerably in importance during the past three decades due to its Trade Fairs, which attract native and foreign interests alike. The Nature Show of Vorarlberg acts as a complement to the Fairs, and affords the visitor a glimpse of the animal and plant life in the area. The radio station is also to be found in Dornbirn. And then there is Feldkirch, a historical town of 24,000 citizens, which together with Bregenz forms the administrative hub of the land. It is the seat of the Provincial Court of Justice, the Revenue Office, and the Chambers of Commerce and Labour, but the town also holds a unique position in ecclesiastical matters in that, if only since 1968, it is also the seat of the diocesan bishop of Vorarlberg. Last comes Bludenz, the smallest in the civic quartet, with a population of 13,000, and various small industries. This ancient settlement, being situated at the intersection of four alpine valleys (the Brandnertal, the Montafon, the Klostertal and the Grosse Walsertal), is quite naturally a centre for mountaineering.

The Earliest Settlements

Present findings would suggest that hunters were roaming the Vorarlberg mountain forests as early as the Ice Age, but settlement did not take place until the Stone Age. The Proto-Illyrian urnfield culture, which can also be documented, dates from the Bronze Age until c. 800 B.C. By the time of the primitive Raetian Melaun culture there are signs of a fairly advanced agricultural system, involving division of labour as well as evidence of mining and trade routes over the passes. In the following centuries before Christ, the Celtic Brigantians settled in the north around Bregenz, where the Celtic La Tène Culture developed, and the Raetian Calucons made their home in the south and west. The latter were soon forced to defend themselves against the invading Romans and, suffering severe losses in battle, had to withdraw from the valleys and lowlands favoured by the intruders. Even in the fourth century, according to the Roman, Ammianus Marcellinus, Vorarlberg must have been marked by virgin forests and an unfriendly climate. So, the Roman cohorts derived very little pleasure from the land; nevertheless, they went to the trouble of laying roads.

The "Flying Dutchman" performed on the lake at Bregenz, which has the largest floating stage in the world. This theatre festival takes place in summer every year.

The four towns of Bregenz, Feldkirch, Dornbirn, and Bludenz became the focal points of this new industry, each one being assigned a certain responsibility. This division of labour demonstrates a canny sense of economics, in that instead of concentrating everything on the capital as is customary, Vorarlberg nurtured a decentralized structure that is both homogeneous and functional. Bregenz, the cultural magnet, draws many visitors due to its ideal position and, furthermore, to its *Spiele auf dem See*, an annual occasion of theatrical and musical performances on Lake Constance. With a population of only 26,000, however, it is not the largest town in Vorarlberg. This position is held by Dornbirn with its 38,000

They erected their strongholds and dwellings on the eastern shores of Lake Constance, Brigantium in their tongue, and now Bregenz, as a Latin loan. The importance of Brigantium as a Roman fort became apparent to posterity only gradually, through excavations by archaeologists. So they dis-

Martin's Tower, built in Bregenz in the fourteenth century, rests on Romanesque foundations; its dome was added in 1701.

Cruising in a stylish boat on Lake Constance is bound to leave lasting impressions on any carefree newcomer to the "Swabian Sea."

Austria has a great number of beautiful and romantic landscapes to choose from and enjoy. This snapshot was taken in the Bartholomäberg area of the Montafon Valley, southeast of Bludenz.

covered the *municipium* by the Ölrain, the Late Roman citadel in the upper part of town, the harbour installations on the Leutbühel, a forum, a temple, several thermal springs, covered markets and villas, and indeed the operating-room of a Roman surgeon. All the finds have been collected in the Vorarlberg Provincial Museum. Brigantium, along with the entire province of Raetia, was governed from Augusta Vindelicorum, now Augsburg, which was also the military headquarters. Yet, under Roman rule, the land witnessed marked improvements: the network of roads was enlarged, estates and farms were built to maintain the Roman garrison and the civilian population, and proper residential towns came into being. Of course, Romanization went hand in hand with these developments, and in 212 A.D. all the inhabitants of Raetia were granted Roman citizenship.

However, in the third century A.D. the Germanic tribes from the north began their invasion of the Roman Empire, crossing the *limes*, the fortified border, several times. Southern Germany was soon overrun, first by the Alemanni, then by the Goths and Franks. Meanwhile Christianity was taking hold of the Province, which under Frankish sovereignty

enjoyed a great measure of independence. The Udalriching family, related to Charlemagne, gained domain over the lands around Lake Constance, and established their ancestral seat at Friedrichshafen. By this time the Magyars had begun their incursions and continued to harass the settlers of what is now Vorarlberg until their utter defeat in the Battle on the Lechfeld, in 955. Mention should here be made of the Benedictine Monastery at Mehrerau-on-the-Lake, founded by Count Ulrich of Bregenz, which

The cross-gabled "Red House" of Dornbirn, built in 1639 by the famous Rhomberg family, is typical of the old architecture in the Upper Rhine valley. *Das rote Hüs*, a brick and half-timber house in Strassburg, was the model for its red coat of paint.

The hillside village of Blons, in the Grosse Walser valley, stirs specific interests in historians and in etymologists. The place-name element *Walser*, after all, is a rather clear indication that centuries ago there must have been one or several waves of immigrants known as *Walcher*, i.e., 'foreigners.'

Players of the alpenhorn show their respect for age-old melodies by cultivating them even today.

"Mary of the Snows," a little Baroque church erected near Gaschurn, in the Upper Montafon area, in 1637. This high-lying valley nestles among the Verwall Group in the north-east, the Rhaetian Alps in the west, and the Silvretta Group in the South.
The name of the chapel derives from the widespread legend according to which a Roman nobleman once had a vision of the Virgin Mary directing him to build a church at a site where, in a verdant summerscape, he would find a mound of snow.

contributed significantly to the spiritual and cultural life of the area. The Counts of Montfort, from whom Vorarlberg derives its coat of arms, deserve to be remembered for the devoted part they played in developing a system of government which in those days was only at its formative stage. Their successors were the Habsburgs, who seized power stroke by stroke over a period of two hundred years.

Union with Appenzell and St. Gallen

Once again, however, the local people showed themselves to be concerned about their freedom and ancestral privileges. Repeatedly they were inspired by their westerly neighbours, who were members of the Helvetian Confederation. No one in his right mind would want to be ruled without being consulted as to his wishes and opinions, and in this attitude the tradition of the Raetian past has been well preserved. Initially it was the independent farmers and, in particular, the Valaisans who, vested with special rights to settle and cultivate the high mountain regions (an arduous task), refused to be treated like vassals without a will of their own by the new lords. There were charters of liberty which awarded the bearers a number of concessions; and the citizens of Feldkirch set the pace, having these guaranteed and sanctioned by the new lord before they acknowledged and duly paid homage to him. Their rights included election of their city bailiff, restriction of the overlord's financial suzerainty, consultation of the citizens in matters

of legislation, and the right to free emigration, marriage and inheritance. These advancements in civil rights gained in 1376 were followed, in 1391, by the union of the citizens of Feldkirch and Bludenz thus forming the Vorarlberg Confederation.

From now on no fort or castle was to be occupied without the consent of the people, which meant that military installations were under their control. The beginnings of the country's corporative constitution can be seen in the establishment of such legal provisions. Afterwards, however, an armed rebellion against the aristocracy began, supported by the Swiss towns of Appenzell and St. Gallen; it was joined by Feldkirch, which was a partner with equal rights. Castles were taken by storm and reduced to ashes; and these early successes incited to more and more daring ventures. The Leaguers crossed the Arlberg mountains, invaded Tyrol, and finally attacked Bregenz, the seat of Count William of Montfort. Since there was danger of the rebellion spilling over into Swabia and Bavaria, an army of knights was mustered from all over Southern Germany. Bregenz was eventually delivered from the besiegers, and this was the beginning of the end of the *Bund ob dem See*, which had once been considered invincible. Austria consolidated her authority, and in the following decades took possession of the whole of Vorarlberg, including Bregenz, by either force, negotiation, or purchase. In the interest of protecting the unity of their native soil, the people of the country supported the Habsburgs, thereby safeguarding their privileges for the time being.

A medal struck in honour of Count Hugo of Montfort-Bregenz. In 1523 he sold the rest of his Bregenz estates to Austria, and died in 1536 as a Bavarian trustee of Höchstädt on the Danube.

The Reformation and the Peasants' Revolts

In 1415, a fire blazed forth like a beacon out of Constance: the religious rebel John Huss (or Hus), who had fought for a Czech National Church, was burnt at the stake as a consequence of a decision made by the Church Council. However, the turbulent movements which were kindled a century later by the Reformation and peasant uprisings passed over Vorarlberg without any lasting effects. The Knights of Ems, in their office as Austrian governors, prevented the Reformation from gaining a foothold in the land, despite the fact that it was encroaching on two fronts, from the south and from the west where Zwingli and Calvin were once again waving the banner of revolt with renewed vigour. In any case, the peasants, who had their rights and liberties guaranteed, had no reason to take up arms like their Swabian and Bavarian brothers who were still under the thumb of the nobility.

Nevertheless, in the period leading up to Luther's fastening his Ninety-Five Theses on the door of All Saints Church in Wittenberg (1517), there were several natives of Vorarlberg among his stalwart collaborators, especially the brothers Bartholomäus and Johannes Bernhardi from Schlins, and Johannes Dölsch and Jodok Mörlin from Feldkirch. In Lindau, Zurich, Basel, Mühlhausen (Mulhouse), and Strassburg (Strasbourg), Vorarlbergers were busy preaching the new ideas. The name of Johannes Dölsch stood beside that of Luther's on the papal bull threatening excommunication.

Quite possibly, this new approach to spiritual and religious matters had its origins in Humanism, which had already begun to attract the attention of the townsfolk in Feldkirch and Bregenz. The most prominent representatives of this movement were Ludwig Rad, an early humanist philosopher; Hieronymus Münzer, or Monetarius, a bibliophile; Jakob Mennel, or Manlius, the ex-officio historiographer at the Imperial Court; and Georg Joachim Rheticus, a pupil of Copernicus. The book trade and libraries thrived. Hohenems Palace, the seat of the Counts of Ems and a centre of cultural endeavours, became the home of a rare and precious collection of Middle High German manuscripts, including the A and C Manuscripts of *The Lay of the Nibelungs* which attained such fame in the eighteenth century. The Counts of Ems commissioned Italian architects to build a stately Renaissance mansion with zoological and pleasure gardens. They set up a Jewish community, and Hohenems remained the seat of a rabbinate into the nineteenth century. Enlightenment and tolerance were demonstrated at a time when, in a good many other places, the spirit of the Middle Ages still prevailed.

Of course, the land was not spared the oppressive shadows of the Thirty Years' War. The border of Graubünden (or, the Grisons) remained a troubled area for two decades. The inhabitants from Prätigau, a Swiss side-valley of the Rhine, south of the Rätikon mountain range, attacked Vorarlberg, and drove away large herds of cattle. Peasants, fired with religious fervour, did not hesitate to commit gruesome felonies. One of their victims was the Capuchin Father Fidelis of Sigmaringen, who was mercilessly slaughtered. The natives found themselves under duress to provide for the troops passing through their land, which imposed an unbearable burden upon them. Often, one household was expected to feed between ten and thirty soldiers for weeks on end. Many farms were destroyed, and it was invariably the Imperial troops that performed these cruel acts. As a consequence of the war the Black Death raged

A nineteenth-century view in watercolour of Hohenbregenz Castle before being destroyed by the Swedes in 1647. It belonged to the Counts of Montfort-Bregenz until 1451, when they shared it with the Austrian governor until 1523. In 1723 the ruins were made into a pilgrimage chapel.

The fortified pilgrimage church of St. Mary's, a Gothic shrine towering above the city of Rankweil.

The daily life of that rural community around the steep Liebfrauenberg, incidentally, is well described in Edith O'Shaughnessy's Other Ways and Other Flesh, a captivating microcosm of Vorarlberg and its people.

through the valleys, demanding its high tribute in the form of a sharp decline in the population; alone in Dornbirn, Altenstadt, Feldkirch, Frastanz, Bregenz, Hörbranz, Mellau, and Egg the plague claimed more than 2,500 victims. Just before the end of the war, when peace negotiations were already under way, both sides were still striving to improve their positions through military victories. General Wran-

The Renaissance palace of the Counts of Ems at Hohenems, on the eastern side of the Rhine valley. The noblemen of Ems, who were raised to the dignity of counts in 1560, had the palace built by the Italian architect Martino Longo to flaunt their new status.

gel invaded Vorarlberg with the Swedish Protestant army and brought Bregenz, which was reputedly invulnerable, to its knees. Fort Hohenbregenz on Mt. Gebhardsberg was blown up, the town subjected to pillage, while the whole land lay prostrate with heavy war indemnities.

Cultural Life Develops

Another wave of emigration was set in motion; now the destination was largely Upper Swabia, which had lost so many of its inhabitants through the war. Although this consequence must have been grimly inconvenient for the Vorarlbergers, it did have its positive side when considered as a whole. Some artisans of the building trade from the Bregenzerwald formed a guild whose members, made up of builders, plasterers and sculptors, poured across the border into neighbouring lands and left to posterity many fine examples of the Baroque style. Franz Beer and Peter Thumb played important rôles in this dissemination of creativity. As for poetry in the spirit of the age, Laurentius of Schnifis became well-known

for his writing; his Baroque diction, and the good things of life he portrayed in song and story, represented an avenue of escape from the misery of everyday existence. At the same time Absolutism was celebrating its final triumphs. The eighteenth century as a whole is characterized by the attempt of those with any form of authority to stave off the winds of change that blasted keen and cold against their faces. Indeed, in 1722 the Vorarlberg Council of Estates had accepted the Pragmatic Sanction of 1713 in return for a confirmation of its privileges, yet the people waited in vain for their superiors to offer them a glimpse of charity or grace. Feldkirch, a champion of Home Rule, which had never been high in Vienna's favour, was gradually and, as it were, surreptitiously replaced by Bregenz as the capital: this lakeside town first became the seat of a Directorate which exercised authority over the surrounding bailiwicks; it was then allowed the honours of accommodating a Regional Office and, later still, a District Office.

In that century, too, the senior administrative centre for Vorarlberg was transferred from Inns-

Schattenburg Castle above Feldkirch, one of the most attractive and well-preserved strongholds in Central Europe, has offered 'shelter' (<MHG *schate;* hence the name) to the town and the surrounding border country since the Middle Ages. Belonging to the Counts of Monfort-Feldkirch, it was the seat of the Austrian protector of Feldkirch since 1390. There is Gothic wainscotting in some of the rooms (now housing the Regional Folklore Museum), and the Chapel contains frescoes from the sixteenth century.

bruck to Freiburg-im-Breisgau, which in those days was part of Further Austria. Moreover, the towns in Vorarlberg lost a great deal of their autonomy, and as a consequence the judicial system was reorganized in such a way that professional judges replaced the lay magistrates. Unpopular reforms alternated with desirable improvements, in accordance with Viennese notions of diplomacy prevailing at the time. Thus, after repeated and severe political interference, there followed a period of great social progress: a fair system of general and equal taxation came into use; the textile industry received support; schools and schooling were modernized; a national postal system was introduced and the road network enlarged. The Vorarlbergers contributed an astoundingly great share towards German Classicism, as is apparent in the work of Josef Anton Brentano, an indefatigable printer from Bregenz, who published hundreds of contemporary works of literature. Angelika Kauffmann, an artist from Schwarzenberg who also belongs to this period, received recognition throughout Europe.

The Franco-Bavarian Interlude

The Napoleonic Wars shook the very foundations of Europe. The Corsican Corporal directed his main offensive against Austria, because he was in no position to challenge England and had no desire to challenge Russia as yet. The Battle of Austerlitz (1805) was a decisive victory for him and led to the peace treaty of Pressburg, in which Austria was forced to cede both Vorarlberg and Tyrol to Bavaria: the Alpine provinces had thus become pawns in the game of power politics and coalition. Bavaria had proved her loyalty to France, and was duly rewarded with new lands. (Incidentally, Bavaria was quick enough to change sides ten years later when Napoleon's star began to pale!) Napoleon's major intention behind the peace treaty was, of course, to weaken Austria and curtail her territorial dominions. Maximilian I of Bavaria, like his counterpart in Württemberg, Frederick I, was made King by Napoleon, but was little more than a puppet in the hands of his chief minister, Count Montgelas. The latter had relentlessly pursued a policy of secularization, seizing and in many cases destroying the treasures of the Church; moreover, when he had subjected Bavaria (now much greater by the inclusion of Franconia) to a territorial reorganization, the methods resorted to were no less draconic. As a corollary, and of no surprise, the Vorarlbergers forfeited their independence only a few weeks after having paid homage to their new sovereign in Bregenz-Vorarlberg became a part of the Bavarian province of Swabia. As if that was not enough, Montgelas' policy of centralization, with the focus on Munich, demanded further sacrifices for the sake of uniformity within the state and its administration. In Vorarlberg seven Provincial Courts under the authority of the Court of Appeal at Memmingen replaced the traditional jurisdictions, which had been considered the keystone of the Constitution. Towards the end of 1806 the Provincial Council of Estates assembled for the last time; two years later it was dissolved. The new Bavarian administration incorporated the province into the Iller District, with Kempten as the county seat. The dissolution of the parish councils was an integral part of this reorganization, their duties being taken over by the central government.

The new sovereign did not exactly make himself popular with the inhabitants of Vorarlberg and Tyrol in his treatment of their regional institutions. It was not long until the bond with Bavaria, through the continual and rigorous interference of the Munich authorities, was felt to be quite unreasonable, and indeed intolerable. The Bavarians levied heavy taxes upon the occupied territories. They introduced conscription in order to further the French war of conquest, they continued to confiscate Church property, and Napoleon's imposed Continental Blockade made life a big misery. It was the policy towards the Church, however, which aroused the most discontent, because it meant that the Vorarlbergers were no longer able to obtain credit at favourable rates of interest from the collected wealth of the Church. There was never any open rebellion, but the Bavarian thorn in Austria's side continued to fester. In 1809, Austria renewed her war effort, penetrating as far as the Bavarian capital. This was the signal for armed revolt which the Tyroleans, under the leadership of Andreas Hofer and Josef Speckbacher, and the Vorarlbergers had been waiting for. The fighting was directed first and foremost against France, rather than her dependent ally, Bavaria. But only a temporary success was granted to the uprising, despite the fact that there was fierce resistance in Tyrol and that the Vorarlbergers advanced as far as Constance and Kempten. The French, Bavarian and Württemberg allies proved far superior both in number and munitions, and soon reconquered the land they had so recently relinquished. Austria found herself once again under French rule, and Vorarlberg became a possession of Bavaria. Those who had fought for their freedom and had been captured were carried off into enemy territory as hostages - a measure which was repeated in 1813 when a similar uprising was feared.

Great rejoicing was made over the reunification of Vorarlberg with Austria, in July 1814: The citizens of Bregenz duly celebrated the occasion by drinking the health of Emperor Francis I at a fountain that liberally dispensed wine free of charge (*left*). Three weeks later, a Thanksgiving Mass was held, to which the Bregenzers were known to have carried in procession the Emperor's effigy with great pomp and circumstance (*right*).

Mercurial Viennese Policy

After Napoleon's downfall Bavaria was no longer in a position to retain Vorarlberg, and consequently had to give up all claim to this territory. On 7 July 1814, Austria took possession again, but left Bavaria the provincial court of Weiler and subsequent access to Lake Constance. The old Corporative Estates, which had been dissolved in the interim, reassembled in the hopes of gaining recognition of the former constitution. But Austria now also had a Montgelas, in the person of Chancellor Metternich, who had risen to act as the all-powerful advocate-general of the Habsburgs in home and foreign affairs. He tended towards a policy of centralization and, as a matter of

fact, he meticulously followed in the footsteps of the Bavarian administrative reformer. The corporative constitution was not reinstated, and those changes which Bavaria had introduced were generally upheld. Even the resumed endeavours to provide Vorarlberg with the status of a bishopric met, as usual, with rebuttal; the land, which had belonged to the dioceses of Chur, Constance and Augsburg, was passed on to the bishopric of Brixen, with a vicar-general responsible for matters concerning Vorarlberg.

During the nineteenth century the textile industry, which had been in existence for little less than a hundred years, was further developed with the financial assistance of the state, enabling Vorarlberg

The Vorarlberg Fair of 1887 at Bregenz, as shown in a contemporary, and rather naive, painting. For the first time a comprehensive picture of the province, its economy and culture was offered on occasion.

to become a major centre for textile production within the Danubian Monarchy. Of course, there were no large factories, yet these sound small and medium-scale enterprises did the area a great economic service. However, such development also brought about unprecedented social problems, especially in regard to child labour. Because the land simply could not cope with the natural increase in numbers, another major shift in population gradually began. Many left their native Vorarlberg and settled in Swabia and Bavaria, or emigrated overseas. Then, at the turn of the century, a serious social situation was caused by the immigration of South Tyrolean labourers of Italian descent, who sought employment in the building of the Arlberg railway. A similar situation occurred later when, before the Second World War, more than five thousand Germans left their homes in South Tyrol to settle in Vorarlberg following the Hitler-Mussolini Agreement.

Vorarlberg was also to feel the effect of the riotous events which struck Vienna and other large towns in Austria in 1848, if without the same amount of bloodshed. A great deal of bitterness, however, had built up through contentious police harassment and pettifogging censorship, which duly found a vent in tumultuous rallies and wild speeches warning against a return to the "old tyranny." At Frastanz a revenue officer was chased away by the mob in no uncertain terms, and a pamphlet which took up this incident lashed out against the "reactionary powers": "Frastanz stands for Vorarlberg, and Vorarlberg for all Austria! Give up your ridiculous hopes of forcing us back into the old yoke, and don't imagine we are still blinkered! We, the peasants, know only too well that we are the largest and most indispensable social class in the state, and that united we can easily withstand your assaults upon our freedom. Frastanz is living proof of the people's determination never again to submit to the old tyranny!"

Standing on Her Own Two Feet

German Austria was the name given to the remains of the Monarchy after the War; and as early as November 1918 the Vorarlbergers were claiming recognition as a Federal State. This unequivocal decision by the people, supported by the constituent Provincial Assembly, met no opposition, and thus the first Governor of the new Federal Province, Dr. Otto Enders, was inaugurated in Vienna. Then came the difference of opinion regarding a possible union with Switzerland during the chaos and hardship of the post-war period; this "flirt," however, was more an act of defiance than a serious proposition,

and nothing came of it. Vorarlberg, the geographically most unprotected province, readily accepted her status of vulnerability on the periphery of the new Austrian Federation: she confirmed her acceptance by passing a Provincial Constitution in 1923 (still valid to this day) and set about making the best of a situation which was, for all of Austria, unpleasant. In any case, the tiny *Ländle* was not as deeply affected by the crisis as were the larger provinces situated in the centre or, for that matter, Vienna. In spite of prolonged financial straits, the Vorarlbergers did not allow a sense of resignation to get the better of them, and they accomplished a considerable task of fine reconstruction work. The use of hydro-electric energy from such projects as the Ill Plants and the Vorarlberg Power Stations created the basis upon which industrialization could be continued and developed. The principal railway line through the Arlberg was electrified; cable-cars were "threaded" to the top of Mt. Pfänder, the pre-Alpine playground so dear to lakeside dwellers (3,488 ft.); and a scenic mountain road built across the Hochtannberg Pass (5,589 ft.) - achievements which proved invaluable in promoting the tourist trade.

Similarly, Vorarlberg was spared the degree of political turbulence which affected the other federal provinces. All the same, its people were to learn through bitter experience that its union with the German Reich was by no means all wine and roses. Once again the coveted regional independence was lost, with the province being governed from Innsbruck, while the Kleinwalser Valley was annexed to the Bavarian administrative district of Swabia. Then came the Second World War with all its anguish and a loss of some eight thousand Vorarlberg soldiers, who were killed in action. After the War the land was occupied by French troops, and the economy and administration were in a state of total collapse. All trade ceased, and the courts, police stations, and post-offices, including telephone and telegraph services, were closed down. The following assessment, which is as concise as it is revealing, appeared in one French report from those gloomy days: "The zone which we have the honour of occupying is in complete chaos!" What followed was a period of joint Franco-Austrian administration which led to a confusing and often awkward overlapping in their separate spheres of responsibility, as well as other unpleasant side effects. Only after the successful appointment of Ulrich Ilg as Governor in 1945 did the conditions gradually begin to normalize.

A free press was again established, housing and roadworks were given priority, the birth-rate rose, and, recognizing the benefits to be had from tour-

Opposite:
The Alpine road winding its way up the pass near Schröcken.

This small church in the tiny village of Schröcken on the Hochbergtann Pass has a tall, slim spire which can be seen from afar by people walking across the pass.

ism, the necessary conditions for its anticipated revival were created. No one could claim that this effort has not been amply rewarded. Without any outside help, Vorarlberg has stood up economically to all the obstacles and adversity in its path, and has developed its potential to the full. Yet one thing cannot be overlooked: the inhabitants continue to oppose all suggestions at centralization which Vienna might make. They have fought too long for their independence (consider the period from 1806 to 1918) to relax their vigilance even now. The long years of political difficulties and conflicts have tempered their will to the strength of steel, and to this day they consider a pinch of suspicion appropriate.

Vienna. The name of this city has a pleasant, friendly ring about it, and holds a certain fascination for us, today more than ever. The word resounds with history; the idyllic tranquillity of the Biedermeier period fills our imagination; great names which have gone down in musical or theatrical history spring to mind in a striking and confusing fashion. We are captivated by the prosperity, glory, and decline of a great dynasty. Here we have the gloomy mists of a tragic destiny which overshadowed the entire area under Viennese domination, between the Adriatic and Galicia, from the River Inn and the Bavarian Alps to the Carpathians and the German-settled country full of fortified churches, and even beyond.

Here, irrepressible cheerfulness and a likeable easy-going disposition go hand in hand with the engaging, warm-hearted life-style of the Viennese. The Prater, Grinzing, Nussdorf, and Heiligenstadt continue to act as the traditional centres of bibulous fun and gaiety, as expressed in innumerable delightful melodies.

But Vienna, like all the other provinces, is also bound by the harsh laws of economic survival. One cannot get something for nothing in this world; the laws of success call for achievement, enterprising imagination, and adventurousness. Vienna has displayed an admirable degree of productivity and has vigorously fulfilled its function as an intermediary in the economic sphere, above all with regard to south-eastern Europe. Vienna Fair, with its many exhibits, and visitors from far and wide, is famous throughout Europe and overseas, and the international character of the city on the Danube is revealed, quite apart from the influx of tourists from all over the world, by the presence of supranational bodies working for international cooperation.

The Lure of the Vienna Basin

The beginnings of settlement in the basin surrounding the Danube and Vienna go beyond recorded history. In the course of thousands of years, the area has developed its own firm laws in relation to man. It has attracted, absorbed and rejected. We do not know to what races the people belonged who first settled this region thousands of years before Christ, although only sporadically. Prehistorians are still feeling their way from one culture to another with the aid of what has been excavated so far (finds are made occasionally even today).

This region did not remain unaffected by the Great Migration of the Peoples and the attendant wars and upheavals. The Indo-Europeans who penetrated the vastness from the north and drove out or killed the original population were followed by the Illyrians, a race whose past is enveloped in myth. Then the sphinx-like Celtic people, roused both by restlessness and by the desire to form the beginnings of a state, floundered along through the fog-patches of prehistory, which were ever so slowly now starting to lift. About the time of the birth of Christ, under Augustus, the boundary of the Roman Empire was

Opposite:
In the *Prater*, the huge Ferris Wheel, 220 ft. high, was designed by an English engineer and inaugurated by the wife of the then British ambassador in 1897.

A wreath of quaint little villages (or suburbs now, rather) have faithfully preserved, along with their pristine simplicities and *Gemütlichkeit*, the art of making good wine... call them Grinzing, Sievering, Nussdorf, Stammersdorf, or whatever. You sit there on fine summer evenings, inhale your glass of the new vintage, and listen to a *Schrammel* quartet intoning winey songs in the vernacular.

extended from the south as far as the Danube. Vindobona was the name the Romans gave to their fortified, carefully consolidated Danubian base. Emperor Marcus Aurelius, who died in A.D. 180, was forced to defend this territory against the Marcomanni and the Quadi, who repeatedly invaded the Danube Basin. The belligerent tribes continued to advance, laying Pannonia waste and eventually destroying Vindobona as well; so after nearly four centuries, the Romans withdrew. Attila and his Huns stepped forth into history. But only a few decades were to pass before Attila's star faded, extinguished by his sudden death. The vacuum attracted the Ostrogoths, who now established themselves in Pannonia; they turned Vindobona into Vindomina, which in the course of time eventually became Wenia - a name already similar to the present-day form, and first documented in 881.

But long before this the light of the cross erected by St. Severinus was beginning to disperse the gloom which concealed the surging throng of peoples. Under the new symbol of salvation that law-giving power which had developed in the west under Charlemagne, and which caused the onslaught of the Avars to crack straight away, pressed downstream along the Danube. The Babenbergs, enfeoffed with

Austria by Emperor Otto II, carried on the work of ruling and organizing; they reached out for Vienna, which by then had become a city. Monasteries arose, which undertook not only religious, but also cultural and civilizing tasks. The Knights of the Cross, made up of militant Christian standard-bearers as well as of adventurers greedy for plunder, passed through the Vienna Basin by land and water. When the last Babenberg succumbed at the Battle of the Leitha against the Hungarians, Vienna fell into the hands of the Bohemian king, Otakar.

A quarter of a century later, however, on 12 August 1278, the first Habsburg, Rudolph, made his definitive entry in Vienna after his victory over the Bohemians on the Marchfeld, where Otakar lost his life. Despite all the vicissitudes of history, the banner of this dynasty remained hoisted over the country as it steadily expanded. Today we admiringly contemplate this fact, for which - quite unique in history, it would be unfair not to say so - the Babenbergs did much to pave the way by their energy, their circumspection, and their skill. Continually acquiring new territories in the south, east and north, the Habsburgs reigned for six and a half centuries, attaining both royal and imperial status; from Vienna they ruled a major European power, before history finally

made them capitulate. With the collapse of the Dynasty, the multiracial empire, too, crumbled and disintegrated. "Austria - that's what's left over," commented a Frenchman, Georges Clemenceau, laconically after the spoils had been divided up at Saint-Germain. It was Rump Austria, with Burgenland as a sop. When the succession states soon began to grow restless, Churchill quickly realized that it was quite wrong to demolish this historic, harmonious political structure. As is generally known, he was struck by similar thoughts after the Second World War as well.

The Great Calamities

What was then left to the German-Austrians, as they now called themselves, with their two million inhabitants, their claim to represent the capital and seat of government of the once so powerful Danubian Monarchy, and their faded imperial glory, was that Vienna which, in the course of fifteen hundred years of development, most visibly reflected the various local Central European developments in the political, military and intellectual fields. The city both survived the Hungarians' craze for conquest and first successfully resisted the Turks in 1529 under Count Niklas von Salm.

The only Habsburg to become a world-dominating figure was Charles V, who resided in Spain and the Netherlands, and who sent out his conquerors across the Atlantic to South and Central America. Although he enjoyed the glory of an empire on which the sun never set, he too departed from the international political scene as a tragic figure. Fame, and the gratitude of a relieved Western Europe, were granted to his illegitimate son, Don Juan d'Austria, whose mother was the daughter of a citizen of Regensburg. As commander of the combined fleets he destroyed the Turkish armada off Lepanto. While his father retired to a monastery as a recluse, the young war hero died at Namur at the early age of thirty-one - another tragedy of the House of Habsburg. The Reformation and Counter-Reformation duly cast their gloomy shadows. The Swedes conquered Korneuburg and Kreuzenstein, but as they approached Vienna the force of their assault slackened. In 1679, the plague raged horribly among the inhabitants. Those strong enough worked night and day transporting the dead. No fewer than sixty thousand people fell victim to this infestation, and Abraham a Sancta Clara himself, the militant man of God, interpreted it as a divine punishment. In a penitential sermon entitled *Mercks Wienn* ("Watch out, Vienna!"), he waved the scourge of conscience

Opposite:
Charles V, Holy Roman Emperor of the German Nation (1519-1556), with his Great Dane. A painting by Jakob Seisenegger (1515-1567).

The Babenberg Family Tree. Its golden trunk puts forth branches bearing 27 medallions, each for a male offspring of the dynasty.

For a close-up view of one of these exquisite miniatures, see p. 14.

at the Viennese, whose unrestrained joie de vivre clearly displeased him. Outside the gates of Vienna, again and again, there cropped up cohorts of Hungarian insurgents whose name, *Kuruzzen* (a corruption of the German word *Kreuz[fahrer]*), suggests their religious rancour towards the Habsburgs, against whom they therefore felt called upon to "crusade." Then, in the summer of 1683 the Turks, under the Grand Vizier Kara Mustafa, tried their luck at conquest once again. For two months they camped outside the city gates and, apparently convinced of the ultimate success of their enterprise, flung libellous pamphlets over the wall directed against the Emperor and against Ernst Rüdiger von Starhemberg, who was in charge of Vienna's defence arrangements.

But the hardships of siege came to an end at last on 12 September 1683. A relief force under Karl von Lothringen and John Sobieski, the Polish king, had arrived, and put the two hundred thousand besiegers to flight. The rich stock of booty they left behind included the Grand Vizier's ceremonial tent, bagfuls of coffee beans and other delicacies from the East. Once more Vienna had defended its position as an outpost of Western Europe and thereby done the whole of Europe an invaluable service. But the rest of Europe and its princes were too concerned with

The interior of a Turkish tent, about the time of the Second Siege of Vienna, 1683 (exhibited in Cracow's Wawel Castle, the former residence of the Polish kings).

themselves and their own petty jealousies and quarrels to appreciate this fight for freedom properly. Abraham a Sancta Clara, in his inimitable style, offered his "sinful" contemporaries the following thought for the day:

What's the good of drumming up whole armies and not stamping out Sin? Don't we realize that the Turk and his wars are the scourges of God? Who drew the Turks, our sworn enemy, to Asia, to Europe, to Hungary? None other than Sin itself! In the alphabet S is followed by T; similarly, Sin is followed by Turk.

"The Relief of Vienna, 1683." Painting by an unknown master (Museum of Army History, Vienna). The Turks were taken by surprise when an army led by King John III Sobieski of Poland swooped down on them from the slopes of Mt. Kahlenberg (*top left*).

As William Wordsworth, the English poet, exulted in a sonnet, in 1816, King Sobieski "conquered through God, and God through him."

The picture gives "the Deliverer" due pride of place: he is the elderly mustachioed knight with the plumed helmet in the centre foreground, to the left.

And in the diary of the Siege of Vienna kept by the Master of Ceremonies of the Sublime Porch we can read:

Finally the Giaours[1], with the infantry in front and the cavalry behind, charged at our forces like enraged pigs and forced them downhill as far as the devastated village[2]. There the battle continued for some time, and then the scoundrels, charging in closely-packed units, managed to break through on the left and right and now attacked the warriors of Islam from all sides. They had their Sahi cannons with them, already primed, and with these they showered balls and stones upon the army of Islam.

When the Grand Vizier's troops saw how the enemy, charging on both flanks, was advancing and how the army of Islam was beginning to take to flight, every man lost the energy and the will to fight, and there emerged the first signs of that confusion which always ends in defeat. As the Polish king and his troops were advancing directly on the Holy Banner, the Grand Vizier mounted his horse, and on his right and left his retainers, Sheikh Vani Efendi and also the Sipah and Silihdar, held themselves in readiness. Although the pashas were already beginning to yield on both flanks, the Grand Vizier and those around him stood firmly and imperturbably at the centre of the army. But the Giaours' attacks became more forceful, the battle was becoming increasingly violent and had raged on for some five or six hours. The missiles from the guns and muskets of the enemy came down on the army of Islam like rain. The Muslims then realized that everything was lost and that disaster was inevitable. Battling and fighting, the mass of warriors in the area took to flight; most of them, as they fled, thought only of preserving their lives and property.

Vienna and the Tragedy of German-Austrian Dualism

Meanwhile the star of a new military commander had risen over the Danubian Monarchy; the scion of Savoy, Prince Eugene, displayed notable circumspection and energy, in the eastern borderlands down as far as the Carpathians, in removing the military threat to the rising Habsburg empire. Considering himself unfairly treated in Paris, he entered the service of Austria. He was a cultivated cosmopolitan, but was, nevertheless, well versed in the arts of war. His military exploits were crowned by the capture of the city and fortress of "Belgerad" (1717). He was generously honoured for his services, acquired art collections of great value and built Belvedere Palace, for which he was envied even by leading members of

[1] Turkish name for infidels, especially Christians.

[2] The reference is to Nussdorf, the modern Mecca of New Wine.

The Karlskirche, the most important example of Baroque church architecture in Vienna. It was built because of a vow made by Emperor Charles VI to the patron saint of the plague, Carlo Borromeo.

the Imperial house. It is to this aesthete with the handy sword that the credit is due for decades of peace on the eastern flank of the Empire.

After the Habsburgs, under Charles V's feeble successors, had attained their greatest territorial expansion, the military advances of the cultivated Prince of Savoy, who resided in splendour on the then outskirts of Vienna, extended the borders of the Empire far out to the east.

The first coffee-houses opened their doors; the first newspaper to appear was the *Wienerisches Diarium*, which later became the *Wiener Zeitung*. Emperor Leopold I received the most interesting European ruler of that period, Peter the Great, Tsar of All Russia, as a guest in Vienna. Churches, theatres and palaces were built, the Imperial Palace was made bigger and more beautiful, and quite some promising intellectual and artistic activity began to flourish. The city attracted musicians, writers, sculptors and architects of standing.

Liberality and tolerance, however, remained subject to restriction. True, witches and Jews were no longer burnt at the stake, but Protestants, as long as they were still within the national frontiers, were well advised not to reveal themselves as such. The Pragmatic Sanction had placed Maria Theresa on the throne when she was only twenty-three years

A detail from the Upper Belvedere, the summer seat of Prince Eugene (cp. p. 16). Built by Johann Lukas von Hildebrandt in 1714-1724, it is one of the most splendid examples of Baroque architecture.

At the Battle of Königgrätz on 3 July 1866 the Prussians, under William I and Moltke, scored a victory over the Austrians and Saxons (Museum of Army History, Vienna).

old. The House of Habsburg once again became involved in armed conflicts. The Dynasty was dogged by the fact that throughout the centuries of its rule there were either no far-sighted politicians available to exploit what brilliant commanders had achieved with the sword, or else weak military leaders threw away what had been attained and built up for the future by gifted statesmen. And the fact that a woman had acceded to the Habsburg throne may well have had a stimulating effect on Austria's rapacious neighbours.

The great Frederick of Prussia was not actively involved when the Empire was threatened by external danger. But he took the risks involved in wresting Silesia from the Habsburgs in three sanguinary wars. Dynastic rather than national interests were the usual basis of orientation, and like his ancestors Frederick the Great was only a product of his times. Things were not much different a hundred years later, when Prussia and Austria clashed at Königgrätz (Sadowa) and set the final seal upon German-Austrian dualism. Occasionally, it is true, Austria and Prussia did fight side by side in the Napoleonic Wars - but only at the decisive stages. Earlier they had allowed themselves to be played off against each other without seeing through Napoleon's strategy of eliminating one adversary after another, and preventing the formation of a united enemy front.

But let us return to the great Empress to whom Vienna owes so much. With one hand she waged the wars which were forced upon her, and with the other she regulated and reformed many matters of public business. She commissioned the Frenchman Jadot to rebuild the University of Vienna, ordered censuses to be taken, and introduced postal deliveries; she had an inventory made of all the houses in Vienna and introduced a standardized system of numbering them by streets. She founded the College of Veterinary Science, but she also put a ban on the Jesuit Order, whose aid had been energetically enlisted in the course of the Counter-Reformation. Later she also dissociated herself from the activities of the "Chastity Commission" she had set up; by Imperial order, minions of the law were obliged to harass not only the women of the streets, but also perfectly virtuous girls who merely happened to be out walking alone. The entire project thus ran the risk of exposing the rising young metropolis to ridicule.

The Shortcomings of a Great Empress

How was it possible for such an extraordinary woman as Maria Theresa to permit herself to hound

the young ladies of Vienna with spies and snoopers? The Empress was, in fact, a very puritanical woman with pietistical tendencies. It may also have been the case that she trusted her husband no farther than she could see him. Her "lord and master," Emperor Francis, left the job of running the country to her, and guaranteed a continual supply of offspring. It is to the actor Iffland, with whom the presentation of the coveted Iffland Ring for the best actor in the German tongue originated, that we owe the following insight into the Empress's sensitivity in the matter of feminine charms:

In Vienna they say that the Empress remains in the next room during audiences, and there is no doubt that she takes charge of him immediately afterwards and does not let him go. If the Emperor looks at one particular spot for a long time during a play, or at one dancer during a ballet performance, the Empress directs his

Empress Maria Theresa (1717-1780) on Coronation Hill at Pressburg (Bratislava), then the Hungarian capital. Painting by Philipp Ferdinand von Hamilton (1664-1750).

The military Maria Theresa Order being awarded, for the first time, by Emperor Francis I to Field Marshal Count von Daun. In the Seven Years' War, Count Leopold von Daun scored victories over Frederick the Great at Kolin (1757) and Hochkirch (1758), and forced the Prussian general Finck to surrender at Maxen (1759). Painting by Karl von Blaas (1815-1894); Austrian Gallery, Vienna.

attention to something in a completely different place; and when he looks back again, she takes him by the arm as if she wanted to protect him. Then he often becomes very peevish, but he acquiesces.

Furthermore, even high-ranking gentlemen were often more interested in pert servant-girls and chambermaids than in the wives of society hosts and other leading figures. It was, unsurprisingly, the Venetian Giacomo Casanova, womanly virtue's classic stumbling-block, who expatiated indignantly on Her Majesty's "vice squad" and wrote:

Because of the Empress's pietism it was extremely difficult, particularly for visitors, to indulge in the pleasures of Aphrodite. A band of wretched snoopers, glorified with the title of "Chastity Commission," relentlessly persecuted the girls. The Empress lacked sovereign tolerance with regard to so-called illicit love; pious to the point of bigotry, she imagined she was chalking up good marks in Heaven by her petty persecution of the natural urges of both sexes. At all hours of the day and everywhere in the streets of Vienna, unaccompanied girls, who had frequently only gone out to earn an honest living, were arrested and dragged off to prison. The police had whole hordes of such spies in their pay, who

followed the girls at a distance, and as these blackguards wore no uniform it was impossible to spot them. The result was that every stranger became an object of suspicion.

Whenever a girl entered a house, the spy trailing her waited outside the door, stopped her as soon as she came out again, and began questioning her. If the poor creature looked embarrassed, or delayed only a moment in giving an answer satisfactory to the snooper, the fellow took her to gaol, after first taking away all her money and jewellery. These valuables were gone for good, for no one ever managed to get them back. In this respect Vienna was a veritable robbers' den, full of privileged rogues...

There was only one way for the girls to escape this molestation. They had to walk along the street with bowed heads, carrying a rosary; if they did this, the loathsome brood could no longer risk arresting them without further ado. They might have been on their way to church, and then Maria Theresa would have had the Chastity Commissioner hanged.

But long after Maria Theresa's death, an incomprehensible reversion to police-state practices, took place; on 11 July 1837, for instance, smoking in public was prohibited in Vienna "under pain of fine or imprisonment."

With the death of Francis of Lorraine, a new era was at hand; its most prominent representative was the heir to the throne, the future Emperor Joseph II. He reduced the vast number of monasteries, legalized the lodges of the Freemasons, instituted freedom of the press, and granted the Protestants religious liberty and equality before the State. Mozart and Haydn, as well as the rather fickle Beethoven, whose impulsiveness even led him to produce a hymn to Napoleon, developed their fertile creative powers, and theatres sprang up everywhere. Pope Pius VI made an arduous journey to the Danube in order to talk the Emperor out of his enlightened plans for reform and his enthusiasm for tolerance, but Joseph II would not allow himself to be persuaded.

The Corsican and the Congress

But then Vienna held its breath once more: all of Europe echoed with the marching feet of the Napoleonic armies. The bloody confrontation in Habsburg-dominated Northern Italy began. Meeting hardly any resistance, the Juggernaut ground relentlessly from west to east. The princes in the German territories bordering on Austria were treated to the iron hand in the velvet glove; the Corsican made sure of their support by granting them more territory to rule over and by promoting dukes and electoral princes to kings. Matters did not end with Napoleon's advance to Vienna and the latter's unresisted occupation in November 1805. In May 1809 the conqueror once more marched into Vienna. Revolutionary armies possess a dynamism of their own, and Napoleon's opponents - inexcusably - were for a long time unwilling to admit that they were dealing with a genius equipped with an unusually precise, quick-thinking mind as well as tremendous energy. The prematurely celebrated 'victory' of Archduke Charles at Aspern was followed six weeks later by Austria's defeat at Wagram.

The Peace of Vienna, officially signed and sealed in the autumn, cost Austria no fewer than forty-two thousand square miles of territory, i.e., Salzburg, the Inn region, Galicia, and the Illyrian provinces. And yet, at the Erfurt princes' conference of 1808 Napoleon had already passed the peak of his power. He had been forced to bring the war in Spain to an inglorious end, as he was in acute danger of being attacked from the rear by Tsar Alexander. In Austria the Emperor's brother Archduke Charles, together with Count Stadion, a high-ranking minister, had by now initiated reforms, based on the Prussian model. They had been urging the people to serve in the territorial army and trying to instil a sense of civic responsibility. But these precautions had been taken too late; Wagram could no longer be averted, and the sun of Aspern was now in eclipse.

"Napoleon as King of Italy." Painting by Andrea Appiani (Museum of Art History, Vienna).

The Maria Theresa Order, the highest Austrian and Hungarian military decoration, instituted by the Empress in 1757 for acts of personal bravery performed in the face of the enemy above and beyond the call of duty (Museum of Army History, Vienna).

But in Vienna one item of news after another was received with the same equanimity. People floated happily in a sea of diversions, thronged to newly-opened places of entertainment, and amused themselves at the theatres - let someone else get on with the wretched wars. The Viennese had always been in full agreement with the Habsburg principle that conflicts should be settled in other ways, and therefore considered the marriage of the Emperor's daughter Marie Louise to the famous Corsican, who was anxious for a son and heir who could succeed him, to be a splendid piece of statesmanship. When the state went bankrupt and the currency, as a result, was devalued by eighty per cent, the Viennese, it is true, grumbled all the time and gave vent to their resentment in politically dangerous diatribes. But even this painful development did not really affect them, especially as a ray of hope was now visible on the horizon. Napoleon's Grand Army, which had marched off to knock some sense into the rebellious Tsarist empire, was broken, buried in snow and ice; all that came back was a wretched, ragged, sickly apology for an army.

Matters were concluded on the battlefields of Central Germany by Napoleon's opponents, whose armies were marching in concert at last. And, since to err is human, it disturbed neither the crowned heads (or their representatives) gathered round the conference table at Vienna, nor the Viennese themselves, that the very Beethoven who only a few years previously had honoured the "Corsican monster" with a hymn, was now entertaining his vanquishers as the conductor of a mammoth orchestra at the Congress. Austria's Chancellor Metternich raided the ailing treasury for all he could get in order to provide first-class food and drink and magnificent entertainment for his honoured guests, who came from nearly all over Europe, and thus to put them in a mood favourable to his intentions. Side by side with him, Talleyrand, as the representative of defeated France, quickly became the leading figure of the Congress. Together the two of them advocated the principle of legitimacy. The hereditary ruling houses, particularly the Bourbons, must not, by loss of territory or other hardships, be held responsible and punished for all the mischief committed by a usurper against a dynastically assured and therefore well-ordered world. The Viennese Court spent nearly thirty million florins on the Congress, at one stage of which the participants, when Napoleon was on his way from Elba to Waterloo, scattered like a bunch of hens attacked by a hawk.

A member of the House of Habsburg, Archduke John, is on record to have made the following comment on the Congress:

This is a lamentable bartering of people and territories. We cursed Napoleon and his system, and rightly so, for he degraded mankind; and now the very princes who fought against all that are following in his footsteps. So we have only been fighting against his person, and not against his system. Russia is pushing westwards - can this be allowed? Prussia does nothing about it; she allows herself to be appeased with Saxony and falls back into her old grasping ways, learning nothing from the hard lessons she has just been through and capable, if need be, of making common cause with Russia against the others and against Austria in order to retain her territory. Austria had always candidly suggested a partition; only the word 'yes' would have been required to win the aid of Russia and Napoleon in extinguishing Prussia as a power. Instead, Austria merely opted for a general recovery and thus re-established the critical situation.

The real winner was ultimately Talleyrand with his thesis that it was all Napoleon's fault, not France's, which meant that territorially his country came out almost unscathed from the wrangling at Vienna. His co-operation with Metternich had paid off.

When it was all over, there was a gaping hole in the public treasury, but Prince Metternich, the pivot

Prince Clemens von Metternich (1773-1859), nicknamed "The Coachman of Europe," was at the helm of Austria's Foreign and Home Affairs through eventful forty years. He fiercely opposed the new ideas of democracy, liberalism, and nationalism, and relied on the police and the army to assist him. Painting by the English artist Sir Thomas Lawrence (1769-1830).

of the whole thrilling spectacle, was able to rub his hands with great pleasure and satisfaction. The Privy Councillor von Gentz could now once more indulge in his romance with the dancer Fanny Elssler at leisure. And Vienna's female population cast admiring glances at the sole surviving remnant of the Franco-Austrian liaison, the young Duke of Reichstadt out at Schönbrunn. Handsomely melancholy and deeply unhappy, he was a meteorite cast off by a comet which had now plunged out of sight. In Vienna, ten years after Napoleon's death on the inhospitable island of St. Helena, this young man, too, died. It was not until one hundred and eight years afterwards that the remains of Napoleon's son were conveyed to Paris. The Duke of Reichstadt was provided with a suitable last resting-place beneath the dome of the Invalides.

The Secrets of the Ballhausplatz

At the Ballhausplatz, where the threads of the complicated web of government converged, some rather odd methods of acquiring information were already common under Prince Eugene, and particularly so under Prince Kaunitz. The diplomat, who stood high in Imperial favour, began acting as a kind of state chancellor under Charles VI after laying aside his sword. However, as he did not trust the Imperial chancelleries an inch, he set up his own intelligence network - it is not known whether he did this with or without "top-level" approval. This secret was only discovered when building work was carried out at the state chancellery for about one hundred years ago. The workers stumbled across whole piles of carefully stored secret intelligence, most of which concerned the Congress of Vienna and had been gathered by Metternich - all, of course, very near the brink of legality. Prince Eugene had instructed the ambassadors at Vienna to supply him with special information supplementing the official reports. Berlin's ambassador to Vienna, Count Seckendorff, seems to have done an uncommonly good job in this off-beat sphere. A mighty boozer before the Lord, and at the same time one well versed in the pose of acting out his histrionics on the diplomatic stage, he used drinking-bouts to pump information out of the Prussian king Frederick William I and August the Strong of Saxony; here he was aided by the Prussian minister Grumbkow and the Saxon minister von Manteuffel. These two men received 6,000 florins annually from Vienna for their valuable services.

The extremely whimsical though highly-qualified Prince Kaunitz, Maria Theresa's foreign affairs adviser, was even worse. By means of his good relations with Marquise de Pompadour (1721-1764), King Louis XV's mistress, established when he was ambassador in Paris, he managed to bring the French over to Austria's side. Prince Eugene's confidant and private secretary, Ignaz Koch, extended the existing European network of intelligence and espionage. A whole staff of decoders, whom nobody knew and who worked somewhere or other behind carefully sealed doors, was kept busy under Koch and, after the latter's death, worked for the benefit of Emperor Francis. These decoders enjoyed privileges most other mortals were allowed but to dream about: they were not only granted tax exemption and handsome pensions, but also received special bonuses of up to a thousand florins if they pulled off something really big in the course of their deciphering work. For they had already discovered ways and means of tampering with foreign diplomats' mail, and all the juicy bits were served up to the Emperor every morning along with his breakfast.

The job of the so-called "postal lodges" was to make a mockery of the principle of postal privacy. The lodge officials carried out their much-appreciated disgusting activities at all important post offices. With wily dexterity the interesting-looking letters were nimbly made to disappear, undone, hastily copied, and then as nimbly restored to their pristine-looking envelopes. Eagle-eyed snoopers were waiting in Trieste and Milan, in Klausenburg (Cluj) and

Lemberg (Lwów), in Budapest and Prague. In Vienna itself, the above-mentioned decoding staff dealt with the mail from abroad. In Wenzel Löschner, who died in 1818, Metternich had his own personal decoder. Such an exalted position was Löschner's reward for having succeeded in cracking the toughest Russian code after years of effort. At the Vienna headquarters up to a hundred letters were "processed" in this manner every day, and the team slaved away at full blast during the Congress of Vienna, when Metternich, understandably, displayed a virtually unquenchable thirst for knowledge. Not even the

Imperial postal system managed by the House of Thurn and Taxis was spared Metternich's curiosity. Here too, appointed lodge officials were found slogging away for the Viennese state chancellery, and not merely as a thank-you job, either.

The Great Gallery at Schönbrunn Palace, modelled on the Hall of Mirrors at Versailles. The central fresco depicts the glorification of Maria Theresa.

Vienna Has Its Share of Unrest and Agitation, Too

Times changed, and the tranquil, pleasant decades of the Biedermeier period followed. External danger no longer posed a threat and nobody considered the possibility of internal unrest. The playwright Grill-

A glimpse at Franz Schubert's birth-place, which was opened as a memorial to the great composer in 1912. Those rooms, with the cherished exhibits, the garden, the court, the "Trout" Well on the right - all help to conjure up the brief span of years, 1797-1828, which that genius, and most modest of men, was allowed to walk on earth.

Opposite page, below: Emperor Francis Joseph I (1830-1916) and Empress Elizabeth (1837-1898). Both portraits are by Franz Xaver Winterhalter.

The Vienna State Opera belongs to the select group of the world's best opera houses.

parzer was approaching the height of his creativity; Raimund and Nestroy had the Viennese at their feet; Schubert completed his great Symphony in C major, his final one, not performed until ten years after his death. In Vienna's streets the postman, with his alarming wooden rattle, was joined by the official figure of the lamplighter pacing solemnly along. In 1829, The Danube Steamship Company came into being, operating between Vienna and Budapest. The Danube, which had once carried the settlers summoned by Maria Theresa and Joseph II from the heartlands of Europe to the south-east, continued to grow in importance as a traffic artery. Then a cholera epidemic descended on the capital, and no fewer than twenty thousand Viennese fell victim to the disease. It was with displeasure and deep antipathy towards new-fangled devices that horse-cab drivers registered the coming of the horse-bus and the horse-tram. As soon as the Emperor Ferdinand Northern Railway, with its trains drawn by steaming, puffing monsters, came bursting in on the Biedermeier idyll between Floridsdorf and Deutsch-Wagram, making nervous wrecks of men and animals alike, the Viennese were no longer in any doubt. A new age had dawned - the party was over.

All at once there were shrill yells of discord everywhere. The wheels of progress were not turning fast enough for the intelligentsia. The breeze of liberty was blowing across the German-speaking territories, and it did not stop at Vienna. Viennese writers protested against the censorship which was still in force at the Burg Theatre. Karl Ferdinand Gutzkow expressed his displeasure in bold terms as follows:

Every serious approach to the solution of social problems is looked upon with suspicion. History, politics, and religion are completely out of bounds. That would be fair enough. But morals, too, are involved here and remain dependent on class prejudice. There must be no illegitimate children on the stage; fathers must not fall out with their sons, and sons must not fall out with their fathers; kings must always be perfect, bad presidents and ministers are designated as incompetents, and all the rest of the rubbish that Viennese audiences manage to think up. Here, the president in 'Kabale und Liebe' is Walter's uncle, not his father. "I've got a spot in my heart," says Ferdinand here, "where the title of uncle has not yet penetrated." I would be ashamed to be the ruler of a state, or a minister in a government, which gave its blessing to such silliness.

In short, signs of unrest could be seen everywhere. Students, professors, liberal-minded citizens and, of course, the rabble adopted a threatening attitude.

And it was the rabble which, as is usually the case in such situations, seized the initiative when it came to action.

The reigning emperor had left town, and Archduke Ludwig, by now in a state of fear, thought he could pacify the seething masses by sacrificing Metternich, who, it should be remembered, had been serving the dynasty and his country for nearly half a century and was in large part responsible for the fact that the Congress of Vienna had provided Austria, and also Europe, with a long-lasting New Order. The storm continued to rage, reaching its climax in a most shocking act of lynch law against Count Theodore Latour, the then Minister of War, and in various other atrocities, in 1848. The acts of retribution committed by the advancing forces of Prince Windischgrätz appear no less formidable and gruesome. In the annals of the Danubian metropolis there are phases and episodes which display similarities to Prague, involving tempests of unleashed passions and bloodthirstiness which culminated in inconceivable atrocities.

Ferdinand I gave up in despair, and the final remnants of Imperial absolutism now vanished; the Viennese optimistically cheered Francis Joseph I, who was firmly committed to constitutionalism. In the young and extremely pretty Elizabeth of Bavaria he offered them just the sort of empress they were after. The city grew and expanded; the bulwarks erected against the threat of enemy attack, those dismal memorials of gloomier times, disappeared, and so did the nastier features of the more recent past Vienna could now relax. And horse-racing provided the Viennese with a new attraction. Then, out of the blue, the Austro-Prussian War of 1866 hit the Danubian Monarchy just at a stage when sunny harmony seemed to be the keynote everywhere.

The Austro-Prussian agreement following their common war against Denmark in 1864 did not wear very well. The spoils, consisting of the twin duchies of Holstein and Slesvig which had been taken from Denmark, promptly caused the two allies, who had charged side by side at the Düppel entrenchments, to turn against each other. Bismarck, who was trying to make Prussia the leading power within Germany and, in the process, had been following more and more closely in Frederick the Great's footsteps, felt that the time had come to thrust Austria back a little more with the aid of the new Prussian breech-loading rifles. The quarrel over Holstein, which eventually fell to Prussia in 1866, was only an excuse for the passage at arms from which Austria emerged the loser. This was the breakthrough for Prussian supremacy, finally acknowledged a few

years later in the Hall of Mirrors at Versailles after the Franco-Prussian War of 1870-71. For Emperor Francis Joseph this defeat was the first of a whole series of personal and political blows, each received with the long-suffering comment: "Nothing in this world has been spared me."

But the military disaster, which appeared to have no drastic political consequences, did not particularly worry the Viennese, whose zest of life was indomitable. The Imperial Opera House opened its doors, to be followed by the Imperial Museum, the New Town Hall, the University, the Burg Theatre, and the Stock Exchange. The Viennese were drawn to the Prater World Fair. Johann Strauss was in the lime-

Emperor Francis Joseph I and Empress Elizabeth of Austria travelling in a phaeton, a light, four-wheeled open carriage, and pair with rider (called *Mylord* in Austria). Coloured lithograph by Ignaz Sonntag, after a drawing by Alexander von Bensa, c. 1855 (Austrian National Library, Vienna).

job that the first fruits of their devoted efforts on behalf of the languages and the repressed national consciousness of the Habsburg-dominated peoples began to burst forth in a rather disquieting fashion. In the ethnic cocktail that Vienna had by then become, the response was not really virulent, but it was certainly noticeable.

Shadows were now descending about the ageing, lonely man in the Imperial Palace, and the Dynasty

St. Stephen's Cathedral, Vienna, the see of bishops since 1469 and of archbishops since 1723.

The pulpit in the Cathedral was created by mastersculptor Anton Pilgram in 1515.

light of general popularity with *Die Fledermaus* (The Bat), and Verdi conducted his Requiem at the Imperial Opera House. The Viennese, being by now used to the hot-and-cold treatment, were not disconcerted for long when the Stock Exchange crashed and the Ring Theatre burnt down (killing more than three hundred people).

Meanwhile the humanistic romanticists devoted to Slavonic civilization had done so thorough a

– and with it the Danubian Monarchy as a whole – began progressing towards its doom. At Mayerling House, Rudolph, the Crown Prince whose relationship with his father was one of latent tension, committed suicide with Baroness Mary Vetsera. The remaining steps along the downward path of personal, dynastic, and national tragedy are now well known. At Miramare Castle outside Trieste, the Emperor's brother, Archduke Maximilian, was urged on by his ambitious Belgian wife and got Napoleon III to appoint him Emperor of Mexico; and he died facing a firing-squad. Empress Elizabeth, who spent most of her time abroad and therefore at some distance from her overworked husband, was killed in Switzerland by an Italian anarchist. Finally, the Heir to the Throne, Francis Ferdinand, and his wife were murdered at Sarajevo by a Serbian nationalist - the First World War had begun, and the Danubian Monarchy was finished.

throughout the musical and theatrical worlds of Europe as well. However, following the annexation of Bosnia and Herzegovina, unrest and agitation were back again, in the former Cordon, elsewhere along the Old Military Frontier, and even in Vienna - all before a single shot had been fired. And four and a half years later the wings of the double eagle were broken. Charles I, the last Emperor, abdicated; the Danubian Monarchy, which for centuries had been a stabilizing force in Central Europe, crumbled; the much-maligned multiracial state, with fourteen nations within its borders, ceased to exist. But the euphoria which accompanied the exodus from the "black and yellow nick for naughty nations" soon gave way to deep disappointment among a number of its former inmates. The fact still remains that this state was ground down not merely by the superior power of its enemies, but also by its own internal condition, i.e., by the heterogeneous forces at work in it whose capacity for centralized loyalty had been somewhat overtaxed.

Resignation, want, distress, and despair were at the bedside when the new republic was born. But what was left of Austria, after all her neighbours had generously helped themselves, was at least fortunate

Austria and the Vienna Waltz are one; and Johann Strauss, "The Waltz King," is gratefully given pride of place - in the people's hearts, and in the Vienna City Park.

Vienna Town Hall is one of the typical buildings lining the Ring, for they share one thing - they are all imitations of architectural styles of bygone years.

Francis Joseph, full of good will and highly respected by his subjects, had been unable to change the course of events. The Crown Prince, who had seen trouble brewing for the Empire and the Dynasty and had been thinking in terms of a settlement with the Czechs and Hungarians, was dead and buried. The Heir to the Throne was not a bit popular in multiracial Austria; the dislike people felt for him was intensified to the point of hatred. When the Emperor lay dying one dismal wartime November day in 1916, not only his closest relatives, but also Katharina Schratt, a former actress at the Burg Theatre, were summoned to his deathbed. This was the woman who had brightened the monarch's final years. His nephew and successor, Charles, acted for all practical purposes as nothing more than an official receiver. Neither he nor his consort, the ambitious and controversial Bourbon-Parma princess Zita, could do much about his fits of despondency and faint-heartedness.

The Pioneers of 1918 and 1945

Karl Kraus and, on another plane, Arthur Schnitzler made their mark as the champions of decadence and dissolution. But suddenly Franz Lehár arrived on the scene and, with his *Merry Widow*, generated a good deal of ecstasy not only among the Viennese, but

Opposite –
Above left:
A detail from the *Hofburg*, formerly the Emperor's residence (cp. pp. 182f.).

Above right:
The Museum of Art History will always be mentioned in one breath with the Prado and the Louvre. Its main attractions are the paintings by Dürer, Rubens, Titian, and Velázquez, and it in fact possesses the largest Brueghel collection in the world.

Below left:
The Providentia Fountain on the New Market, by Georg Raphael Donner (1693-1741), is a symbol of Austria's principal rivers.

Below right:
"UNO City", on the north bank of the Danube, represents the modern city of Vienna and at the same time underlines Vienna's function as a mediator between East and West.

Parliament House, on the Ring, completed in 1883, is today the seat of the *Nationalrat* ('National Assembly') and the *Bundesrat* ('Federal Assembly'). In its architectural design, it is dominated by a gabled portico and the Fountain of Athene outside the main entrance - a clear tribute to Greece, the cradle of democracy.

enough, both in 1918 and in 1945, to be able to drum up men possessed of energy and circumspection who guided the country out of the mess it had drifted into and showed the people the way to a brighter future.

Vienna, which in the autumn of 1918 had been transformed pretty well overnight from the centre of government of a major power to the oversized capital of a country that had dwindled to one eighth of its former area, was in something of a predicament. A large-scale suburban housing programme was carried out in the face of numerous difficulties, and the "swollen head," as people in the various provinces tended to call it, developed during the twenties into the best-governed European capital as regards public welfare, and served as a model for other countries. There was, of course, no lack of political problems, triggered off by the ever-increasing feeling of resentment which had been piling up. Soon there were two major political camps, but they were too busy hating each other to join forces and meet the danger pressing in from the west. Once more there was a civil war, with its attendant bloodshed, but the attempt to block the pull of National Socialism by establishing a conservative, class-based social order failed, and Austria was dragged into totalitarianism, and with it into the Second World War. Again it was Vienna which, as a prime target, got the worst of it. The city suffered no fewer than fifty-two air raids; something like twelve thousand buildings, including St. Stephen's Cathedral, the Opera House, the Burg Theatre, and the University were destroyed or gutted or otherwise badly damaged; nearly eleven thousand inhabitants of the city were killed in the indiscriminate bombings. Later on, the division of the city into four zones of occupation (plus one international zone) caused nothing but friction: difficulties regarding authority and responsibility, problems of communication, and various hold-ups in the work of reconstruction which was undertaken with indomitable vigour.

Nevertheless, the rebuilding of the city was carried out with admirable gusto in the face of seemingly insuperable difficulties. Helpers and well-wishers appeared on the scene; Vienna was caught up in a wave of good will and sympathy which lifted it out of its chaos and desolation. The result was a synthesis worked out with admirable far-sightedness as well as a sense of reality. Historic neo-Gothic build-ings, memorials enshrining the city's great past, Baroque palaces, unassuming Biedermeier dwellings and all the monumental residential blocks along the Ring were joined by high-rise flats and modern functional structures set there by first-rate architects, both native and foreign, all without seriously disturbing the harmony of the urban scene. All this thought and activity was guided by the far-sighted perception that, in the line-up of European capitals, Vienna had a specific part to play, namely that of mediator and clearing-house between Western and Eastern Europe, serving as a focus of contact, discussion and insight in the fields of politics, economics, scholarship and culture. This has been the development, during the last decades, of a city whose history ranges from the Golden Fleece to the Atomic Energy Commission, from the Imperial Insignia to international fairs - a modern city of growing importance. Austria's capital is doing a great job as a bridge between the past and the future and as a cultural and intellectual centre of fame and repute. If you want Europe and its history in a nutshell, this is it.

Post-war rebuilding made Vienna, federal capital and federal province in one, rise like a phoenix from the ashes of a huge conflagration. And every Austrian knows: this popular city has a worldwide reputation both for being a cultural focus and the seat of major international organizations; and those attending any of the numerous conferences and meetings there are sure to carry away with them that awareness of Vienna's rôle to all the parts of the globe.

The Imperial Orb, 8 1/4 ins. high, gold-plated resin, surmounted by a jewelled cross, dates from the Hohenstaufen period and forms part of the Nuremberg Imperial Insignia - so-called because they were kept at Nuremberg from 1424 to 1796. The Imperial Orb, in the shape of the globe, signifies world-wide power.

The Republic of Austria

Coat of arms: An eagle displayed argent, with a mural coronet masoned proper Or, and charged on the breast with an inescutcheon gules a fess argent; encircling both pounces a chain proper, now broken.
Official colours: red, white, and red

There are two distinct components in the Austrian coat of arms - the eagle, and the red-white-red striped breast-plate -, and the difference between them lies in their origin.

The eagle was a well-known sign of power in Roman times, the symbol of Jupiter, father of the gods, and also a prevalent emblem adapted by the Roman legions for their standards. Following the decline of the Roman Empire, it was first introduced by Charlemagne in a deliberate attempt to portray himself as a worthy successor to the Imperial throne. From then on, the eagle continued to symbolize the Holy Roman Empire of the German Nation, and after 1430 A.D. appeared regularly as a double-headed eagle. With the establishment of the Austrian Empire in 1806, this double-headed eagle became the main feature in the new state arms and was thus later recognized as the standard symbol of royalty. When the Republic of Austria was created in 1918, this traditional heraldic figure was therefore replaced by the original single-headed eagle. The other symbols of royalty - the Emperor's crown, the sceptre, and the orb - were ousted by those typical of the social classes which came into their own with the democracy: since that time, the mural coronet, the sickle, and the hammer have represented the middle class, the peasantry, and the working class, respectively. This coat of arms had to lie dormant for the duration of an authoritarian regime in 1934, and also when Austria was under the rule of the German Third Reich, between 1938 and 1945. When the Republic was re-established in 1945, the broken chain was added to mark the freedom regained.

Since the end of the fifteenth century, the Imperial eagle had borne the dynastic arms of the ruling royal family on its breast. In the nineteenth century, the shield was composed of the arms of Austria, Lorraine, and the Habsburg family. In 1915, it was replaced by the striped Austrian shield still to be seen in the present Republican coat of arms, which can incontestably be traced back as far as 1230. This simple design may well have originated several decades earlier, but lack of adequate sources of information before that time preclude the possibility of more precise dating (cp. p. 70). At any rate, the moving and often-told legend of the shield's origin should be regarded as mere fable according to which the arms date from the time of the siege of Acre, in the Holy Land in 1190, when the Duke of Austria took off his scabbard belt to reveal a white stripe in his otherwise blood-soaked tunic.

The Austrian flag, whose origin can be traced back for seven hundred years to that early coat of arms, may well lay claim to being the oldest of all national flags, most of which did not come into existence until the end of the eighteenth century.

Burgenland

Coat of arms: Or, an eagle recursant with wings displayed gules, crowned with a ducal coronet of the first, on a rock sable, charged on the breast with an inescutcheon paly gules and vairé, all within a bordure of the first; in dexter and sinister chief two crosses pattée sable.
Official colours: red and yellow

A new coat of arms had to be created for this youngest province, which became an indisputable part of Austria only in 1923. Incidentally, the name "Burgenland" (literally, 'castle province') does not stem from the many fortresses once built there, but from the German name given to the West Hungarian districts of Press*burg* (Bratislava), Wiesel*burg*, Öden*burg*, and Eisen*burg*. It was originally proposed that the coat of arms of Ödenburg (Sopron) be used, the town designated to be capital. However, the idea of using its civic device, a fortified gateway with turrets, was abandoned when it became clear that Ödenburg would remain part of Hungary. Instead, in 1922 the heraldries of the two most powerful provincial dynasties of the Late Middle Ages - the Counts of Mattersdorf-Forchtenstein and Güssing-Bernstein (which both had become extinct in the course of the fifteenth century) - were combined to form the new coat of arms.

In early times, the Forchtenstein bore a black eagle with a golden crown on a silver field, as recorded in the *Arlberg Books of Heraldry*, a unique collection of Austrian arms dating from around 1400. Later, however, the eagle stands on a crag, and there is now a small cross in each upper corner. The Bernstein arms, with their shield divided in four vertical fields, have never varied, and their simplicity was well-suited for placement on the Forchtenstein eagle's breast.

The Vandals, the main branch of the East Germanic Lugi, originally coming from Scandinavia in the third century, resided in Western Hungary for an extensive period. In 1920, the new official colours were taken from their legendary coat of arms, a red dragon on a golden field. Of course, the province's coat of arms had to be adapted to these colours; so the black Forchtenstein eagle on a silver field became a red eagle on a golden field. These colours, together with the black crag, were reminiscent of the then highly esteemed black, red, and gold colours of Germany.

Carinthia

Coat of arms: Or, three lions passant sable, impaling gules a fess argent.
Official colours: yellow, red, and white

Beginning in the twelfth century, with the introduction of the very first coats of arms by the ruling families, the Dukes of Carinthia had apparently always borne a black shield charged with a silver panther. Then, in 1247, a completely new coat of arms appeared in the seal of the Carinthian duke's son, Ulrich, who resided in Bohemia: on a cleft field, three lions on the dexter, or right half (when seen from the point of view of the person carrying the shield), and a fess, i. e., a horizontal stripe, on the sinister. He probably intended to announce thereby his claim to the Duchy of Austria, which had been vacant since the death of the last Duke of Babenberg the previous year. One half of the shield bears the lion from the coat of arms of the family resident at Mödling, a collateral line of the Babenbergs, and the other half displays the striped shield of Austria itself. When Ulrich became the Duke of Carinthia he reverted to the old arms depicting the panther. The cleft shield became the arms proper of Carinthia when it was used in the royal seal in 1269 by King Přemysl Otakar of Bohemia, who was then ruler of the province. These arms were retained by the subsequent dukes, even by the Habsburgs, who in 1335 succeeded in adding Carinthia to their patrimonial dominions. Carinthia is the only Austrian province to possess a tricoloured flag, and whose official coat of arms bears a helmet, with crest and mantling, above the shield. This form was stipulated by a constitutional act passed by the Provincial Diet in 1930.

Lower Austria

Coat of arms: Azure, five eagles respecting each other, two, two, and one, all Or; the whole ensigned with a mural coronet masoned proper of the second.
Official colours: yellow and blue

In the fourteenth century, the practice of devising *Kunstwappen*, i.e. new coats of arms for saints or for distinguished forebears of the ruling families, came into fashion. One such fabricated shield, in honour of the Babenberg Margrave Leopold III (d. 1136), who was later canonized and made the patron saint of the country (cp. pp. 69f.), has been known since 1335. It depicts five, at one time even six, eagles on a shield. Thus it revives the traditional eagle of the Babenberg arms, which first appeared in 1176, but also seems to have been inspired by the contemporary royal arms of France, a blue field ornamented with several golden fleurs-de-lis.

The ambitious Duke Rudolph IV gave this shield a prominent position among the Habsburg arms around 1360, with the result that from then on Austria as a whole, and the land below the River Enns in particular, possessed two equally important coats of arms: the red, white, and red striped shield of Austria, and the blue and golden shield portraying the five eagles. In 1805 the latter was selected as the sole symbol of Lower Austria, and has remained so to this day. Originally the eagles' heads all faced in one direction, but in the modern, official arms they face each other.

On the strength of the Provincial Constitution Act of 1920, the shield is surmounted by a mural coronet, which is actually a burghal crown, but was decided upon in this case in order to signify the transfer of power, by free elections, to the middle class during the transition from a monarchy to a republic.

Upper Austria

Coat of arms: Sable, an eagle Or, impaling argent two pallets gules; the whole ensigned with a ducal coronet.
Official colours: white and red

Originally, this land above the River Enns had no coat of arms entirely its own since it was annexed to Austria in several stages - the Traungau district as early as 1192, and the Innviertel in 1779. The region did not receive arms until about 1360, when the present-day arms of Lower Austria were also created. In this instance, too, the new device was based on a fabricated shield, one that had been foisted on the Lords of Machland, a family long since extinct, from the north of the province. The shield illustrates, as do the two related arms of Carinthia and Salzburg, the fusing of two fields, quite a rare phenomenon in early heraldry.

The Austrian ducal coronet, like the new coat of arms, owes its origin to the aspirations of Duke Rudolph IV. Possibly the most peculiar of the more famous Habsburgs, he wished upon his Duchy the elevated dignity of an electorate, not content with the *Privilegium minus*, which had raised Austria to a duchy in 1156, Rudolph bestowed upon himself a *Privilegium maius* in 1359, granting Austria a great increase of both privileges and power. In accordance with that enhancement of status, he had the traditional ducal coronet of ermine embellished with points and a rim set with precious stones, attributes which at that time were regarded as suitable only for a royal crown. In addition, Rudolph strove for the title of an Archduke Palatine, a distinction that did not receive Imperial sanction until a century later. Thus the term "archducal coronet" is not often used. However, the Upper Austrian provincial government did not want to relinquish their singularly ornamented ducal coronet, which had symbolized their province throughout the ages.

Salzburg

Coat of arms: Or, a lion rampant sable, impaling gules a fess argent, the whole ensigned with a prince's coronet.
Official colours: red and white

Looking at the Salzburg arms one immediately notices the striking resemblance to the Carinthian arms. Unfortunately, here too, there is no clear evidence as to its origin. According to some, the Salzburg lion is borrowed from the arms of either the Lords of Peilstein or even the Staufen dynasty; but this claim cannot be substantiated. The explanation following would seem to be quite plausible. The arms of the Archbishopric of Salzburg first appeared on a penny coined at Friesach, Carinthia, in 1287. However, they probably originated earlier than this as it is highly unlikely, towards the middle of the thirteenth century, for an independent territory not to possess its own coat of arms. Philipp, a brother to Duke Ulrich of Carinthia, was Salzburg's ruler until 1256. The device which

subsequently became the official arms of Carinthia was first seen on Ulrich's seal in 1247, and it is almost certain that these arms were adopted by his younger brother, and then continued to be recognized as those of Salzburg ever after. In borrowing the fraternal emblem, Philipp followed a common practice in medieval heraldry. To wit, he personalized the arms by somewhat changing the pattern; a single lion replaced the original three Carinthian lions on the dexter flank. The arms retained this form throughout the centuries of the archiepiscopal principality which existed until 1803, and indeed up to the present day.

In 1850, the crownland of Salzburg, now separated from Upper Austria, obtained the rank of an independent duchy, and was awarded a heraldic prince's coronet to symbolize the distinction. Vanity, proverbially having been "given to us as a sixth sense," readily ignores barriers of nobility: in more recent, Republican decades, following the example of their Upper Austrian colleagues, the Government of Salzburg did not want to part with their coronet, and so officially declared it a permanent feature of the Province's coat of arms.

Styria

Coat of arms: Vert, a panther rampant and incensed argent, armed of his claws and horns gules, the whole ensigned with the Styrian ducal coronet.
Official colours: white and green

Steyr, or to be exact *Stirapurch*, family seat of the ruling margraves, was the name given to the entire country south and east of it; the castle itself and the territory to the south of it were later incorporated into Upper Austria. These margraves had the same flame-tongued silver panther in their arms as did their rulers, the Carinthian dukes. The earliest evidence is

provided by a seal from the year 1166. After the margraviate was elevated to a duchy in 1180, and was handed over to the Austrian Babenbergs in 1192, the panther device nevertheless continued in use; and its colours have been traditional since 1246. As it is, very few of the old historical arms display a green shield and the choice of this colour in Styria is probably derived from the abundant woodlands there.

While in earlier heraldic versions, flames issued from every orifice of the panther's body (as can also be seen in the present civic arms of Graz), an act passed by the Provincial Diet in 1926 restricted them to the jaws only. As in Upper Austria and Salzburg, the Styrian ducal coronet has been retained; it was copied from a fifteenth-century original which is still to be seen at Graz.

Tyrol

Coat of arms: Argent, an eagle displayed gules, crowned with a ducal coronet Or, charged with two trefoils of the third, and gorged with a laurel wreath proper.
Official colours: red and white

The first evidence of the Tyrolean arms, about the year 1205, can be traced to the seal of a prince of that province. It was later found attached to a document of Count Albert dating from the last decade of the twelfth century. A life span after, the eagle began to wear the wing decorations; the oldest coloured version of the arms is met with in the Zurich Arms Scroll credited to have been compiled between 1330 and 1340. When Tyrol was taken over by the Habsburgs from Countess Margarete Maultasch in 1365, there were no imme-

diate changes in her heraldic bearings; however, after 1411, the eagle was often portrayed with a small crown on its head.

In the sixteenth century a final addition was made; it was a Renaissance custom to place a wreath of laurel over heraldic shields, or over figures volantes (i. e., in flight). This custom was also accepted in Tyrol, and gradually the *Ehrenkränzl*, or 'wreath of honour', behind the eagle's head became a regular part of the arms. The earliest examples of this date from around 1560; but the coronet, in contrast, was not accepted into the official description until the matter was approved by the Provincial Diet in 1921.

The figures that appear in the arms of other provinces, apart perhaps from those of Styria and Vorarlberg, are hardly suitable for presentation without a surrounding shield. The Tyrolean eagle, however, stands beautifully by itself, and is therefore often seen in all parts of the country devoid of any restricting borders of the shield.

Vorarlberg

Coat of arms: Argent, a gonfanon gules, charged with five barrulets, two, two, and one, all sable; in chief three annulets of the second.
Official colours: red and white

History had its first view of the Vorarlberg coat of arms when it appeared on the seal of a Count Palatine of Tübingen, in 1181. It was under a branch of the Tübingen family, the Counts of Montfort, that Vorarlberg began to develop into a sovereign province. The Tübingen banner was used, with varying colour combinations, in the arms of the many influential families descended from the ancestral dynasty. With the Counts of Montfort it was red on a gold or silver field.

After most of the country had been united under Habsburg rule, the Montfort arms were re-introduced as the emblem of the whole area. Yet only in 1863 were they officially recognized in an Imperial arms charter. No fewer than eight further fields were united around the Montfort shield, in the arms which were awarded to the Province at that time.

Eventually, under the Province's Constitution Act of 1923, the original Montfort shield was left to stand by itself. The Act also laid down the shape of the banner, which was an exact replica of the version in the so-called Zurich Arms Scroll from around 1340, except that in place of the triangular shape to be found in the scroll, a rounded shield was decided upon. And finally, a brief comment is due concerning the unusual motif. Although the object depicted on the coat of arms may well remind the layman of a war banner, the description is not strictly correct in heraldic terms. Whilst in fact the banner should be made of a simple square cloth, this version with its loose hanging flaps must be called a gonfanon, or gonfalon. (Linguistically, these are Romance doublets, but go back to a West Germanic etymon meaning 'war banner.') Such gonfanons served in large engagements to indicate the leaders' positions on the battlefield. Apart from that, they were also used as symbols of large feudal tenures handed over by the king. In this case, the gonfanon was referred to as a *vexillum* in contemporary documents and chronicles. The Counts Palatine were probably thinking of such a *vexillum* when they chose their motif. During the nineteenth century, experts in heraldry thought of it in more peaceful terms, as a church banner.

Vienna

Coat of arms: Gules, a cross argent.
Official colours of both the city and the province: red and white

The City of Vienna originally had the single-headed eagle of the Babenberg rulers on its seal. This most likely goes back to the Civic Charter of 1221. A new seal in 1327 was the first to show the coat of arms with a cross laid on the eagle's breast. Other towns adopted the cross as part of their arms to indicate their capacity as a market town. Of course, it is also possible that the Municipality of Vienna took the white cross on a red ground - the same colours as the royal flag of the Holy Empire - when it was granted a charter as a Free Imperial City,

for the cross was first struck on Viennese pennies around that time, provably between the years 1278 and 1281.

The oldest depiction of the arms in colour stems from the last decade of the fourteenth century. In an Imperial arms decree of 1461, Vienna was awarded a golden double-headed eagle on a black ground. In 1464, the shield with the cross upon the breast was added. The Municipality used these arms until 1925. Vienna has had the rank of a Federal Province since 1920, and in 1925 an act by the Regional Diet determined that the city and provincial coat of arms should be based on the seal of 1327. The former arms with the double-headed eagle were used again between 1934 and 1945, but since 1946 the legal ruling of 1925 has been re-enforced.

Thus, the Viennese coat of arms consists of the cross on the shield only; in the seal, however, the shield is laid on the breast of a single-headed eagle.

© Helmut Schmid Publishers, Salzburg, Vienna, and Regensburg
Production: Helmut Schmid Publishers
Planning and lay-out: Peter Stemmle, Technical Consultant
Computer typeset: Rotaplan Offset Kammann Druck Ltd.
Paper: MAGNOMATT SATIN 150 g/m^2
Printer: Aumüller Druck KG
Binder: R. Oldenbourg Graphische Betriebe GmbH

ACKNOWLEDGEMENTS

Abbreviations used: o < oben, 'above'; u < unten, 'below'; r < rechts, 'right'; l < links 'left'.

Amt NÖ Landesregierung, Bildstelle: 67, 187 o; Anrather, Oskar, Salzburg: 111 o, 119, 124 u; Bayerisches Hauptstaatsarchiv, München; Hochstift Freising Urkunde 14 (früher: Kaiserselekt 859): 6/7; Bregenzer Festspiele GesmbH: 168; Bundesdenkmalamt, Foto, Wien: 30; Burgenland Tourismus/Berger: 34; Burgenland Tourismus/Chesi: 33 u, 35, 37, 41; Burgenland Tourismus/Liszt: 31 o, 39; Burgerbibliothek, Bern: 72 u; Carolino Augusteum, Salzburger Museum für Kunst- und Kulturgeschichte: 113, 116 o+u, 118, 120 l; Chorherrenstift Vorau: 138 r; Damm, Fridmar, Köln: 42/43, 57, 84/85, 87, 96, 104/105, 117, 123 r, 126/127, 128, 136, 137 o+u, 142, 146/147, 154, 158 o+u, 180, 181, 182/183, 184, 185, 189, 190 o, 196 u, 198 l, 199 u, 200 lo, 200 ru, 201; Daume, Helfried, die Fotoschaffer, A-4020 Linz: 91; Eisriesenwelt GesmbH, Werfen: 108; Fremdenverkehrsbetriebe der Stadt Salzburg: 124 o; Fürböck, Fotoarchiv: 130; Fürstliche Fürstenbergische Hofbibliothek, Donaueschingen 12; Heeresgeschichtliches Museum, Wien: 16, 18, 188, 190 u, 192, 193 l; Historisches Museum der Stadt Wien: 19, 28, 196 o; Hofstetter, Kunstverlag, Ried im Innkreis: 103, 120 r; Hofstetter, Kunstverlag, Ried im Innkreis, Foto: M. Oberer, Wien: 101; Jungwirth, Christian, Graz: 134 u; Keltenmuseum Hallein: 8 (4x), 110; Kleinwalsertal Tourismus: 171 ru; Kunsthistorisches Museum, Wien: 11, 13, 17, 46 u, 52 u, 186, 193 r, 194, 197 u (2x), 203; Landesbildstelle Kärnten: 48, 52 o, 54, 58/59; Landesmuseum für Kärnten, Klagenfurt: 46 o, 61; Landesverband Burgenland Tourismus, Eisenstadt: 31 u; Landesverband für Tourismus in OÖ/Pochletko: 88 u; LFVA Steiermark : 129, 139 o; Mader, Fritz, Barsbüttel: 49, 51, 109, 114, 143, 148; Marionettentheater Salzburg: 124 r; Mathis, Peter, Hohenems: 164/165, 170 o, 171 o, 172, 176; Meyer, Albrecht, Wien: 75 u, 195, 198 r, 200 ro; Mozarteum Salzburg: 121; Museen der Stadt Regensburg, Historisches Museum: 115; Österreichische Galerie Belvedere Wien: 60, 81; Österreichische Nationalbibliothek, Wien: 15, 24, 27, 53, 68, 89, 138 l, 152, 197 o; Österreich Werbung: 9, 32 u, 47 o, 50 o, 140; Österreich Werbung/Ascher: 162 l; Österreich Werbung/Bohnacker: 170 u, 174 u; Österreich Werbung/Jezierzanski: 171 lu; Österreich Werbung/Kneidinger: 63; Österreich Werbung/Loebl/Schreyer: 162 o; Österreich Werbung/Mallaun: 45; Österreich Werbung/Markowitsch: 22/23, 47 u, 50 lu+ru, 125, 135 u; Österreich Werbung/Panagl: 79 u; Österreich Werbung/Ramstorfer: 33 o; Österreich Werbung/Storto: 161; Österreich Werbung/Trumler: 62, 66, 78, 83, 88 o, 94, 98 lo, 98 u, 99, 131 l, 139 u, 157 o+u; Österreich Werbung/Wahrmann: 79 o; Österreich Werbung/Wiesenhofer: 44, 98 ro, 131 r, 134 o, 135 o, 162 ru; Osttirol-Werbung/Berger: 151 u; Pirker, Herbert, Bad Aussee: 64/65; Primus, Wilfried, Innsbruck: 159, 163; Probst, Siegfried, Pressefoto: 107; Rastl, Ingrid: 141; Schloßverwaltung zu Innsbruck und Ambras: 156; Schmidt-Glassner, Helga, Bildarchiv, bei Callwey Verlag, München: 71; Steinmann, Foto, Innsbruck: 149 r, 150 r; Stiftsmuseum Klosterneuburg: 14 o; Stift Zwettl: 72 o; Tiroler Landesmuseum Ferdinandeum, Innsbruck: 153; Tiroler Volkskunstmuseum, Innsbruck: 149 l, 150 l; Tourismusverband Steyr: 93; Trumler, Gerhard, Wien: Umschlagbild vorne, 29, 32 o, 73, 74, 169, 175; Truöl, Hans, Sonthofen: 167; Universität Heidelberg: 14 u, 133 o+u; Verlag St. Peter, Salzburg: 111 u, 112 o+u; Verlagsarchiv: 25, 36, 69, 70, 75 o, 76, 95, 100, 123 l, 144/145, 151 o, 155, 160, 166, 173, 174 o, 187 u, 191, 199 o, 200 lu; Vorarlberger Landesmuseum Bregenz: 178 o+u. In a few cases, the Publishers did not succeed in establishing the respective copyrights, and owners are therefore requested to get in touch.

ISBN
3-900284-60-1

Index

Page references for names and subjects in captions are indicated by italics.

Agilolfing dynasty, 89, 101

Alpine foreland, or foothills, 7, 9, 10, 24, 80, *80*, 86, 94, 106, 162

Alps, 9, 17, 25, 44, 66, 86, 97, 106, 110, 123, 128, 141, *145*, 142, 154, *158*, 162, 184

Art:
  Baroque, 16, 31, 32, 33, *33*, 38, 78, 82, *90*, 92, 93, 102, *112*, *116*, 120, 136, 138, 162, *172*, 175, *190*, 202 / Biedermeier, 17, 30, 82, *112*, 184, 195, 196, 202 / Classicism, *18*, 177 / Empire, 92 / Gothic, *31*, 40, *75*, 78, *87*, 102, *102*, *116*, *151*, 162, *174*, *176* / Neo-Gothic, 202 / Realism, 80 / Renaissance, 28, 79, 92, 120, *135*, 162, 174, *175*, 206 / Rococo, 156 / Romanesque, 49, *51*, 69, 70, *75*, 114, 120, *154*, *169* / Romanticism, 17, 123

Arthur, King, a British hero of legendary fame, 131, *149*, 150

Aspern, Battle of, 16, *18*, 82, 122, 193

Avars, Asiatic invaders in the early Middle Ages, 10, 25, *25*, 26, 69, 87, 88, 89, 111, 129, 185

Babenberg, House of, a Franconian dynasty ruling the margraviate (976-1156) and duchy (1156-1246) of Austria, 13, 14, *14*, 15, 30, 49, 69, *69*, 70, 72, 75, 76, 77, 89, 130, 131, 132, 138, 185, *187*, 205, 207

Barbarossa → Frederick I

Beethoven, Ludwig van, a German composer, last of the Vienna classics, 17, 192, 194

Brucker Libell, a legal document (dim. of L *liber* 'book') of religious toleration, laid down by the Provincial Diet of Bruck-on-Mur, Upper Styria, 61, 136

Bruckner, Anton, an Austrian composer of symphonies and religious music, *98*, 99

Catholicism, the doctrine and practice of the Roman Catholic Church, 26, 38, 46, 61, 80

Celts, *8*, 9, 25, 44, 45, 46, 56, 66, 86, 94, 97, 110, *110*, 128, 129

Charlemagne, or Charles the Great, King of the Franks and Emperor of the West, 10, *11*, 26, 69, 87, 88, 89, 101, *112*, 114, 115, 129, 170, 185, 204

Charles V, Roman Emperor, founder of the Spanish colonies, 15, 151, 186, *187*, 190

Charles VI, Roman Emperor (Charles III, King of Hungary), more a Spaniard than an Austrian, *33*, *62*, 136, *138*, *189*, 194

Charles I, Emperor of Austria (Charles IV, King of Hungary), *27*, 83, 199

Charles II, Archduke of Austria, son of Emperor Ferdinand I, 136

Charles, Archduke of Austria, Field Marshal, *18*, 82, 193

Christianity and Christianization, 9, 10, 26, 38, 46, 49, 89, 97, 101, 102, 111, *111*, 114, 129, 156, 170

Congress of Vienna, 1814-15, aimed at territorial resettlement and restoration to power of the crowned heads of Europe, 63, 82, 106, 192, 194, 195, 197

Counter-Reformation, a reform movement within the Roman Catholic Church in opposition to the Protestant Reformation (*see also* Protestantism), 15, 61, 79, 80, 92, 135, 136, 186, 191

Crusades and Crusaders (or Knights of the Cross), 72, 75, 92, 131, 185

Cultic sites, ancient, 46, 102, 148

Dürer, Albrecht, 1471-1528, a German painter and engraver, *11*, *46*, *201*

Elizabeth, Empress of Austria, 83, 94, *95*, *196*, 197, *197*, 198

emigration from:
  Burgenland, 41 / Salzburg, 118, *118*, 119 / Tyrol, 162 / Vorarlberg, 179

Esterházy, a dynasty of Hungarian magnates, 30, 31, 34

Eugene of Savoy, Prince, an Austrian general, born in France, *16*, 28, *119*, 188, *190*, 194, 195

Eugippius, an ecclesiastical writer, died c. 533, an African, ordained priest at Rome, a companion of St. Severinus of Noricum → saints

Ferdinand I, Roman Emperor (1556-64), 78, 136, 151

Ferdinand II, Roman Emperor, "Advocatus ecclesiae," 61, 136

Ferdinand I, Emperor of Austria (1835-48), 197

Ferdinand II, Archduke of Tyrol, *157*

festival performances in:
  Bregenz, 168 / Salzburg, 124, *124*

Francis I, Duke of Lorraine, Emperor, husband of Maria Theresa, 191, 192, 192

Francis II (I), Emperor: of the Holy Roman Empire (1792-1806); = of Austria, Francis I (1804-35), 16, 63, 106, 122, *178*

Francis Joseph I, Emperor of Austria, 83, *83*, 93, 94, *95*, 153, *196*, 197, *197*, 198

Francis Charles, Archduke of Austria, father of Emperor Francis Joseph I, 93

Frankish Empire, or Realm of the Franks, a united monarchy until 887, 10, 87, 114

Frederick I, German Emperor, nicknamed Barbarossa, 92, 119, 130

Frederick II, Duke, The Quarrelsome, 14, 15, 76, 77, 132

Frederick II, The Great, King of Prussia, *17*, 89, *89*, 191, *192*

Frederick III, King of Austria and Roman Emperor, 77, 78, 92, 133

Great Migration of the Peoples, The, 9, 13, 25, 46, 69, 86, 110, 111, 129, 156, 184

Grillparzer, Franz, the greatest dramatic poet of Austria, 2, 17, 50, 77, 195f.

Habsburg (or Hapsburg), House of, a German princely family ruling Austria (1273-1740) [afterwards, until 1918: House of Habsburg-Lorraine] and Spain (1516-1700), 10, 15, 53, 55, 61, 79, 132, *150*, 158, 185, 186, 191, 194, 204, 206

Hallstatt Culture (or Age, or Period), 9, 66, 86, *96*, 108

Haydn, [Franz] Joseph, a classical Austrian composer, 32, *32*, 82, 192

Henry II Jasomirgott, a Babenberg Margrave (and later, Duke) of Austria, 14, 156

Hofer, Andreas, a Tyrolean patriot, 122, 140, 152, *152*, 153, 158, *160*, 177

Hungarians → Magyars

Huns, a nomadic and warlike Asian people, 9, 10, 25, 26, 98, 185

Illyrians, ancient inhabitants of the east Adriatic coast and its hinterland, 8, 9, 110, 184

John, Archduke of Austria, Field Marshal, the most popular member of the Habsburg dynasty, 122, 140, *141*, 194

Joseph II, Roman Emperor, King of Hungary and Bohemia, the oldest son of Maria Theresa, 89, *141*, 166, 192, 196

Knights of the Cross → Crusaders

Königgrätz (or Sadowa), Battle of, deciding the Austro-Prussian War of 1866, 19, 191

Kuenring, Lords of, a knightly dynasty in the Wachau, *72*, 76

Lay of the Nibelungs → Nibelungenlied

Lechfeld, Battle on (or of) the, 10, 26, 69, 115, 170

Leitha, Battle on (or of) the, 15, 132, 185

Leopold I, Roman Emperor, 15, 30, 82, 190

Leopold III, The Saint, a Babenberg Margrave of Austria, 13, *14*, 30, *69*, 70, *75*, 102

Leopold V, The Virtuous, a Babenberg Duke of Austria, 72, 75, 130, 131

Leopold IV, a Habsburg Duke of Austria, 55

limes, or fortified border, of the Roman Empire, along the Danube, 25, 97, 129, 170

lines of communication, ancient and modern:
Alpine highways, 106, *109* / Amber Road, 25 / Roman roads, 9 / Salt Road, 97

Luther, Martin, the leader of the German Protestant Reformation, 61, 79, 118, 133, 151, 174

Magyars (or Hungarians), a race from the Ural Mountains, 10, 15, 26, 69, 76, 82, 89, 93, 115, 132, 170, 185, 186, 199

Marchfeld, Battle on (or of) the, 15, 52, 185

Maria Theresa, Roman Empress, Queen of Hungary and Bohemia, 16, *17*, 31, *138*, 190, 191, *191*, 192, *193*, 195, *195*, 196

Maultasch, Margarete ('Satchel-mouthed Meg'), Countess of Tyrol, *52*, 53, 158, 206

Maximilian I, "The Last Knight", Roman King (and later, Emperor), 60, 78, 94, 120, *148*, 149, *149*, *150*, 151, 158, *158*, 161

Metternich-Winneburg, Clemens Wenzel Lothar, Prince, the Imperial Chancellor of wide repute, 17, 18, 63, 106, 122, 140, 178, 194, *194*, 195, 197

Migration of the Peoples ➡ Great Migration of the Peoples

minnesingers, knightly, 70, 76, *76*, 131, 132

monastic orders ➡ religious orders

mountain passes:
Arlberg, *166*, 167, 173, 179
Brenner, *148*, 156, 161, *161*, *166*
Hochtannberg, 179, *180*
Jaufen, 152, 157
Lueg, 106, 116, 122
Semmering, 17, 40

Mozart, Wolfgang Amadeus, an Austrian musical genius, *121*, 122, 123, 124, *124*, 125, 192

Napoleon I, Emperor of the French, nicknamed "The Corsican Corporal", 16, 17, *18*, 19, 82, 106, 122, 140, 152, 156, 177, 178, 192, 193, *193*, 194

Nestroy, Johann Nepomuk, an Austrian actor and playwright, 17, 196

Nibelungenlied ('Lay of the Nibelungs'), the most famous Austrian medieval heroic poem (ca. 1200), *12*, 13, 92, *138*, 174

Noricum, a Roman province corresponding roughly to modern central Austria south of the Danube and west of Vienna, 9, 45, 46, 69, 97, 98, 110, 128

oppidum (*pl.,* oppida), a Celtic hill fort, 45, 67, 68, 94, 129

Ostarrîchi ('Realm in the East'), the old name of Austria, 7, 10, 50, 69, 131

Otakar ➡ Přemysl Otakar

Otto I, The Great, King of the Germans, Emperor of the Holy Roman Empire, 10, *13*, 26, 69, 102, 115

Pannonia, a Roman province lying east of Noricum and bounded north and east by the Danube, south (against Dalmatia) by the Dinaric Alps, *9*, 10, 25, 26, 69, 114, 185

Paracelsus, Theophrastus Bombast von Hohenheim, a Swiss physician and philosopher, ending his days in Salzburg, 38

pilgrim shrines:
Frauenkirchen, 34, 38 / Gebhardsberg (Bregenz), 175 / Heiligenblut, 56, *57* / Liebfrauenberg (Rankweil), 174 / Maria-auf-der-Heid, 37 / Maria Loretto, 38 / Maria Plain, 120 / Maria Saal, 50, *50* / Mariazell, 137, 138, *140* / Ollersdorf, 37, 38

Prandtauer, Jakob, an eminent architect of the Austrian Baroque, 82, 92, 162

Přemysl Otakar, King of Bohemia, 15, 50, 52, *53*, 77, 130, 132, 185

Pressburg (Bratislava), 10, 24, 82, 115, 177, *191*

Privilegium maius, 78, 205

Privilegium minus, 14, 70, 78, 205

Protestantism, conflicts and compromise (*see also:* Counter-Reformation, Brucker Libell), 63, 79, 80, 90, 118, *131, 134*

quotations, real or apocryphal:
- A.E.I.O.U. (among others, 'Austria est imperare orbi universo'), 77, 133
- "Austria - that's what's left over", 20, 186
- "Bella gerant alii; tu, felix Austria, nube!", 133
- "I would rather perish with my house than sacrifice a single acre of this land!", 153
- "Nothing in this world has been spared me", 197

Raetia (or Rhaetia), a Roman province west of Noricum, 9, 170

Raeti, its inhabitants, 110

Raimund, Ferdinand, an Austrian actor and playwright, 17, 82, 196

Reformation (*see also:* religious reformers, Counter-Reformation), 15, 80, 173, 186

regional customs:
alphorn playing, *171* / carved barrels, *37*, 40 / decorated earthenware jugs, 40, 41, *41* / ornamental bread loaves, 36, *36* / Shrovetide practices, 56, 57, 163, *163* / Sliding down the Barrel, 102

religious orders:
Augustinian Canons, 101, 137 / Benedictines, *48*, 49, *71*, 101, *112*, 136, *139*, 170 / Capuchins, 174 / Cistercians, or White Monks, 9, 70, *70* / Jesuits, 80, 191

religious reformers:
John Calvin (Jean Cauvin), 173 / John Huss (or Hus), 77, 173 / Martin Luther ➡ Luther / Ulrich (or Huldreich) Zwingli, 173

Richard I Coeur de Lion (or the Lion-Hearted), King of England, 72, *72*, 75

Roman Empire and its civilization, 9, *9*, 16, 25, 45, 56, 66, *67*, 69, 76, 87, 97, 106, 110, 129, 156, 170, 184, 204

Rosegger, Peter, a Styrian writer and poet, 141

Rudolph I, founder of the Habsburg dynasty, German King, Emperor of the Holy Roman Empire, 15, 52, *53*, 77, 78, *112*, 132

Rudolph IV, The Founder, a Babenberg Duke of Austria, 77, 78, 205

saints (by approved or by popular cult):
Alcuin, 115 / Boniface, 111, 114 Columban, 111 / Corbinian, 111 / Cyril, 114 / Emmeram, 111 / Erentrudis, 112 / Eugippius, 45, 68, 98 / Florian, 97, *99*, 101 / Hemma, 49, *51*, 102, 130 / Leopold ➡ Leopold III / Mary, the Blessed Virgin, 33, 37, 38, *102*, 137, 138, *172*, *174* / Methodius, 114 / Nonius, 102 / Rupert, 111, *111*, 112, *112*, 114, 122 / Severinus, 46, 68, 69, 98, 110, 185 / Stephen, 10, 26, *27*, *138* / Urban of Langres, 37 / Virgilius, 111, 114 / Wendelin, 37 / Wolfgang, 69, 102, *102*

Schubert, Franz, an Austrian composer, the Viennese incarnation of classic Romantic music, 17, 82, 196, *196*

secularization, 177

Stelzhamer, Franz, a great Upper Austrian dialect poet, 102

Strauss, Johann, Jr., an Austrian composer and director of music, 197, 198, *199*

Tassilo III of the Agilolfing dynasty, Duke of Bavaria, 87, 88, 89, 101, 115

Thirty Years' War, 1618-48, 15, 80, *120*, 174

trade routes ➡ lines of communication

Turkish Peril, the, 26, 28, *28*, 55, 61, 78, 79, 80, 82, *134, 139*, 186, 187, *187*, 188, *188*

universities: Innsbruck, 162 / Salzburg, 122 / Vienna, 78, 191, 197

Venus – an ancient fertility symbol: of Drassburg, 24 / of Willendorf, 66, *66*

Viennese Waltz, 17, *199*

Walther von der Vogelweide, a medieval lyric poet and singer, *14*

Wittelsbach, House of, a Bavarian dynasty of rulers, 10, 89

World War:
First, 16, 19, 20, 24, 62, 63, 83, 153, *153*, 166, 168, 198
Second, 20, *27*, 33, 45, 63, 106, 119, 120, 154, 166, 179, 186, 202